LEARNING APL

D0077751

LEARNING
APL

AN ARRAY
PROCESSING
LANGUAGE

James A. Mason
York University

HARPER & ROW, PUBLISHERS, New York
Cambridge, Philadelphia, San Francisco,
London, Mexico City, São Paulo, Singapore, Sydney

1817

To my parents, Lucile and Keith

Sponsoring Editor: John Willig
Project Editor: David Nickol
Text Design: Betty L. Sokol
Cover Design: Betty L. Sokol
Production: Delia Tedoff
Compositor: Computer Data Systems, Inc.
Printer and Binder: R. R. Donnelley & Sons
VAX is a trademark of Digital Equipment Corporation.

Learning APL: An Array Processing Language
Copyright© 1986 by Harper & Row, Publishers, Inc.

Library of Congress Cataloging in Publication Data

Mason, James A.
    Learning APL.

    Bibliography: p.
    Includes index.
      1. APL (Computer program language) I. Title.
II. Title: Learning A.P.L.
QA76.73.A27M37 1985   001.64'24   84–25151
ISBN 0–06–044243–3

85 86 87 88 9 8 7 6 5 4 3 2 1

Contents

Preface

A typical programmer first learns computer programming in a language like
BASIC, COBOL, FORTRAN, Pascal, or PL/I, in which data manipulations are
performed in many small steps, each described by a separate statement. Usually
even the simplest tasks to be performed in such a language require programs of
more than ten statements, and most tasks require much longer programs.

APL is a very different programming language, since it permits the
programmer to perform complicated data manipulations with extremely short
programs and even with one-line expressions. The need for the programmer to
write explicit loops, conditional statements, and assignment statements is
minimized by the power of the functions that APL provides for manipulating
arrays of data. Of all the common general-purpose programming languages,
APL is the one in which application systems can be implemented fastest.

The main ideas of APL were developed by Kenneth Iverson and presented in
his book *A Programming Language* (John Wiley & Sons, 1962), although the
notation of APL has changed from Iverson's original version and many features
have since been added to the language. The acronym APL comes from the title
of Iverson's book. The subtitle of this book (*An Array Processing Language*)
suggests a more specific interpretation of the acronym.

The goal of this book is to help the reader to acquire fluency in APL by
learning to think in terms of arrays of data and by learning the large vocabulary
of APL functions that operate on arrays. That learning is best accomplished by
solving problems in APL. Hence, the most important parts of this book are the
exercises. They have been chosen carefully to be short, but interesting and
challenging, and to be cumulative in their effect. In order to be accessible to the
widest possible readership, the exercises have been designed to require only

high-school mathematics, for the most part, and to involve character data as much as numerical data. Many of the exercises suggest practical applications.

This book is intended primarily for readers who already have some experience with computer programming in a language other than APL. For such readers it is suitable either for self-study or for use in a one-semester course. The book may also be used in a course for novice programmers if it is supplemented with introductory material on the elements of computer usage and programming.

The book should be read as much as possible in sequence from beginning to end, although parts involving three-dimensional and higher-dimensional arrays may be skipped over on first reading, if desired. As many of the exercises as possible should be solved, and the answers tested on a computer. (Suggested answers to some of the exercises are given in an appendix.) Each exercise should be solved using only those features of APL that have been introduced up to that point in the book. In classroom use it is appropriate for some of the exercises to be used as examples in class and the rest to be assigned as homework.

The first six chapters cover most of the standard features of the APL language as well as some common extensions. The coverage is reasonably comprehensive but not exhaustive. In addition to this book it is desirable to have a reference manual for whatever implementation of APL is being used. That will provide details of features of APL that are beyond the scope of this book and that may differ from one version of APL to another. (Those include certain system commands, system variables, system functions, and file-accessing functions that are not part of standard APL.)

Chapter 7 illustrates a way of making APL expressions look like English sentences, a technique that has not been presented in other books on APL. It also provides a case study of how an application can be implemented quickly and easily as a workspace of many small, cooperating APL functions.

Having used and taught APL and other general-purpose programming languages for over 10 years, I have found APL about the most pleasant and easiest-to-use language of all. I am confident that after reading this book and working the exercises, the reader will have acquired fluency in APL and will have come to share my enthusiasm for this interesting and powerful programming language.

I would like to thank the following people for their help in producing this book (my sincere apologies to anyone I have overlooked): Lewis Baxter, Allan Cobb, Eric Drumm, Richard Levine, and Peter Roosen-Runge for their comments on earlier versions of the book; my students, especially George Stephen who contributed several exercises; my editors, John Willig and David Nickol, and sales representative Ellen Graca at Harper & Row, and the prepublication reviewers, for their helpful suggestions for improving the manuscript; my friends Beatrice and Marvin Mandelbaum, Jane and Lawrence Muller, and P. Rajagopal for their encouragement; Donald Solitar for his comments and for his invaluable help in producing the final copy of the manuscript; York University for providing computing facilities; and the staff of the Atkinson College Duplicating Centre for their careful and speedy work. Special thanks go to Thomas Plum for a conversation that inspired me to develop Chapter 7. Finally, I would like to thank Saundra, Eric, and Allan for their patience and support.

James A. Mason

Chapter 1

USING APL

1.1 The Unique Nature of APL

APL is a language of a very different sort from the more well-known programming languages COBOL, FORTRAN, BASIC, PL/I, and Pascal, and it is generally easier to use than any of them. The main power of APL resides in its functions for manipulating arrays of data. In many cases they eliminate the need for explicit step-by-step programming. In APL, short expressions can often be written to do what would require many statements in one of the more conventional programming languages.

Unlike most other popular languages, APL is a highly interactive language, designed to be used conversationally at a typewriter terminal or video display terminal. The APL user types one-line expressions and receives immediate responses from the computer. Data values are entered at the terminal and can be used immediately for computations or can be stored in a permanent *library* for later use. Programs, called *functions,* are also typed at the terminal and can be executed immediately or saved in the user's library. Because of its conversational nature and its conciseness, APL is a very pleasant language to use.

The next section of this chapter gives some short examples of sessions at an APL terminal. One thing you will notice from the example sessions is that APL uses an unusual set of characters. Except for its system commands, APL has no English keywords, and each primitive function in the language is represented by a single symbol (or in a few cases, two). The use of symbols rather than words makes APL expressions very concise, and understandable internationally. However, it does take some time and effort to get used to the APL symbols. So we will learn the meanings of the various symbols gradually. Appendix A shows where the APL characters are found on a normal APL keyboard.

1

1.2 Example APL Sessions

In the following pages examples of two APL sessions are presented. These sessions should be read not for full understanding, but to get an initial idea of how APL is used.

Lines typed by the person who was using the computer have been underlined for clarity. Also, some explanatory comments have been added.

After you have finished reading Chapter 1, you should try to recreate parts of the example sessions on your computer. Consult Appendix A for help in typing the special characters used in the examples.

Session 1

Sign on to the computer and entry to the APL system. (Exact details vary from one system to another.)

CLEAR WS   —The initial *workspace* is *clear* (empty).

       HIGHS←3 ¯1 8 15 27 25 32 35 24 18 10 6   —assigning an array of high temperatures for the months of a year, in degrees Celsius

Note the raised negative sign (¯), not to be confused with the minus sign (−).

    HIGHS
3 ¯1 8 15 27 25 32 35 24 18 10 6 —displaying the array of
                            high temperatures

    HIGHS[6 7 8]   —displaying the highs for June, July, and August

25 32 35

    LOWS←¯25 ¯22 ¯8 ¯3 ¯1 5 15 18 2 ¯4 ¯2 ¯10   —assigning an array of low temperatures for the months of the year

    ⌈/*HIGHS*   —finding the highest of the highs
35

    ⌊/*LOWS*   —finding the lowest of the lows
¯25

    (+/*HIGHS*)÷12   —computing the average of the highs
16.83333333

    ∧/*HIGHS≥LOWS*   —testing that each high is at least as large as the corresponding low
1   —1 means *true.*

    (*HIGHS*>25)/ι12   —finding the months with high temperatures greater than 25 degrees Celsius
5 7 8

RANGE←HIGHS−LOWS —finding the difference between the high and
low temperatures for each month

RANGE —displaying the temperature ranges for the 12
months

28 21 16 18 28 20 17 17 22 22 12 16

(RANGE=⌈/RANGE)/ι12 —finding the months with the maximum
temperature range

1 5

∇F←FARENHEIT C —defining a new function
[1] ⍝*CONVERTS TEMPERATURES FROM CELSIUS TO FARENHEIT* —a comment
[2] *F←32+C×1.8*
[3] ∇ —end of function definition

FARENHEIT HIGHS —applying the function to the vector of highs

37.4 30.2 46.4 59 80.6 77 89.6 95 75.2 64.4 50 42.8

)WSID TEMPS —giving the workspace a name (*TEMPS*)
WAS CLEAR WS

)SAVE —saving the workspace on disk
13:24:16 18−*FEB*−84 3 *BLKS TEMPS*

)LIB —listing names of workspaces in the user's
disk library

GRADES
PRICES
TEMPS

)OFF —signing off

Sign off messages.

Session 2:

Sign on.

CLEAR WS

)LIB —Listing the names of workspaces in the
user's disk library

GRADES
PRICES
TEMPS

```
    )LOAD PRICES          —loading a workspace from the library
SAVED 19:56:50 17-FEB-84 2K

    )FNS                  —listing the names of user-defined functions
                           in the workspace
LIST
    ∇LIST[☐]∇             —displaying the definition of the LIST
                           function
    ∇ QUANTITIES LIST PRICES;EXT

[1]     ' '
[2]     EXT←QUANTITIES×PRICES
[3]     '          UNIT   EXTENDED'
[4]     'QUANITITY PRICE      PRICE'
[5]     ' '
[6]     5 0 9 2 10 2 ⍕QUANTITIES,PRICES,[1.5]EXT
[7]     ' '
[8]     'TOTAL:          ', 10 2 ⍕+/EXT
    ∇

    )VARS                 —listing the names of variables in the
                           workspace
P       Q

    P                     —displaying the value of variable P
1.75 0.59 3.98 17.25 32.98 2.99 19.95

    Q                     —displaying the value of variable Q
3 8 ¯12 2 9 0 1

    Q LIST P              —applying the LIST function to Q and P
          UNIT   EXTENDED
QUANTITY PRICE      PRICE

    3      1.75       5.25
    8      0.59       4.72
   12      3.98      47.76
    2     17.25      34.50
    9     32.98     296.82
    0      2.99       0.00
    1     19.95      19.95
TOTAL:            409.00

    ∇LIST[.1]             —inserting some new lines into the LIST
                           function
[0.1]      ⍝ COMPUTES EXTENDED PRICES AND TOTAL PRICE
[0.2]      ⍝ FROM GIVEN QUANTITIES AND UNIT PRICES
[0.3]      ∇
```

```
      ∇LIST[□]∇              —displaying the revised definition of LIST
    ∇  QUANTITIES LIST PRICES;EXT
[1]    ⍝ COMPUTES EXTENDED PRICES AND TOTAL PRICE
[2]    ⍝ FROM GIVEN QUANTITIES AND UNIT PRICES
[3]    ' '
[4]    EXT←QUANTITIES×PRICES
[5]    '          UNIT   EXTENDED'
[6]    'QUANTITY PRICE      PRICE'
[7]    ' '
[8]    5 0 9 2 10 2 ⍕QUANTITIES,PRICES,[1.5]EXT
[9]    ' '
[10]   'TOTAL:            '; 10 2 ⍕+/EXT
    ∇
```

```
      )ERASE P Q              —erasing variables from the workspace

      )VARS                   —checking whether any variables remain

      )WSID                   —displaying the name of the current active
                               workspace
PRICES

      )SAVE                   —saving the workspace in the disk library
14:39:52 19-FEB-84  4 BLKS PRICES

      )LOAD TEMPS             —loading the workspace saved in Session 1
SAVED    13:24:16 18-FEB-84 2K

      )VARS                   —listing names of variables in the workspace
HIGHS   LOWS    RANGE

      HIGHS                   —displaying the value of HIGHS
3 ¯1 8 15 27 25 32 35 24 18 10 6

      LOWS                    —displaying the value of LOWS
¯25 ¯22 ¯8 ¯3 ¯1 5 15 18 2 ¯4 ¯2 ¯10

      MONTHS←ι12              —creating an array of month numbers

      MONTHS                  —displaying the value of variable MONTHS
1 2 3 4 5 6 7 8 9 10 11 12

      MONTHS[▲HIGHS]          —displaying month numbers in order of
                               increasing high temperatures
2 1 12 3 11 4 10 9 6 5 7 8

      MONTHS[▲LOWS]           —displaying month numbers in order of
                               increasing low temperatures
1 2 12 3 10 4 11 5 9 6 7 8

      )CLEAR                  —clearing the active workspace
CLEAR WS
```

⍝ *SOME SHORT EXAMPLES*: —a comment

⍝ *POWERS OF TWO*:

```
×\16ρ2
```
2 4 8 16 32 64 128 256 512 1024 2048 4096 8192 16384 32768 65536

⍝ *A MULTIPLICATION TABLE*:

```
TABLE←(ι10)∘.×(ι10)
TABLE
```

1	2	3	4	5	6	7	8	9	10
2	4	6	8	10	12	14	16	18	20
3	6	9	12	15	18	21	24	27	30
4	8	12	16	20	24	28	32	36	40
5	10	15	20	25	30	35	40	45	50
6	12	18	24	30	36	42	48	54	60
7	14	21	28	35	42	49	56	63	70
8	16	24	32	40	48	56	64	72	80
9	18	27	36	45	54	63	72	81	90
10	20	30	40	50	60	70	80	90	100

⍝ *BIG LETTERS*:

```
BIGO←10 10ρ'O'        —creating big letter 'O' in a 10-by-11
                         character matrix

BIGO[2+ι6;2+ι6]←' '
BIGO[1 10;1 10]←' '
BIGO←BIGO,' '

BIGF←10 11ρ'FF',9ρ' '   —creating big letter 'F' in another 10-by-11
                         character matrix
BIGF[1 2;ι10]←'F'
BIGF[6 7;ι6]←'F'

BIGO,BIGF,BIGF        —printing a word made from the big letters
```

```
OOOOOOOO    FFFFFFFFFF  FFFFFFFFFF
OOOOOOOOOO  FFFFFFFFFF  FFFFFFFFFF
OO      OO  FF          FF
OO      OO  FF          FF
OO      OO  FF          FF
OO      OO  FFFFF       FFFFF
OO      OO  FFFFF       FFFFF
OO      OO  FF          FF
OOOOOOOOOO  FF          FF
 OOOOOOOO   FF          FF
```

```
)OFF                 —signing off
```

Sign off messages.

1.3   System Commands

Before we get into the APL language itself, you must know a few things about the APL system environment: how to sign on and off from APL, and how to save and retrieve things in your private library for permanent storage of programs and data (which is usually on a disk storage device). Many of the system commands summarized in this section have already been illustrated in the sample terminal sessions.

A key element of the APL system is the *workspace*. When you sign on to an APL system you are given a clear workspace into which you can enter data and functions, and in which you can perform computations. The workspace you are using at any one time is called the *active workspace*. Whenever you wish you can save the entire active workspace, including the data and functions in it, in your library. The library can contain many workspaces, which remain stored when you sign off from the computer. At any time when you are signed on, it is possible to *load* a workspace from your library. The workspace loaded will then become the active workspace.

A typical APL session consists of the following sequence of steps:

1.   Sign on to the computer and enter the APL system.
2.   Use the initial clear workspace, or load a workspace from your library.
3.   Enter data, enter function definitions, and do computations in the active workspace.
4.   Repeat as often as desired:
     a.   Save the active workspace in your library (if you want to keep it).
     b.   Obtain a new clear workspace or load another workspace from your library.
     c.   Enter data, enter function definitions, and perform computations in the active workspace.
5.   Save the active workspace in your library (if desired).
6.   Sign off from the computer.

To use APL you need to know the following system procedures and commands. System commands begin with a right parenthesis to distinguish them from names of variables or functions.

How To Sign On   The procedure for signing on to APL varies from one computer to another. Generally the procedure is quite simple, but you will have to learn it from manuals for your particular computer and terminal.

How To Sign Off   Signing off is easier than signing on but no less important. If you forget to sign off, and instead simply turn off your terminal, various undesirable things may happen: You may lose data, or you may incur extra usage charges if you are paying for computer usage. To terminate an APL session properly you should type the system command

        `)OFF`

In reply the computer will type an appropriate message, perhaps including some job statistics, such as the cost of the session and the balance remaining in your account.

How To Get a Clear Workspace   When you sign on to APL the active workspace is initially clear, containing no data or functions. If at some other time you want to replace the active workspace by a clear workspace, type the system command

        `)CLEAR`

That command will destroy all user-defined functions and data currently in the active workspace.

How To Give a Name to the Active Workspace   Workspaces stored in your library must have distinct names, called *workspace IDs*. You can give a workspace a (new) name when it is active by typing

        `)WSID` name

including the name which you have chosen, as in this example:

        `)WSID PROJECT`

In reply, the system will give the old name for the workspace, or will type `WAS CLEAR WS` if the workspace was unnamed. Different versions of APL have different rules regarding what are acceptable workspace names. Usually a workspace name can consist of at least six letters and/or digit characters, beginning with a letter. Consult the reference manual for your APL system for details.

How To Find out the Name of the Active Workspace   The `)WSID` command without a name after it can be used to find out the name of the currently active workspace. The system will type the name as in the following example:

        `)WSID`
`PROJECT`

How To Save a Workspace in Your Library   The active workspace, including all data and functions in it, can be saved, under its current workspace ID, by typing the command

        `)SAVE`

Note: The saved workspace will replace in the library any other workspace which has previously been saved with the same name.

How To Load a Workspace from Your Library   The command

        `)LOAD` name

will cause the workspace with the specified name to be loaded from your library and to become the active workspace. The previous contents of the active workspace will be destroyed. A copy of the loaded workspace will remain, unchanged, in the library.

How To Eliminate a Workspace from Your Library   To delete a workspace from your library, type the command

        `)DROP` name

using the workspace ID of the workspace to be dropped. This command should be used with care, because a workspace cannot be recovered once it has been dropped.

How To List the Names of All Workspaces in Your Library   In response to the command

        `)LIB`

the APL system will list the names of all workspaces currently saved in your library.

The following schematic diagram may be helpful for remembering the system commands:

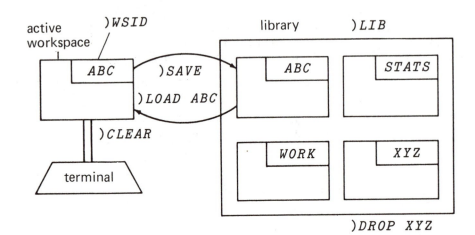

1.4 Typing APL

Once you have signed on to APL and the workspace you want is active, the system is in what is known as *calculator mode* or *immediate mode*. That means that you can type an APL expression and the system will reply immediately by typing the value of the expression. For example, if you type

        2+3

and press the RETURN key, APL will respond by typing

5

After the system has typed its reply it will advance the output medium (paper or display screen) to a new line and indent six spaces as a way of prompting you to type another line.

Before you press the RETURN key it is possible to make corrections to a line which you have just been typing. This is done by backspacing to the position at which the mistake began, pushing the INDEX, LINEFEED, or ATTENTION key (depending on the version of APL and the kind of terminal which you are using), and retyping the portion of the line to the right of that position. For example,

              BACKSPACEing to here and pressing INDEX, LINEFEED,
          ┌─ or ATTENTION key
          │
          ▼
    532+20
        ¯200   ← then retyping this and pressing RETURN

yields the value

332

Backspacing is also used to produce certain *overstruck* characters like ⍋ (Δ over |) and ⍀ (∩ over ○). Not all pairs of characters may be overstruck, but those that can be may be overstruck in either order. That is, either Δ BACKSPACE | or | BACKSPACE Δ will produce the character ⍋. The valid overstruck characters are listed in Appendix A.

It is also possible to BACKSPACE to insert omitted characters in blank spaces. APL interprets a line as it finally appears when RETURN is pressed, not according to the order in which keys were pressed while the line was being typed. Thus, APL is said to interpret lines of input with *visual fidelity*.

Lines beginning with the *lamp* symbol ⍝ are interpreted as comments and are not evaluated as APL expressions. APL displays no response to them but simply indents six spaces on the next line and waits for another expression.

EXERCISE

Recreate parts of the example sessions from Section 1.2 on your computer.

Chapter 2

APL Expressions and Arrays

2.1 Variables and Assignment (←)

Assignment of a value to a variable in APL is done with the left arrow symbol
(←). For example, typing

    A←23

will cause the number 23 to be assigned to the variable *A*. APL does not print
anything in response to an assignment. In calculator mode it simply indents six
spaces on the next line and waits for the user to type something else.

   APL does not require variables to be declared before they are used. The first
assignment to a variable both creates the variable and assigns it a value. Once a
variable has been created in calculator mode, it remains in the active workspace,
and it is saved, together with its current value, whenever the workspace is
saved in the user's library. Of course, the value of a variable can be changed in
the active workspace at any time by assignment of a new value to it. Furthermore, the new value can have different dimensions and be of a different type
than the old value: A variable can have a character string as value at one mo-
ment and a matrix as value the next.

   The name of a variable can consist of letters, digits, and the delta symbol (Δ).
It must begin with a letter or delta. Letters in the name of a variable can also be
overstruck with the underscore symbol (_). In that case they are treated as different from letters that have not been underscored. The maximum length of a

variable name depends on the particular version of APL which is being used. Most versions allow variable names of up to 30 characters or more. The following are examples of variable names:

$$A$$
$$\Delta$$
$$SUM\Delta OF\Delta LENGTHS$$
$$\Delta 37$$
$$PRODUCT$$
$$\underline{PRODUCT}$$

A list of all variables which exist in the active workspace can be obtained by typing the system command

$$)VARS$$

Variables, along with their values, can be deleted from the active workspace by typing

$$)ERASE$$

followed on the same line by the names of the variables, separated by blanks, as in

$$)ERASE\ SUM\ PRODUCT\ A\ \Delta 37$$

2.2   Numbers

Numbers in APL may be typed with or without decimal points. The maximum number of digits allowed depends on the particular version of APL which is being used. A number can also have an exponent part to indicate scaling by a power of 10. This is written as an E followed by the value of the exponent. The following are some examples of numbers in APL:

$$2.718281828$$
$$375000$$
$$2.1896E12 \quad \text{(which is equal to 2189600000000)}$$

The sign of a negative number or of a negative exponent is indicated by the raised negative symbol (¯), found above 2 on the keyboard. It is a different symbol from the minus symbol (−) found near the right end of the top row of the keyboard. The minus symbol represents a function which computes the negative of a number or subtracts one number from another, while the raised negative symbol is considered to be part of a numeric constant, just as a decimal point is. Thus one can write

¯8	(the number negative 8), or
−¯8	(an expression to compute the negative of the number negative 8, which yields the value 8), or
−A	(an expression to compute the negative of the value of the variable A)

but it does not make sense to write $^-$−8 or $^-$A.

The distinction is made between the raised negative sign and the minus function to avoid ambiguity when arrays of constants are written. For instance,

        6   5   4 $^-$3   2   1

is a one-dimensional array, or vector, of six numbers (one negative and five positive), whereas

        6   5   4   −3   2   1

is an expression to subtract the vector 3   2   1 from the vector 6   5   4 (yielding the vector 3   3   3).

2.3   Characters

Character string constants in APL are written between single quotation marks ('). If a single quotation mark is itself to be quoted, it must be typed twice. For example, if

        'DON''T FORGET!'

is typed in calculator mode, APL responds by typing

DON'T FORGET!

This example also illustrates the fact that valid APL overstruck symbols can be included in quoted strings (! is . overstruck on ').

Character values are assigned to variables in the same way that numbers are, by use of the assignment arrow:

        STRING←'A SHORT LIST OF WORDS'

Subsequently, typing the name of the variable in calculator mode causes the string to be printed:

        STRING
A SHORT LIST OF WORDS

2.4   Arithmetic Functions

The APL symbols for the basic arithmetic functions are the ones used in ordinary arithmetic:

- \+ is the symbol for addition
- − is the symbol for subtraction (with two arguments) or for negation (with one argument)
- × is the symbol for multiplication
- ÷ is the symbol for division (/ has other meanings in APL)

The asterisk character (*) is the symbol for exponentiation (i.e., raising to a power).

Some examples are

        1÷3
0.3333333333   —one-third approximated by a finite decimal
                                   fraction
        2*3
8   —the cube of 2
        2*.5
1.414213562   —the square root of 2 (2 to the ½ power)
        ¯4*2
16   —the number ¯4 squared
        −4*2
¯16   —the negative of the square of 4
        2*¯20   —2 raised to the ¯20 power
9.536743164E¯7   —a very small value expressed in scaled form

If you have used other programming languages, many of which use * for multiplication and / for division, you will have to get used to APL's different, but really more correct notation.

2.5 Comparison Functions; True (1) and False (0)

APL has symbols < ≤ = ≥ > and ≠ (not overstruck) for comparisons. They have their usual mathematical meanings:

    < means "less than"
    ≤ means "less than or equal to"
    = means "equal to"
    ≥ means "greater than or equal to"
    > means "greater than"
    ≠ means "not equal to"

All of them can be applied to numbers, but in some versions of APL only = and ≠ can be applied to character data.

The result of a comparison is a number, either 1 or 0. 1 represents *true* and 0 represents *false*. For example, the expression

        5≥2+3   yields the value
1

while the expression

        'A'='B'   yields the value
0

A comparison applied to character strings does not yield just one number, as you might expect, but rather a one-dimensional array of numbers, one for each position in the strings being compared. For example,

        'CAT'='CAR'   yields the array of three numbers
1 1 0

since the two strings agree in the first two character positions but differ in the third position. (In APL character strings are treated as one-dimensional arrays of individual characters.)

The fact that *true* and *false* are represented by numbers in APL means that the results of comparisons can be used in arithmetic expressions. For example, suppose *HOUR* is a number from 0 to 23, representing an hour on a 24-hour clock. Then the following expression gives the equivalent hour on a 12-hour clock:

$$HOUR+(12\times(HOUR=0))-12\times(HOUR>12)$$

That is, the *HOUR* zero becomes 12, and *HOUR*s greater than 12 are reduced by 12.

2.6 Arrays, Shape, and Reshape (ρ)

As was mentioned earlier, APL is particularly good at operating on data in the form of arrays. An array is a collection of either numbers or characters and has zero, one, two, three or more dimensions.

A single number, like 375, or a single character, like 'X', is called a *scalar*. It is considered to be a zero-dimensional array, analogous to a point in geometry.

A list of numbers, such as

    12 ‾0.75 9E7 3.14159 (typed with spaces between them)

or a string of characters, like

    'THIS EXAMPLE' (typed between single quotation marks)

is a one-dimensional array, or *vector*, analogous to a line segment in geometry. A vector has a length equal to the number of elements that it contains.

Matrices, or two-dimensional arrays, of numbers are commonly used in mathematics. APL provides those and also permits two-dimensional arrays of character data. Character matrices can be used to represent pictures, or lists of words, or pages of text, among other things. A two-dimensional array is analogous to a rectangle in geometry, having a height (number of rows) and a width (number of columns).

APL also allows the creation of three-dimensional, four-dimensional, and higher-dimensional arrays of either numbers or characters. In all cases an array may contain either numbers or characters, but not both numbers and characters in the same array.

The length of a vector can be measured by a function called *shape*, represented by the Greek letter rho (ρ). For instance, if the following assignments are made,

    A←'WORD'
    B←1982 12 31
    C←'1982 12 31 '

then application of the shape function will yield the lengths of *A*, *B*, and *C*:

ρ*A*	will yield
4	because the value of *A* has 4 characters.
ρ*B*	will yield
3	because the vector *B* contains 3 numbers: 1982, 12, and 31.
ρ*C*	will yield
11	because vector *C* contains 11 characters.

Notice that C is a character vector, even though it contains digits and looks almost like the numeric vector assigned to B. Notice also that the blanks in C, including the one at the end, are counted in its length.

Matrices are created in APL by *reshaping* scalars or vectors into desired numbers of rows and columns. For example, to create a three-row by four-column matrix M containing nothing but zeros one types the assignment statement

      $M\leftarrow3$ $4\rho0$

Here the rho symbol represents the reshape function. At its left is the desired shape for the matrix: a vector 3 4, indicating 3 rows and 4 columns. At its right is the scalar number 0, which is to be used to fill the array. If the value of M is printed, by typing

      M

the matrix will appear as

```
0  0  0  0
0  0  0  0
0  0  0  0
```

The shape of M, ρM, will be the vector 3 4 which was specified when the matrix was created.

If a matrix is created by reshaping a vector, the elements of the vector are put into the matrix one row at a time, as in the following example:

      3 5ρ*'ABCDEFG'*

ABCDE
FGABC
DEFGA

The given vector fills the first row of the matrix and overflows into the second row. Notice that the elements from the vector are reused as often as necessary to fill the matrix completely to the shape specified. That fact can be exploited to create repetitious patterns like the following checkerboard array:

      5 5ρ'×o'

```
×o×o×
o×o×o
×o×o×
o×o×o
×o×o×
```

Reshape can also be used to create vectors, as the following examples illustrate:

      25ρ1 0
1 0 1 0 1 0 1 0 1 0 1 0 1 0 1 0 1 0 1 0 1 0 1 0 1
      11ρ*'ABRACAD'*
ABRACADABRA
      4ρ*'FOURTEEN'*
FOUR
      40ρ*'OVER AND '*
OVER AND OVER AND OVER AND OVER AND OVER

The reshape function always uses just as many elements as it needs from its right argument to fill the array it is creating.

A three-dimensional array can be created by using reshape with a three-element vector on the left to indicate the desired shape. For example,

$$A \leftarrow 2\ 3\ 4\rho'ABCDEFGHIJKLMNOPQRST'$$

will create an array consisting of two *planes*, each with three rows and four columns. Such an array can be visualized as a rectangular solid divided up into cells:

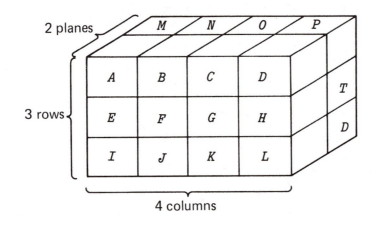

When the array is printed, each of its planes is printed like a matrix:

```
        A
ABCD
EFGH              —first plane
IJKL

MNOP
QRST              —second plane
ABCD
```

Notice that the first plane of *A* has been filled first, each plane has been filled a row at a time, and the first four elements of the given vector have been reused to complete the new array. As you might expect, the shape of *A*, ρA, will be the vector 2 3 4.

Similarly, four-dimensional and higher-dimensional arrays can be created, by specifying a desired shape vector with one number for each dimension. In the shape vector of a four-dimensional array, the first number specifies the number of *hyperplanes* or *blocks*, the second number gives the number of planes in each hyperplane, and the third and fourth numbers give the number of rows and columns in each plane. The following example shows how a four-dimensional array is printed:

```
      2 2 2 6ρ'FIRST PLANE SECONDPLANE '
FIRST
PLANE   \
             First hyperplane
SECOND  /
PLANE


FIRST
PLANE   \
             Second hyperplane
SECOND  /
PLANE
```

The shape of any array is itself always a one-dimensional array. Consequently a shape vector has a shape of its own: namely, a one-element vector giving the length of the original shape vector. The following example illustrates this:

```
      A←3 5ρ1 2 3 4
      A
1 2 3 4 1                     A is a 3-by-5 matrix.
2 3 4 1 2
3 4 1 2 3
      ρA
3 5                          The shape of A is a two-element vector.
      ρρA
2                            The shape of the shape of A is 2.
```

Notice that the shape of the shape of A gives the number of dimensions that array A has. In APL that number is called the *rank* of A. A vector has rank 1, a matrix rank 2, a three-dimensional array rank 3, and so on.

It follows that a scalar, having no dimensions, should have rank zero, and that is the case. For example, the rank of the scalar 3, ρρ3, is zero. That means that ρ3, the shape of scalar 3, must be a vector with no elements at all: an *empty vector*. In fact, if you type

```
      ρ3
```

in calculator mode, you will see that nothing is printed.

Although an empty vector does not contain any elements, it is still a legitimate one-dimensional array. Empty vectors are useful as initial values to which elements are to be appended later.

As we have seen, an empty numeric vector can be created by applying the shape function to a scalar. Another way to create an empty vector is to use the reshape function, specifying a desired shape of 0:

```
      E←0ρ1
```

In this case, since the value of the right argument is not needed to fill the array created, the right argument can be any number at all. To create an empty character vector, one can use reshape with a character as the right argument (e.g., 0ρ'X'), or one can simply type two single quotation marks with nothing between them:

```
        E←''
        ρE
0
```

In a similar manner, other kinds of empty arrays can be created. For example, if you wish to represent a page of text by a matrix, and you want to start with an empty page 65 columns wide, you can use the following assignment statement:

```
        PAGE←0 65ρ' '
```

The result will be a character matrix with 0 rows and 65 columns, to which rows can be added later, as we shall see.

Functions like +, −, ×, and ÷, which apply to scalars can also be applied to arrays. For example, the minus function may be used to negate each of the elements of a vector:

```
        A←1 3 5 7
        −A
¯1 ¯3 ¯5 ¯7
        A
1 3 5 7
```

Notice that the minus function applied to A yields a new array; it does not change the value of A itself. Only the assignment operation (←) can actually change the value of a variable.

If a function that takes two arguments is applied to two arrays, it is really applied to each pair of corresponding elements in the two arrays. For example, if A has the value assigned above, then

```
        A+4 5 6 7         yields
5 8 11 14
```

Clearly, the arrays involved must have identical shapes, so that the correspondence between their elements is well defined. The only exception is when one of the arguments has just a single element. In that case that single element is paired with each of the elements of the other argument, as the following examples show:

```
        A
1 3 5 7
        A+3
4 6 8 10
        B←0ρ0
        B+3

        ρ(B+3)
0
```

The last example shows that when a scalar is added to an empty vector, the result is an empty vector.

EXERCISES

2.6.1.   What is the value of the expression $'ABRACADABRA'='A'$?

2.6.2.   What is the value of the expression $ρρρA$? Does it depend on the value of A?

2.6.3.   Write an expression to mark the columns on your terminal paper or display screen with ○'s in columns 5, 15, 25, 35, and so on, and │'s in columns 10, 20, 30, 40, and so on, like this:

    ○   │   ○   │   ○   │   ○   │   ○   │   ○   │

2.6.4.   Write an assignment statement to assign to a variable called *SAILBOAT* the following 4-by-5 character matrix:

Note: The horizontal lines are the underscore character (above *F* on the keyboard).

2.6.5.   Write an expression using reshape to create the 4-by-4 identity matrix

```
1 0 0 0
0 1 0 0
0 0 1 0
0 0 0 1
```

2.6.6.   What are the values of the following expressions?

```
9ρ'HA'
9ρ(3ρ'HA')
3 3ρ'HA'
3 3ρ(3ρ'HA')
5 2ρ(3 3ρ'□ ')
```

Note: If the right argument of reshape is a matrix, its elements are copied out by rows.

2.6.7.   Write an expression to produce the value 1 or 0 according to whether or not the value of a given variable *M* is a matrix. Use parentheses to indicate the scopes of the functions involved.

2.6.8.   Write an expression to create and print a 3-dimensional character array with shape 4 2 3 in which the first plane contains only *A*'s, the second plane contains only *B*'s, the third plane only *C*'s, and the fourth plane only *D*'s.

2.6.9.   Write an expression that will add a given vector V to each row of a given matrix M. Use parentheses to indicate the scopes of the functions in the expression. For example, if the value of M is

```
1    2    3    4
5    6    7    8
9   10   11   12
```

and the value of V is 2 0 ¯1 3, then the value of the expression should be the matrix

```
 3    2    2    7
 7    6    6   11
11   10   10   15
```

(You may assume that V has as many elements as M has columns.)

2.6.10.   Suppose the value of A is an array of arbitrary shape containing only one element. Write an expression using reshape which yields the value of A converted to a scalar.

2.7   Monadic Versus Dyadic Functions

Shape and reshape are a pair of different functions for which the same symbol (ρ) is used. APL has many such pairs and, like shape and reshape, functions represented by the same symbol often have related meanings.

A function like shape with only one argument is called a *monadic* function. Its argument is always written to the right of it. A function like reshape with two arguments is called a *dyadic* function. One of its arguments is written on the left and the other on the right. Except for a few special cases, all functions in APL are either monadic or dyadic.

One can tell whether a function in an APL expression is monadic or dyadic by looking at its left context: Since a dyadic function has a left argument, there will be a constant, a variable, or a subexpression (in parentheses) to the left of it. A monadic function, in contrast, will be preceded by another function, a left parenthesis, an assignment arrow, or nothing at all. For example, in the expression

$$B \leftarrow -C - (\rho A) \rho \rho 1\ 2$$

the first − is monadic (negation) and the second is dyadic (subtraction). Likewise, the first and third ρ symbols represent the monadic shape function, while the second ρ is the dyadic reshape function.

EXERCISE

2.7.1.   In the following expression, which functions are monadic and which are dyadic? Evaluate the expression by hand and determine its value.

$$((\rho 2\ 3) \rho 5\ ^{-}6\ 7) - (2 \rho - \rho 2\ 3\ 4)$$

2.8 Ravel (,)

The monadic function *ravel*, represented by a comma (,), yields a vector obtained by copying the elements out of whatever array has been supplied as its argument. The elements are copied out of the array in the same order in which reshape puts elements into arrays. For example, if M is the numeric matrix

```
16   25    9
36   49   64
```

then the ravel of M

```
     ,M
```

yields the vector

```
16  25  9  36  49  64
```

Ravel essentially undoes the work of reshape: It *unravels* the elements from an array, ignoring the shape of the array.

If ravel is applied to a scalar, the result is a one-element vector. For example, while the shape of a single character

```
     ρ'C'
```

is an empty vector, the shape of a raveled character,

```
     ρ,'C'
```

is 1. For that reason, ravel is frequently applied to variables whose values are character strings, so that the shape of one-character strings will be 1 rather than empty.

EXERCISES

2.8.1.   If M is the following 4-by-5 character matrix

```
A
LIST
OF
WORDS
```

what is the value of the expression ,M?

2.8.2.   Suppose A is a variable whose value is an array of arbitrary shape. Write an expression that will tell how many elements there are in A.

2.9 Catenate (,)

The dyadic function called *catenate*, represented by a comma, is used to join arrays together. It combines two arrays of equal rank along one of their dimensions to produce a new array of the same rank. For instance, if A and B are two matrices created as follows

```
A←2 3ρ1
B←2 3ρ2
```

the assignment

$$C \leftarrow A, [1]B$$

creates a new matrix C by combining A and B along their first dimension (vertically):

```
      C
1   1   1
1   1   1
2   2   2
2   2   2
```

A and B can be catenated in this way because they have the same number of columns. The shape of the result, ρC, is 4 3; its first element is the sum of the first elements of ρA and ρB.

Since A and B have the same number of rows, they can also be catenated along their second dimension (horizontally):

```
    A,[2]B
1   1   1   2   2   2
1   1   1   2   2   2
```

The result has shape 2 6.

The dimension along which catenation is done is given in square brackets after the comma. If that dimension is the last dimension of the two arguments, the bracketed number can be omitted. Thus, for the matrices A and B,

$$A, B$$

has the same value as

$$A, [2]B$$

In some versions of APL the overstruck symbol $\ominus$ (− over ,) can be used instead of , [1] to indicate catenation along the first dimension.

When vectors are catenated together, the result is a longer vector:

```
    S←'TWO '
    T←'WORDS'
    S,T
TWO WORDS
```

Scalars can be catenated with scalars, vectors, matrices, or higher-dimensional arrays, as the following examples illustrate:

```
    SCALAR←5
    VECTOR←1 2 3
    MATRIX←2 3ρ6
    HIGHER←2 2 3ρ'A'

    SCALAR,4
```

(Note: When a scalar is catenated with a scalar, the result is a vector, which has higher rank than the scalars.)

```
      VECTOR,4
1  2  3  4
      4,VECTOR
4  1  2  3
      MATRIX,4
6  6  6  4
6  6  6  4
      4,[1]MATRIX
4  4  4
6  6  6
6  6  6

      HIGHER,[1]'B'
AAA
AAA

AAA
AAA

BBB                            ← A plane of B's has been added.
BBB
      ρ(HIGHER,[1]'B')
3  2  3
      HIGHER,[2]'B'
AAA
AAA
BBB                            ← A row of B's has been added to each plane.

AAA
AAA
BBB
      ρ(HIGHER,[2]'B')
2  3  3
      HIGHER,[3]'B'
AAAB
AAAB
                               ← A column of B's has been added to each
AAAB                           plane.
AAAB
      ρ(HIGHER,[3]'B')
2  2  4
      HIGHER,'B'
AAAB
AAAB

AAAB
AAAB
```

when a scalar is catenated with a matrix or higher-dimensional
‫⌐lar is replicated as many times as necessary to fit the face of the
, ⌐o which it is being catenated.

In many versions of APL, vectors can also be catenated onto matrices, provided that the vector fits the end of the matrix to which it is catenated. Here
are some examples:

```
      MATRIX
6    6    6
6    6    6
      MATRIX,1 2
6    6    6    1
6    6    6    2
      1 2 3,[1]MATRIX
1    2    3
6    6    6
6    6    6
```

Another example involves catenating vectors vertically onto the bottom of an
initially empty character matrix as a step in producing a page of text:

```
      PAGE←0 40ρ' '     —40-column character array with no rows
      PAGE←PAGE,[1]'        THIS IS THE FIRST LINE OF A PAGE.       '
      ρPAGE
1  40

      PAGE←PAGE,[1]'THIS IS THE SECOND LINE FOR THE PAGE.        '
      ρPAGE
2  40

      PAGE
      THIS IS THE FIRST LINE OF A PAGE.
THIS IS THE SECOND LINE FOR THE PAGE.
```

In such cases where the ranks of the two arguments are different, the result of
catenation always has rank equal to the greater of the ranks of the arguments.

Finally, it is important to bear in mind the difference between a constant vector like

```
      1  2
```

and an expression like

```
      1,2
```

which uses catenate to create a vector by joining two scalars. In either case the
result is the same, but the expressions are quite different syntactically. When
variables are involved in catenation, the comma must always be included, as in
the example

```
      A←1
      B←2
      A,B
1 2
```

If you omit the comma, and type

    A B

APL will give a *SYNTAX ERROR* message.

EXERCISES

2.9.1.   Write an expression whose value is the matrix resulting when a border of *'s is put around a given character matrix *C* . For instance, if *C*←2 3ρ*'ABC'* the expression should yield the matrix

    *****
    ABC
    ABC
    *****

2.9.2.   Write an expression involving a variable *N*, whose value is a scalar number, to generate the *N*-by-*N* identity matrix. For example, when the value of *N* is 5, the expression should produce the matrix

    1   0   0   0   0
    0   1   0   0   0
    0   0   1   0   0
    0   0   0   1   0
    0   0   0   0   1

2.9.3.   Write an expression involving a variable *N* and the catenate and reshape functions to generate an *N*-by-*N* checkerboard array of x and O characters. For example, if the value of *N* is 4, the value of the expression should be the matrix

    xOxO
    OxOx
    xOxO
    OxOx

Make sure that the expression works correctly regardless of whether the value of *N* is odd or even.

2.9.4.   Write an assignment statement to change the value of a given variable *LIST* from a vector of numbers to a one-column matrix of the same numbers. For instance, if *LIST*←1 2 3 then the value of *LIST* after the new assignment statement should be the matrix

    1
    2
    3

2.9.5.   Suppose *A* and *B* are two three-dimensional arrays:

    A←2 2 3ρ*'A'*
    B←2 2 3ρ*'B'*

What will each of the following expressions cause to be printed?

```
A,[1]B
A,[2]B
A,[3]B
,(A,[1]B)
,(A,[2]B)
,(A,B)
```

2.9.6.   Let S be a variable whose value is a character vector. Write an expression using reshape, catenate, and ravel to yield a new character vector in which each character from S occurs in triplicate. For instance, if $S\leftarrow'THESE'$ then the result should be

$TTTHHHEEEESSSEEE$

2.9.7.   Suppose $PAGE$ is a 50-column character matrix representing a page of text, and $LINE$ is a vector of 50 or fewer characters. Write an assignment statement to append the value of $LINE$ to the bottom of the $PAGE$ array. If the value of $LINE$ has fewer than 50 characters, put blanks on its right end to make it 50 characters wide. (Note: A single assignment statement, involving the catenate and reshape functions among others, should be written for this exercise.)

2.9.8.   Suppose N is a variable with value 1 or 0, representing *true* or *false*. Write an expression that will generate the word $TRUE$ or the word $FALSE$ as a character vector, according to the value of N.

2.10   The Right-to-Left Precedence Rule

If an expression involves several functions, parentheses can be used to indicate the *scope* of each of the functions: that is, what its arguments are. For instance, the expression

$$(A,B)\rho C$$

indicates different scoping than the expression

$$A,(B\rho C)$$

However, if parentheses are to be omitted, as in

$$A,B\rho C$$

some rule is needed to determine the functions' scopes.

In many languages, rules of precedence are used to determine scope. In normal algebra, for example, multiplication takes precedence over addition, so that

$$a + b \times c$$

is treated as if it had parentheses around $b \times c$:

$$a + (b \times c).$$

But APL has so many unusual functions that rules of precedence would be hard to remember. Instead, APL uses the following simple rule to determine function scope:

Unless parentheses indicate otherwise, the right-hand argument of a function is everything to the right of the function.

Thus, the expression

$A,B\times C\rho D$

has the same value as if it were parenthesized

$A,(B\times(C\rho D))$

The effect of the scope rule is that functions in an unparenthesized expression are applied in right-to-left order. For that reason, the scope rule is sometimes called the *right-to-left rule*. (However, although expressions are evaluated from right to left, they can, with practice, be written and read from left to right. For example, an experienced APL programmer reads the expression $,A,B$ as "the ravel of A catenate B," not as "catenate A and B and then ravel the result.")

APL's scope rule applies to all of its functions, including arithmetic functions. Hence, the value of the expression

$2\times3+5$

is 16 (equivalent to $2\times(3+5)$), not 11 as you might expect. When you are writing APL, you must forget the normal precedences of arithmetic operations and remember the right-to-left rule.

The main advantage of the right-to-left rule is that you do not have to learn precedences for all of the novel APL functions. Furthermore, the rule extends to user-defined functions too, and it can be exploited to make APL expressions look like English. For example, because of the right-to-left rule, it is possible to define functions named *PRINT, LINES, THROUGH, OF, THE*, and *PAGE* in such a way that an expression like

PRINT LINES 2 THROUGH 5 OF THE PAGE

becomes a valid APL expression with an appropriate meaning. This possibility will be explored in detail in Chapter 7.

When you are learning APL, it is important to learn how to evaluate expressions by hand in a systematic way. An example will show how this can be done. Suppose the following assignments have been made:

$A\leftarrow4$
$B\leftarrow2$

and suppose that the expression to be evaluated is

$(B,B\times8\div12-A\times2)\rho3,A$

The first step is to find the subexpressions that must be evaluated, and to number them in the order of their evaluation. Notice that the right-to-left rule applies to the subexpression in parentheses as well as to the expression as a whole:

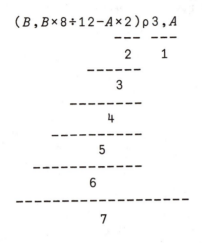

Next, the value of each subexpression is computed and written down. To avoid having to write a subexpression more than once, each subexpression can be represented by a number, which is bracketed here by the symbols ⊂ and ⊃:

Subexpression	composed of	has value
⊂1⊃	3,A	3 4
⊂2⊃	A×2	8
⊂3⊃	12-⊂2⊃	4
⊂4⊃	8÷⊂3⊃	2
⊂5⊃	B×⊂4⊃	4
⊂6⊃	B,⊂5⊃	2 4
⊂7⊃	⊂6⊃ρ⊂1⊃	3 4 3 4
		3 4 3 4

The last value is the value of the entire expression.

EXERCISES

2.10.1.   Evaluate the following expressions by hand systematically:

a.   ,2,3 4ρ5,6
b. 3 5ρρ2 3,[1]3 2ρ4 5 6

2.10.2.   Redo the exercises in Section 2.9, using as few parentheses as possible.

2.11   The Index Generator (ι)

The monadic *index generator* or *integer* function, is represented by the Greek letter
iota (ι). When applied to a positive integer, it yields a vector of the numbers 1,
2, 3, ... up to the given integer. By applying other functions to the result, one
can obtain various useful vectors. The following are some examples:

```
      ι6
1  2  3  4  5  6
      3+ι5
4  5  6  7  8
      ¯ι4
¯1  ¯2  ¯3  ¯4
      3×ι5
3  6  9  12  15
      6.5-ι5
5.5  4.5  3.5  2.5  1.5
```

The expression ι0 generates the empty numeric vector (just as 0ρ0 does).
Negative arguments for the iota function cause a *DOMAIN ERROR*, meaning
that the iota function is not defined on negative numbers.

The first number in a vector generated by iota is normally 1. However, the
origin for index generation can be changed from 1 to 0 by assignment to the
system variable □*IO* (which stands for "index origin"):

```
      □IO←0
```

Then ι6 will yield the vector 0 1 2 3 4 5 instead of 1 2 3 4 5 6.

Zero and 1 are the only two possible settings of the index origin. The value
of the index origin, □*IO*, is local to the current workspace and is saved when
the workspace is saved. (A clear workspace has index origin 1.) Changing the
index origin will affect the behavior of other functions besides iota. (See Appendix B for more details.) In this book the default origin of 1 will normally be
used.

EXERCISES

2.11.1. Suppose N is a variable whose value is a positive integer. Write expressions in terms of N which will generate the following arrays:

    a. A vector consisting of the first N perfect squares, such as

        1 4 9 16 25 36 49 64 81 100

    when N is 10.

    b. An $(N+1)$-by-$(N+1)$ matrix with the numbers 1 through N staggered as in the following example (where N is 3):

```
1   2   3   1
2   3   1   2
3   1   2   3
1   2   3   1
```

    c. An N-by-N matrix containing the numbers 1 through N-squared in reverse order, as in the following example, where the value of N is 4:

```
16  15  14  13
12  11  10   9
 8   7   6   5
 4   3   2   1
```

2.11.2. Write an expression to generate a 6-by-7 numeric matrix to represent the calendar for a month, as follows: Suppose a variable $FIRST$ gives the day of the week on which the month begins (from 1 for Sunday through 7 for Saturday), and suppose a variable $LENGTH$ gives the number of days in the month. Then the expression should generate a matrix like the following example, where $FIRST$ was 7 and $LENGTH$ was 31:

```
 0   0   0   0   0   0   1
 2   3   4   5   6   7   8
 9  10  11  12  13  14  15
16  17  18  19  20  21  22
23  24  25  26  27  28  29
30  31   0   0   0   0   0
```

2.12 Laminate (,)

Lamination is another way of joining arrays together. Like catenation, it is symbolized by a comma in APL, but unlike catenation, lamination results in an array of higher rank than its arguments. An example using vectors will illustrate the difference:

```
        A←1 2 3
        B←4 5 6

        A,B              Catenation yields
1 2 3 4 5 6              a longer vector.

        A,[.5]B          Lamination yields
1   2   3
4   5   6
```

a two-row matrix obtained by putting vector *A* on top of vector *B* like layers in plywood (hence the name *lamination*).

The two vectors can also be laminated in a different way, producing a two-column matrix:

        A,[1.5]*B*
    1   4
    2   5
    3   6

When the laminate function is applied, the number in brackets after the comma is not a whole number. Rather, it is a number that falls between the dimension numbers of the argument arrays. The number indicates where the new dimension is to be inserted into the shape vector to form the shape vector for the new array. In the foregoing examples, both ρ*A* and ρ*B* are one-element vectors with value 3. The number .5 in the expression

        A,[.5]*B*

indicates that the new dimension is to be inserted before the old first dimension, so that the shape of the result will be 2 3. In contrast, the number 1.5 in

        A,[1.5]*B*

indicates lamination with a new dimension after the old first dimension, so that the new shape will be 3 2. The size of the new dimension resulting from lamination is always 2.

Clearly, arrays being laminated must normally have identical shapes. However, as usual in APL, if one of the arguments is a scalar, it is replicated as many times as needed to fit the other argument. Consequently, an expression like

        '*ABC*',[1.5]'*X*'

which laminates a vector with a scalar will produce a matrix

    AX
    BX
    CX

Matrices, having higher rank than vectors, have more possible ways of being laminated together. While vectors can be laminated in two different ways, matrices can be laminated in three ways, as the following examples show:

```
S←3 4ρ'AAAABBBBCCCC'
T←3 4ρ'DDDDEEEEFFFF'
S
AAAA
BBBB
CCCC

T
DDDD
EEEE
FFFF
```

```
S,[.5]T
```
yields a three-dimensional array with two planes
```
AAAA
BBBB
CCCC

DDDD
EEEE
FFFF
```

```
S,[1.5]T
```
yields a three-dimensional array with three planes, two rows, and four columns
```
AAAA
DDDD

BBBB
EEEE

CCCC
FFFF
```

And finally,

```
S,[2.5]T
```
yields a three-dimensional array with three planes, four rows, and two columns
```
AD
AD
AD
AD

BE
BE
BE
BE
```

EXERCISES

2.12.1. Suppose *DATA* is a vector of numbers. Write an expression to create a two-column matrix in which the second column contains the values from *DATA* and the first column contains the numbers 1, 2, 3, and so on. For example, if

        DATA←31 28 31 30 31

then the expression should yield the matrix

        1 31
        2 28
        3 31
        4 30
        5 31

2.12.2. Suppose the assignment

        A←1 2 3

has been made. Then what will be the value of the following expression?

        4,[1.5]A,[1.5]5

2.12.3. Given a variable *S* whose value is an arbitrary character vector, write an expression to produce a new vector twice as long as *S* in which each character of *S* is followed by a blank. For example, if

        S←'ATTENTION'

then the result should be the vector

A T T E N T I O N

with one trailing blank and no leading blanks.

2.12.4. Redo Exercise 2.9.6 using the laminate function.

2.13 Subscripts

Subscripts for an APL array are written in square brackets. For example, if *A* is assigned

        A←1 3 5 7 9

then the value of

        A[2]

is the second element of *A*: the scalar number 3.

When a one-dimensional array is subscripted, there are two arrays taking part: (1) the vector being subscripted, and (2) the array being used as subscript. In APL a subscript can be an array of any rank: a scalar, vector, matrix, or higher-dimensional array. The following examples illustrate some of the possibilities:

$$STRING \leftarrow 'STOPS'$$
$$A \leftarrow 1 \ 3 \ 1$$

$STRING[4]$	—subscript a scalar
P	—result a scalar
$STRING[2 \ 3 \ 4 \ 1]$	—subscript a constant vector
$TOPS$	—result a vector of the same length
$STRING[A]$	—subscript a variable whose value is a vector
SOS	—result a vector of the same length
$STRING[2 \ 3\rho 1 \ 2]$	—subscript an expression whose value is a matrix
STS	—result a matrix of the same shape
TST	

Subscripting of a vector always creates an array with the same shape as the subscript array, but with values taken from the vector being subscripted.

In APL, constant arrays can be subscripted as well as variables. An example is the following expression, which yields the number of days in the month whose number is given by the variable $MONTH$:

$$31 \ 28 \ 31 \ 30 \ 31 \ 30 \ 31 \ 31 \ 30 \ 31 \ 30 \ 31[MONTH]$$

Another example is

$$CODE \leftarrow 19 \ 5 \ 3 \ 18 \ 5 \ 20 \ 27 \ 23 \ 15 \ 18 \ 4 \ 19$$
$$'ABCDEFGHIJKLMNOPQRSTUVWXYZ \ '[CODE]$$
$$SECRET \ WORDS$$

in which subscripting is used to convert a vector of numbers into a vector of characters by their positions in the alphabet.

Furthermore, expressions also can be subscripted in APL. A useful expression, for instance, if M is a matrix is

$$(\rho M)[1]$$

Its value is the number of rows in the matrix. Similarly,

$$(\rho M)[2]$$

gives the number of columns in the matrix.

EXERCISES

2.13.1.   Write an expression using subscripting to yield the last element in a vector V of arbitrary length.

2.13.2. Write an expression using subscripting to yield the reverse of a given vector V (e.g., If V has value 8 2 3, the result should be 3 2 8).

2.13.3. Suppose $DIGITS$ is a vector of decimal digits (numbers from 0 through 9). Write an expression using subscripting to produce the corresponding vector of digit characters. For example, if the value of $DIGITS$ is the numeric vector

9 0 2 3 9

then the value of the expression should be the character vector

90239

2.13.4. Suppose M is a matrix of integers 0 through 4 which represent directions of movement: 0—no movement; 1—up; 2—right; 3—down; 4—left. Write an expression that will produce a corresponding character matrix in which "no movement" is represented by blank and the other movements are represented by arrows. For example, if the value of M is

```
3   4   4   4   4
3   0   0   0   0
3   0   0   4   4
3   0   0   0   1
2   2   2   2   1
```

then the result should be the 5-by-5 character matrix

```
↓ ← ← ← ←
↓
↓     ← ←
↓        ↑
→ → → → ↑
```

2.13.5. Given a character vector ST and a character scalar CH, write an expression to create a two-row character matrix which contains the value of ST in the first row, and in the second row has an arrow beneath each copy of the character CH. For example, if the assignments

$ST←'CONSTANTINOPLE'$
$CH←'N'$

are made, then the expression should yield the 2-by-14 matrix

```
CONSTANTINOPLE
   ↑      ↑   ↑
```

When a two-dimensional array is subscripted, the row subscripts are separated from the column subscripts by a semicolon (;). Each subscript expression can be an array of any rank. For example, let M be the matrix

```
1   2   3
4   5   6
7   8   9
```

Then the following expressions will yield the values shown:

$M[2;3]$

6   —the element in row 2 and column 3

$M[1\ \ 3;1\ \ 2]$

1 2   —the elements in the first and third rows and
7 8   the first and second columns

$M[2;]$

4 5 6   —the second row

$M[;3]$

3 6 9   —the third column, as a vector

$M[;2\ \ 2]$

2 2   —the second column, taken twice to make a
5 5   two-column matrix
8 8

The examples illustrate two further facts about subscripting:

1. If the row subscripts or the column subscripts for a matrix are omitted, all of the subscripts for that dimension are supplied by default.

2. The shape of a subscripted matrix expression is the catenation of the shapes of the two subscript expressions. That is,

$\rho M[R;C]$ has the same value as $(\rho R),(\rho C)$.

Rule 2 explains why $M[;3]$ yields a vector rather than a one-column matrix. To get the third column of matrix M as a one-column matrix, one could write the expression $M[;,3]$ in which the column number 3 is raveled so that the overall shape of the result will be 3 1.

Subscripting of three-dimensional and higher-dimensional arrays is similar to subscripting of matrices: An array is used as subscript for each dimension, and the subscripts are separated by semicolons. The shape of the result is the catenation of the shapes of the subscript arrays. Thus, for a three-dimensional array A, the expression

$A[P;R;C]$

yields a new array composed of elements from the intersection of planes P, rows R, and columns C of A. Its shape is

$(\rho P),(\rho R),(\rho C)$

To take an example, suppose A is the 2-by-2-by-4 character array

$A\leftarrow 2\ \ 2\ \ 4\rho\,'PAGEONE\ PAGETWO\ '$

A

PAGE
ONE

PAGE
TWO

Then the expression

    A[1 2;2;1 2 3]

yields the 2-by-3 matrix

ONE
TWO

composed of elements taken from the first and second planes, the second row, and the first three columns of A.

EXERCISES

2.13.6. Redo Exercise 2.9.8 using subscripting.

2.13.7. Write an expression involving a variable A which will yield the string

SCALAR if the value of A is a scalar,
VECTOR if the value of A is a vector,
MATRIX if the value of A is a matrix, or
HIGHER if the value of A has rank greater than 2.

2.13.8. Let MONTH be a variable whose value is a number between 1 and 12, inclusive. Write an expression that will yield the three-letter abbreviation for the name of the corresponding month: JAN, FEB, MAR, APR, MAY, JUN, JUL, AUG, SEP, OCT, NOV, or DEC. (This can be done in at least two different ways, using subscripting.)

2.13.9. Write an expression to obtain the middle element from a matrix M with an odd number of rows and an odd number of columns.

2.13.10. Suppose the following assignments are made:

    SUITS←4 8ρ'SPADES   HEARTS DIAMONDSCLUBS   '
    VALUES←13 2ρ' A 2 3 4 5 6 7 8 910 J Q K'

Suppose HAND is a matrix with two columns, representing a hand of cards. Each row of HAND represents a card, the first column giving the suit (coded as 1, 2, 3, or 4) and the second column giving the value (between 1 and 13, inclusive). Write an expression using subscripts and involving HAND, VALUES, and SUITS to yield a character matrix which displays the hand. For example, if the value of HAND is the 3-by-2 numeric matrix

    2   8
    1   12
    3   1

then the result should be the 3-by-11 character matrix

    8 HEARTS
    Q SPADES
    A DIAMONDS

2.13.11. Sales of items in a fast-food chain are represented by a three-dimensional array *SALES* with dimensions (1) location (store number), (2) food item number, and (3) month number. Each cell of the array gives the quantity of a particular food item sold at a particular store in a particular month. Write expressions to print the following cross sections of the *SALES* array:

a. For a given item number, *ITEM*, a matrix showing sales by location and month.

b. For a given month number, *MONTH*, a matrix showing sales by location and item number.

c. For a given *LOCATION* and *ITEM*, a two-column matrix showing month numbers and sales for each month, like this:

```
1    3175
2    2926
3    2501
4    2873
```

and so on.

Test your answers using a small number of locations and items.

2.13.12. Let *M* be a matrix, and let *R*, *C*, and *LENGTH* be variables whose values are scalar numbers. Write an expression to obtain, as a vector, the elements of *M* starting in row *R* and column *C*, and extending downward for a total of *LENGTH* elements. For instance, if *M* is the 5-by-5 character matrix

```
A
SHORT
LIST
OF
WORDS
```

and *R* is 2, *C* is 1, and *LENGTH* is 4, then the result should be the four-character vector *SLOW*.

2.13.13. Suppose *M* is the 4-by-5 character matrix

```
PAGES
ONE
TWO
TEN
```

Consider the assignment statement

```
A←M[(3 2ρ1 2 1 3 1 4);ι4]
```

a. What will be the shape of *A*?

b. What will be the value of *A*?

Subscripting can also be used on the left side of an assignment arrow. In that case the value on the right side of the arrow is assigned to the subarray indicated by the subscripts. For example, the following sequence of statements causes the matrix shown to be printed:

```
MAT←5 5ρ0
MAT[2 3 4;3]←ι3
MAT
```
```
0   0   0   0   0
0   0   1   0   0
0   0   2   0   0
0   0   3   0   0
0   0   0   0   0
```

The expression on the right side of the assignment arrow should be either a one-element array (e.g., a scalar) or an array with the same number of elements as the subarray indicated by the subscripts. If a one-element array is used on the right, it is assigned to all of the elements of the subarray, as in the following example:

```
BIGH←5 5ρ'H'
BIGH[1 2 4 5;2 3 4]←' '
BIGH
```
```
H       H
H       H
HHHHH
H       H
H       H
```

If the same cells of the same array are referenced on both the left side and the right side of an assignment, as in

```
VECTOR←'ABCDE'
VECTOR[2 5]←VECTOR[5 2]
```

then the assignment works as it should: First, all of the required elements are selected from the array, and then they are all reinserted in their new places. The final result for the example is

```
VECTOR
```
```
AECDB
```

in which the second and fifth characters of the original vector have been exchanged.

Note the difference between the following two pairs of assignments:

```
A←1 1 1 1
A[1 2 3 4]←0

B←1 1 1 1
B←0
```

The second assignment in the first pair sets each element of the existing array A to 0, leaving a vector of four zeros. The second assignment in the second pair gives B a new value of scalar 0, changing its shape as well as its value. That is, assignment to a subscripted variable requires an already existing array and preserves its shape, but assignment to a nonsubscripted variable gives the variable a new shape as well as a new value.

EXERCISES

2.13.14. Suppose M is a matrix of unknown dimensions. Write a single assignment statement to exchange rows A and B of M, assuming that the values of A and B are valid row numbers for M.

2.13.15. Write a sequence of three assignment statements to produce the following 10-by-14 character matrix as the value of a variable $BIG8$:

```
 x x x x x x x x x x x x
x x x x x x x x x x x x x x
x x                x x
x x                x x
  x x x x x x x x x x x
   x x x x x x x x x x x
  x x            x x
  x x            x x
 x x x x x x x x x x x x x
  x x x x x x x x x x x
```

2.13.16. Let $PICTURE$ be a large character matrix, and let $ELEMENT$ be a smaller character array (for example, the sailboat array of Exercise 2.6.4). Let ROW and COL be variables whose values are scalar integers. Write an assignment statement to copy the value of $ELEMENT$ into the $PICTURE$ matrix so that its upper left corner is in row ROW and column COL of the $PICTURE$. You may assume that the value of $ELEMENT$ will fit within the value of $PICTURE$.

Chapter 3

User-Defined Functions

As we have seen, many things can be done in APL in calculator mode, without writing actual programs. However, APL also provides a facility for creating programs, which are called *user-defined functions*. Such a capability is needed for at least two reasons:

1. To provide a way of giving names to sequences of expressions, so they can be saved in the user's library, and so they can be reexecuted without having to be retyped.
2. To provide a way of extending the language beyond the set of functions which have been defined as primitives.

This chapter will deal with defining, editing, and using *straight-line* functions, without explicit branching or looping. Such functions are quite adequate for many applications of APL because of the power of APL's functions for processing arrays. Straight-line functions also have the advantage that they always terminate when they are executed; they cannot get into unending loops.

Discussion of the branch operation (→), which is used for coding explicit loops and conditional logic, is postponed until Chapter 5. Although branch is ultimately needed, reliance on branch instead of using the power of the APL primitive functions can make user-defined functions unnecessarily long and inefficient. When you are learning APL it is better to concentrate on the primitive functions for array processing, rather than to develop an early dependency on the use of branch.

3.1   Defining Functions

The *del* symbol (∇) is used to go from calculator mode to *function definition mode*. In the latter mode, expressions and statements which are typed are not evaluated immediately, but become part of the definition of a function. They are evaluated only later, when the function is executed.

The name of the function being defined goes in the *header line* of the function, which immediately follows the del for entry to function definition mode. The rules for forming function names are the same as the rules for forming names of variables. (See Section 2.1.) The header line also contains the names of any parameters or local variables for the function. An example is the header line of the *FARENHEIT* function from the first example session in Section 1.2:

> ∇ *F←FARENHEIT C*

It specifies the name of the function and indicates that the function has an input parameter, *C*, and an output parameter, *F*.

After the header line has been typed, APL responds by typing the number 1 in square brackets and waits for the user to type the first line of the function definition. In the case of the *FARENHEIT* function the first line was a comment line (indicated by the lamp symbol ⍝):

[1]   ⍝*CONVERTS TEMPERATURES FROM CELSIUS TO FARENHEIT*

and the second line, typed in response to the number 2 in square brackets, was an assignment statement:

[2]   *F←32+C×1.8*

To terminate a function definition and return to calculator mode, one types another del, as was done in the *FARENHEIT* function in response to the prompt for line number 3:

[3]   ∇ ·

Many versions of APL allow a comment at the end of any line. That is, all characters in a line to the right of a lamp symbol are treated as part of a comment (unless, of course, the lamp symbol is within a quoted character vector).

3.2   Displaying Function Definitions

Back in calculator mode one may print the definition of any function in the active workspace by typing

> ∇ name-of-the-function [□]∇

The two dels cause APL to enter function definition mode before printing the function and to return to calculator mode after printing the function. The *quad, window,* or *box* symbol (□) in square brackets indicates that all lines of the function are to be printed. For example, to display the *FARENHEIT* function, one types

> ∇*FARENHEIT*[□]∇

and the definition is printed as

```
    ∇   F←FARENHEIT C
[1]     ACONVERTS TEMPERATURES FROM CELSIUS TO FARENHEIT
[2]     F←32+C×1.8
    ∇
```

To list the names of all user-defined functions in the active workspace one types the system command

```
    )FNS
```

3.3 Kinds of Functions

A function can have zero, one, or two-input parameters and one optional output parameter. There are thus six possible forms for function headers, as shown in the following chart:

	Functions that return a value	Functions that do not return a value
Functions with no parameters ("niladic" functions)	∇ *RESULT←NAME*	∇ *NAME*
Functions with one parameter ("monadic" functions)	∇ *RESULT←NAME PARAMETER*	∇ *NAME PARAMETER*
Functions with two parameters ("dyadic" functions)	∇ *RESULT←LEFT NAME RIGHT*	∇ *LEFT NAME RIGHT*

Like primitive dyadic functions, dyadic user-defined functions have one argument on the left and the other on the right of the function name.

The restriction to at most two input parameters does not cause a great deal of inconvenience, for two reasons:

1. Since arrays can be used as arguments, many numbers or characters can be supplied to a function in one or two arrays.
2. Global variables and special input functions can also be used to supply data for a function. (These will be discussed later.)

The *FARENHEIT* function is an example of a monadic function that returns a value. An example of a niladic function that returns a value is the following function to create a large letter H in a 10-by-18 character array:

```
      ∇LARGEH[□]∇
   ∇   M←LARGEH
[1]      M← 10 18 ρ'HH',(14ρ' '),'HH'
[2]      M[5 6 ;]←'H'
   ∇

      LARGEH
HH                HH
HH                HH
HH                HH
HH                HH
HHHHHHHHHHHHHHHHHH
HHHHHHHHHHHHHHHHHH
HH                HH
HH                HH
HH                HH
HH                HH
```

The advantage of using a function in this way, rather than simply saving the matrix as the value of a variable, is that the function may require less space for permanent storage than would be required to store the matrix which the function creates. Thus the function can save space at the expense of the time needed to recreate the matrix each time the function is used.

Functions that do not return values are much like programs in other languages. They may call on other functions, and they may cause output to be printed during their execution. For if a line of a function is not an assignment statement, then the value of that line is printed as soon as the line is evaluated when the function is being executed.

For example, one can write a function to print a simple form letter as follows:

```
      ∇LETTERTO[□]∇
   ∇   LETTERTO ADDRESSEE
[1]      'DEAR ',ADDRESSEE,':'
[2]      ' '
[3]      '     YOU ARE INVITED TO OUR GRAND OPENING'
[4]      'NEXT MONDAY AT 9 O''CLOCK.'
[5]      ' '
[6]      (32ρ' '),'ABC COMPANY'
   ∇
```

Then typing

```
      LETTERTO 'MR. MASON'
```

(and pressing the RETURN key after inserting a clean sheet of paper) will cause the following letter to be printed:

```
DEAR MR. MASON:

     YOU ARE INVITED TO OUR GRAND OPENING
NEXT MONDAY AT 9 O'CLOCK.

                                ABC COMPANY
```

On many computer terminals the character set can be switched so that such a letter can appear in normal uppercase and lowercase letters rather than in uppercase only.

To take another example, a common practice for documenting APL workspaces is to include in each workspace a function called *EXPLAIN* or *DESCRIBE* which, when executed, prints an explanation of the workspace. The following is a short example:

```
      ∇ EXPLAIN
[1]     'THIS WORKSPACE CONTAINS FUNCTIONS FOR CONVERTING METRIC'
[2]     'MEASUREMENTS TO THEIR ENGLISH EQUIVALENTS AND VICE VERSA.'
[3]     'FOR EXAMPLE, THE FOLLOWING EXPRESSION CONVERTS TEMPERATURES'
[4]     'FROM THE CELSIUS SCALE TO THE FARENHEIT SCALE:'
[5]     ' '
[6]     '        FARENHEIT ¯40 0 5 10 15 20 25 30 100'
[7]     FARENHEIT ¯40 0 5 10 15 20 25 30 100
      ∇
```

3.4 Invoking Functions

A user-defined function that does not return a value can only be invoked by typing its name and arguments (if any) on a line by themselves, either in calculator mode or as a line in the definition of another function. A function that does not return a value cannot be used as part of a larger APL expression.

But a user-defined function that does return a value can be used in APL expressions in the same way that primitive functions are used. The right-to-left precedence rule applies to user-defined functions just as it does to primitive functions, and parentheses may be employed as usual to indicate scope explicitly.

Using the *FARENHEIT* function again as an example, suppose *HIGHS* and *LOWS* are assigned vectors of Celsius temperatures, as in the first example session of Section 1.2:

```
      HIGHS←3 ¯1 8 15 27 25 32 35 24 18 10 6
      LOWS←¯25 ¯22 ¯8 ¯3 ¯1 5 15 18 2 ¯4 ¯2 ¯10
```

Then, invoked by itself,

```
      FARENHEIT HIGHS
```

will cause the vector

```
37.4 30.2 46.4 59 80.6 77 89.6 95 75.2 64.4 50 42.8
```

to be printed, but if *FARENHEIT* is used in an expression like

```
      (FARENHEIT HIGHS)-FARENHEIT LOWS
```

the values returned by the calls to the *FARENHEIT* function will be subtracted to produce a vector of the differences between the high and low temperatures on the Farenheit scale:

```
50.4 37.8 28.8 32.4 50.4 36 30.6 30.6 39.6 39.6 21.6 28.8
```

Similarly, in the expression

$$HIGHS,[1.5] \; FARENHEIT \; HIGHS$$

the value of the *FARENHEIT* function will be laminated with the given vector *HIGHS* to produce a two-column matrix of the Celsius temperatures and their Farenheit equivalents:

3	37.4
⁻1	30.2
8	46.4
15	59
27	80.6
25	77
32	89.6
35	95
24	75.2
18	64.4
10	50
6	42.8

3.5 Local Versus Nonlocal Variables

Variables that are created by assignment in calculator mode or when a user-defined function is executed are normally *global*: Their values are available to all functions in the workspace, and they are saved when the workspace is saved.

Variables can be made *local* to a function by being listed at the end of the header line, following a semicolon and separated by semicolons, as in the following examples of header lines, in which the variables A, B, SUM, $L1$, and $L2$ are declared local:

$$\nabla \; PROGRAM;A;B;SUM$$

$$\nabla \; R \leftarrow FUNCTION \; V;L1;L2$$

Local variables created within a function are erased, along with their values, upon exit from the function. Hence, a good rule to follow, to avoid cluttering up your workspaces with unnecessary garbage, is:

Always declare variables used within a function to be local unless there is some good reason not to.

As an example, consider the following function. The variables $ROWS$ and $COLS$ have been declared local, since they are used only temporarily, to hold vectors of row and column subscripts. Once exit has occurred from the function, there is no further need for those vectors.

```
      ∇SUPERMATRIX[□]∇
  ∇   R←SHAPE SUPERMATRIX MATRIX;ROWS;COLS
[1]     ⍝ THIS FUNCTION CREATES A LARGE MATRIX COMPOSED OF MULTIPLE COPIES
[2]     ⍝ OF A GIVEN MATRIX. THE SHAPE PARAMETER SHOULD BE A VECTOR OF
[3]     ⍝ TWO NUMBERS INDICATING HOW MANY COPIES OF THE GIVEN MATRIX THERE
[4]     ⍝ ARE TO BE VERTICALLY AND HORIZONTALLY IN THE LARGE MATRIX.
[5]     ROWS←(ρMATRIX)[1]
[6]     COLS←(ρMATRIX)[2]
[7]     ROWS←(ROWS×SHAPE[1])ρ⍳ROWS
[8]     COLS←(COLS×SHAPE[2])ρ⍳COLS
[9]     R←MATRIX[ROWS;COLS]
  ∇
```

Before executing *SUPERMATRIX*, use of the *)VARS* system command indicates that there are no variables in the active workspace:

```
      )VARS
```

Then, creating a matrix *M*, applying the *SUPERMATRIX* function, and repeating the *)VARS* system command shows that the local variables *ROWS* and *COLS* do not remain in the workspace after *SUPERMATRIX* has finished executing:

```
      M←3 4ρ⍳12

      M
 1    2    3    4
 5    6    7    8
 9   10   11   12

      2 3 SUPERMATRIX M
 1    2    3    4    1    2    3    4    1    2    3    4
 5    6    7    8    5    6    7    8    5    6    7    8
 9   10   11   12    9   10   11   12    9   10   11   12
 1    2    3    4    1    2    3    4    1    2    3    4
 5    6    7    8    5    6    7    8    5    6    7    8
 9   10   11   12    9   10   11   12    9   10   11   12

      )VARS
M
```

If a local variable has the same name as a global variable, the global variable is not destroyed when the local variable is created. It becomes inaccessible while the local variable exists, but it and its value are restored when the local variable is destroyed.

Nonlocal variables can be used for communicating data to and from functions, especially in cases where two input parameters and one output parameter are not enough to do the job. For instance, Exercise 2.13.16 of Section 2.13 involved copying a matrix *ELEMENT* into a larger matrix *PICTURE*, with the upper left corner of *ELEMENT* in a specified *ROW* and *COLUMN* of *PICTURE*. Even if *ROW* and *COLUMN* are combined into a single *POSITION* vector, there are still three variables involved in the problem. So to make a function called *INSERT* to do the job, one might leave the *PICTURE* variable nonlocal, and define the function as follows:

```
        ∇   ELEMENT INSERT POSITION;ROWS;COLS
[1]        ROWS←¯1+POSITION[1]+ι (ρELEMENT) [1]
[2]        COLS←¯1+POSITION[2]+ι (ρELEMENT) [2]
[3]        PICTURE[ROWS;COLS]←ELEMENT
        ∇
```

The values of variables that are declared local to a function are also available to any function that is called by the given function, unless the called function declares the same variables to be local to itself. Thus, the following function, which uses the *INSERT* function, communicates with *INSERT* by means of the variable *PICTURE* as well as parameters. Although *PICTURE* is local to *FRAME*, and hence is erased upon exit from *FRAME*, it is not local to *INSERT* and so is available to *INSERT* when it is invoked in line [3] of *FRAME*.

```
        ∇FRAME[□]∇
        ∇   R←FRAME M;PICTURE
[1]        ⍝ PUTS A FRAME OF RECTANGLES AROUND A CHARACTER MATRIX
[2]        PICTURE←(2+ρM)ρ'□'
[3]        M INSERT 2 2
[4]        R←PICTURE
        ∇
```

The following sequence shows the effect of executing the *FRAME* function. Notice that the variables *PICTURE* (local to *FRAME*) and *ROWS* and *COLS* (local to *INSERT*) do not remain after execution of *FRAME*.

```
        )VARS
SAILBOAT

        SAILBOAT
```

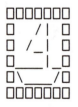

```
        FRAME SAILBOAT
```

```
□□□□□□□
□  /|  □
□ /_|  □
□___|_□
□\___/□
□□□□□□□
```

```
        )VARS
SAILBOAT
```

(Note: The *FRAME* function has been introduced here only to illustrate communication between user-defined functions. Exercise 2.9.1 already indicated a simpler way to do what *FRAME* does.)

3.6 Passing Arguments via Parameters

When a user-defined function is invoked, the arguments supplied for it pass data only into the function. Modifications a function makes to its input parameters are not made to the corresponding arguments of the function call. Hence the input parameters can be used like local variables within the function. (Technically, the input parameters of a user-defined function are called *call-by-value* parameters, since they receive only the values of corresponding arguments, not the actual names or locations of the arguments.)

For example, a function for extracting substrings from character strings might be defined as follows

```
        ∇SUBSTRING[□]∇
    ∇   SUB←STRING SUBSTRING POS
[1]     A EXTRACTS THE SUBSTRING OF STRING CONSISTING OF POS[2]
[2]     A CHARACTERS BEGINNING AT POSITION POS[1].
[3]     A WORKS ONLY FOR POS[1]>0 AND POS[2]≥0.
[4]     A IF POS RUNS OFF THE END OF STRING, AN EMPTY VECTOR IS RETURNED.
[5]     A RAVEL STRING IN CASE IT IS A SINGLE (SCALAR) CHARACTER:
[6]       STRING←,STRING
[7]     A CONVERT POS INTO A VECTOR OF SUBSCRIPTS:
[8]       POS←¯1+POS[1]+ιPOS[2]×(ρSTRING)≥POS[2]+POS[1]-1
[9]       SUB←STRING[POS]
    ∇
```

(Notice how line [8] handles the case in which the substring would run beyond the end of the string.)

```
      ⍝ TEST CASES:
      S←'EXAMPLE'
      S SUBSTRING 3 5
AMPLE
      S SUBSTRING 3 1
A

      R←S SUBSTRING 3 6
      ρR
0

      R←S SUBSTRING 4 0
      ρR
0

      S←'X'
      ρS

      POS←1 1
      R←S SUBSTRING POS
      R
X
      ρR
1
      S
X
      ρS

      POS
1 1
```

As the last example shows, the values of the arguments S and POS remain unchanged despite the changes $SUBSTRING$ makes to its parameters $STRING$ and POS.

3.7   Editing Functions

To edit a function one reenters function definition mode with the del symbol ∇ followed by the name of the function. Lines can then be inserted, replaced, or deleted in the function.

To insert or replace a line one types the desired line number in square brackets, followed by the new contents for the line. Fractional numbers are used to indicate insertions, and the header line can be indicated by typing [0]. To delete a line one types the line number in square brackets and preceded by a delta: [Δ8]. (Some older implementations of APL use a different method for deleting lines; so check your reference manual to be sure.) Lines are automatically renumbered to integers starting at [1] upon leaving function definition mode. (Again, some older implementations are different; they may require you to use a system command to renumber the lines of a function.)

To erase a function entirely from the active workspace, the system command)*ERASE* is used just as it is for erasing variables. For example,

```
)ERASE FUN1 FUN2 VAR
```

will erase the functions or variables named *FUN*1, *FUN*2, and *VAR*.

Function editing will be illustrated by making some changes to the *SUBSTRING* function from the previous section. Before editing, the definition of the function is

```
      ∇SUBSTRING[□]∇
   ∇   SUB←STRING SUBSTRING POS
[1]    ⍝ EXTRACTS THE SUBSTRING OF STRING CONSISTING OF POS[2]
[2]    ⍝ CHARACTERS BEGINNING AT POSITION POS[1].
[3]    ⍝ WORKS ONLY FOR POS[1]>0 AND POS[2]≥0.
[4]    ⍝ IF POS RUNS OFF THE END OF STRING, AN EMPTY VECTOR IS RETURNED.
[5]    ⍝ RAVEL STRING IN CASE IT IS A SINGLE (SCALAR) CHARACTER:
[6]     STRING←,STRING
[7]    ⍝ CONVERT POS INTO A VECTOR OF SUBSCRIPTS:
[8]     POS←¯1+POS[1]+⍳POS[2]×(ρSTRING)≥POS[2]+POS[1]-1
[9]     SUB←STRING[POS]
   ∇
```

Editing of the *SUBSTRING* function is shown below. Portions typed by the user have been underlined for clarity. The editing begins with a del symbol followed by the name of the function. The APL system responds by typing a new line number in square brackets, since it assumes the user may want to extend the function by adding lines to it. That line number is overridden by simply typing another line in square brackets. In the example, [8.1] is typed to indicate that a line is to be inserted between lines 8 and 9. The editing then proceeds:

```
      ∇SUBSTRING
[10]   [8.1]
[8.1] ⍝ EXTRACT THE SUBSTRING AND ASSIGN IT TO THE OUTPUT PARAMETER:
[8.2] [1]⍝ EXTRACTS THE SUBSTRING OF STRING CONSISTING OF
[2]    ⍝ POS[2] CHARACTERS BEGINNING AT POSITION POS[1].
[3]    [7.1]
[7.1] ⍝ (EMPTY IF THERE IS NO SUCH SUBSTRING OF THE GIVEN STRING)
[7.2] [Δ4]
[4]    [□]
```

Line 8.1 has been inserted; lines 1 and 2 have been replaced; line 7.1 has been inserted; and line 4 has been deleted. Then the quad in square brackets, [□], asks for a listing of the function, without leaving function definition mode. That listing shows the line numbers after the changes have been made and before renumbering:

```
        ∇    SUB←STRING SUBSTRING POS
[1]     ⍝ EXTRACTS THE SUBSTRING OF STRING CONSISTING OF
[2]     ⍝ POS[2] CHARACTERS BEGINNING AT POSITION POS[1].
[3]     ⍝ WORKS ONLY FOR POS[1]>0 AND POS[2]≥0.
[5]     ⍝ RAVEL STRING IN CASE IT IS A SINGLE (SCALAR) CHARACTER:
[6]      STRING←,STRING
[7]     ⍝ CONVERT POS INTO A VECTOR OF SUBSCRIPTS:
[7.1]   ⍝ (EMPTY IF THERE IS NO SUCH SUBSTRING OF THE GIVEN STRING)
[8]       POS←¯1+POS[1]+⍳POS[2]×(⍴STRING)≥POS[2]+POS[1]−1
[8.1]   ⍝ EXTRACT THE SUBSTRING AND ASSIGN IT TO THE OUTPUT PARAMETER:
[9]       SUB←STRING[POS]
        ∇
[10]    ∇
```

Notice that the system has typed line number 10 in square brackets after print-ing the listing of the function. That means that the system is still in function definition mode. So a del is typed on that line to leave function definition mode and return to calculator mode.

Finally, the edited function is listed again to show that the changes have been made and the lines have been renumbered:

```
        ∇SUBSTRING[⎕]∇
        ∇    SUB←STRING SUBSTRING POS
[1]     ⍝ EXTRACTS THE SUBSTRING OF STRING CONSISTING OF
[2]     ⍝ POS[2] CHARACTERS BEGINNING AT POSITION POS[1].
[3]     ⍝ WORKS ONLY FOR POS[1]>0 AND POS[2]≥0.
[4]     ⍝ RAVEL STRING IN CASE IT IS A SINGLE (SCALAR) CHARACTER:
[5]      STRING←,STRING
[6]     ⍝ CONVERT POS INTO A VECTOR OF SUBSCRIPTS:
[7]     ⍝ (EMPTY IF THERE IS NO SUCH SUBSTRING OF THE GIVEN STRING)
[8]       POS←¯1+POS[1]+⍳POS[2]×(⍴STRING)≥POS[2]+POS[1]−1
[9]     ⍝ EXTRACT THE SUBSTRING AND ASSIGN IT TO THE OUTPUT PARAMETER:
[10]      SUB←STRING[POS]
        ∇
```

The header line of a function may be replaced just like any other line. If the name of the function is changed when the header line is replaced, then the function is renamed within the workspace, as the following sequence shows*:

```
        )FNS
SUBSTRING

        ∇SUBSTRING[0]
[0]     SUB←STRING EXTRACT POS —the new header line
[1]     ∇

        )FNS
EXTRACT
```

---

* In some versions of APL, changing the name of a function by editing the header line creates a new function without destroying the old one.

```
      ∇EXTRACT[□]∇
  ∇   SUB←STRING EXTRACT POS
[1]    ⍝ EXTRACTS THE SUBSTRING OF STRING CONSISTING OF
[2]    ⍝ POS[2] CHARACTERS BEGINNING AT POSITION POS[1].
[3]    ⍝ WORKS ONLY FOR POS[1]>0 AND POS[2]≥0.
[4]    ⍝ RAVEL STRING IN CASE IT IS A SINGLE (SCALAR) CHARACTER:
[5]     STRING←,STRING
[6]    ⍝ CONVERT POS INTO A VECTOR OF SUBSCRIPTS:
[7]    ⍝ (EMPTY IF THERE IS NO SUCH SUBSTRING OF THE GIVEN STRING)
[8]     POS←¯1+POS[1]+⍳POS[2]×(⍴STRING)≥POS[2]+POS[1]-1
[9]    ⍝ EXTRACT THE SUBSTRING AND ASSIGN IT TO THE OUTPUT PARAMETER:
[10]    SUB←STRING[POS]
  ∇
```

Most versions of APL also have a facility for making changes within a line of a function. This is invoked by typing the line number followed by a quad symbol (□) and a number indicating the approximate position in the line at which the change is to be made, all in square brackets. For instance,

$$\nabla EXTRACT[\,4\,\square\,20\,]$$

indicates that line 4 of the $EXTRACT$ function is to be edited at about column 20.

The APL system then prints the line and waits below the indicated column for editing characters. These can be typed at any positions below the line, by use of the space bar and BACKSPACE key. Slash characters (/) indicate that the characters above them should be deleted. Digit characters or letters indicate that blank spaces should be inserted before the characters above them, as shown by the following table:

Character	indicates insertion of
1	1 space
2	2 spaces
3	3 spaces
4	4 spaces
5	5 spaces and so on
A	5 spaces
B	10 spaces
C	15 spaces
D	20 spaces and so on

An example is the following editing of line 4 of $EXTRACT$:

```
      ∇EXTRACT[4□20]
[4]    ⍝ RAVEL STRING IN CASE IT IS A SINGLE (SCALAR) CHARACTER:
                          //////////////////8
```

After the deletions and insertions have been indicated, the APL system types the modified line and waits for the user to type any desired characters in the blank spaces or at the end of the line:

```
[4]      ⍝ RAVEL STRING IN CASE IT IS              CHARACTER:
```

The user types the desired insertion characters and presses the RETURN key, which completes the editing of the line:

```
[4]      ⍝ RAVEL STRING IN CASE IT IS ONLY ONE CHARACTER:
```

A del may then be typed to leave function definition mode.

Even the numbers of lines can be edited. The effect is to create a new line without destroying the old one. That provides a way of moving lines, as shown below:

```
        ∇EXTRACT[7⎕2]
[7]      ⍝ (EMPTY IF THERE IS NO SUCH SUBSTRING OF THE GIVEN STRING)
        /3
[2.5]     ⍝ (EMPTY IF THERE IS NO SUCH SUBSTRING OF THE GIVEN STRING)
[2.6] [∆7]
[7]      [⎕]∇
     ∇    SUB←STRING EXTRACT POS
[1]      ⍝ EXTRACTS THE SUBSTRING OF STRING CONSISTING OF
[2]      ⍝ POS[2] CHARACTERS BEGINNING AT POSITION POS[1].
[2.5]  ⍝ (EMPTY IF THERE IS NO SUCH SUBSTRING OF THE GIVEN STRING)
[3]      ⍝ WORKS ONLY FOR POS[1]>0 AND POS[2]≥0.
[4]      ⍝ RAVEL STRING IN CASE IT IS ONLY ONE CHARACTER:
[5]       STRING←,STRING
[6]      ⍝ CONVERT POS INTO A VECTOR OF SUBSCRIPTS:
[8]       POS←¯1+POS[1]+⍳POS[2]×(⍴STRING)≥POS[2]+POS[1]-1
[9]      ⍝ EXTRACT THE SUBSTRING AND ASSIGN IT TO THE OUTPUT PARAMETER:
[10]      SUB←STRING[POS]
     ∇
```

(As usual the lines will be renumbered automatically upon leaving function definition mode.)

EXERCISES

3.1.   Write a function with header line ∇ $R←M$ *LINES* L to return the matrix consisting of the rows of matrix M indicated by the numbers in the vector L . You may assume that each number in L will be a valid row number for M.

3.2.   Write a function with header line ∇ $V←A$ *THRU* B which, given integers A and B where B is greater than or equal to A, will generate a vector V of the integers from A to B, inclusive. For instance,

```
     ¯2 THRU 3
```
should produce the vector

```
¯2 ¯1 0 1 2 3
```

Notice that this function, together with the one in Exercise 3.1, will permit one to write an APL expression like

```
     PAGE1 LINES 2 THRU 5
```

3.3. Write a function with header line ∇ $R \leftarrow QUOTE$ S which will return the string that results when a pair of quotation marks are catenated onto the ends of a given string. For example, if S is assigned

$$S \leftarrow 6\rho' \; '$$

then $QUOTE$ S should yield the string
'   '   (including the quotes)

This function is useful for testing other functions that yield character strings as values, since it shows exactly where a string begins and ends, including any leading or trailing blanks.

3.4. Write a function ∇ $BORDER$ CM to print a character matrix with a border of horizontal and vertical lines around it. (Like $QUOTE$, $BORDER$ is useful for testing other functions.) For example,

$$BORDER \;\; 2 \;\; 3\rho'ABC' \;\; \text{should print}$$

```
 ─────
|ABC|
|ABC|
 ─────
```

3.5. Redo Exercise 2.13.12 as a function ∇ $R \leftarrow M$ GET P which will extract from a matrix M the elements starting in row $P[1]$ and column $P[2]$ and extending downward for a total of $P[3]$ elements. For instance, if M is the 5-by-5 character matrix

```
A
SHORT
LIST
OF
WORDS
```

then

$$M \;\; GET \;\; 2 \;\; 1 \;\; 4 \;\; \text{should yield the four-character vector}$$
$SLOW$

You may assume that the elements specified by P lie entirely within M.

3.6. Consider the following sequence of function definitions and statements. What values will be printed in the places indicated by underlines? Explain.

```
      ∇FUN1;A
[1]   A←2
[2]   FUN2
[3]   ∇
      ∇FUN2
[1]   A
[2]   A←A+3
[3]   ∇
      A←1
      FUN1
      ___
```

A

3.7.   Write functions ∇ $L \leftarrow LENGTH$ A and ∇ $W \leftarrow WIDTH$ A which
will return the following values:
a. If A is a scalar, then both functions should return the value 1.
b. If A is a vector, then both functions should return the length of
the vector.
c. If A is a matrix, then $LENGTH$ should return the number of rows
in A and $WIDTH$ should return the number of columns in A.
You may assume that the rank of A is at most 2.

3.8.   Write a function ∇ $V \leftarrow M$ $ELEMENTS$ P to yield a vector V consisting of those elements of matrix M whose rows and columns are
given by the values in a two-column matrix P. Each row of P will
give the position of one desired element of M: $P[J;1]$ will give the
row number and $P[J;2]$ the column number of the Jth desired element. For example, if M is the matrix

```
1    2    3    4
5    6    7    8
9   10   11   12
```

and if P is the matrix

```
2   3
3   4
1   4
```

then

```
    M  ELEMENTS  P
```

should yield the vector

```
7  12  4
```

(*Hint:* Use ravel.)

3.9.   Write a function ∇ $R \leftarrow ADDLINENUMBERS$ A which will add a
column of sequence numbers to a numeric vector or matrix, as shown
by the following examples:

```
    ADDLINENUMBERS  8  12  ¯3
1    8
2   12
3   ¯3

    ADDLINENUMBERS  3  4ρ6
1   6   6   6   6
2   6   6   6   6
3   6   6   6   6
```

You may assume that the function will be applied only to vectors or matrices. The result should be a matrix, with the sequence numbers in the first column. (*Hint:* When catenate or laminate is used, an expression can appear in the square brackets following the comma.)

Chapter 4

More APL Primitive Functions

4.1 Additional Numeric Functions

The multiplication and division functions have monadic counterparts: The monadic *signum* function (×) yields a representation of the sign of its argument:

    1 if the argument is greater than zero
    ⁻0 if the argument is zero
    ⁻1 if the argument is less than zero

The monadic *reciprocal* function (÷) yields the result of dividing its argument into one. That is, the expression $÷A$ is equivalent to $1÷A$.

The monadic functions *floor* (⌊) and *ceiling* (⌈) round fractional numbers downward and upward, respectively, to the nearest whole number, as the following examples illustrate:

```
      ⌊2.01
2
      ⌊¯2.01
¯3
      ⌊¯2
¯2
      ⌈ 2.01 ¯2.01 ¯2
3 ¯2 ¯2
```

The function | used monadically yields the absolute value of its argument. For example,

```
      | ¯3 ¯2 ¯1 0 1 2 3 yields
3 2 1 0 1 2 3
```

Used dyadically, the | symbol represents the *residue* function. In its simplest use, with positive integers as arguments, the residue function yields the remainder when the right argument is divided by the left argument. For instance,

     5 | 13   yields
3

The number on the left is called the *modulus*, and the result is said to be the value of the right argument *modulo* the left argument (e.g., 3 is 13 modulo 5). In general, the value of $A \mid B$ is equal to the value of the following expression:

     $B - A \times \lfloor B \div A + A = 0$

For example, if A is $^-5$ and B is $^-17$ then tracing the expression yields the value $^-2$ for $A \mid B$, as shown below:

Expression	composed of	has value
⊂1⊃	$A = 0$	0
⊂2⊃	$A + $ ⊂1⊃	$^-5$
⊂3⊃	$\lfloor B \div $ ⊂2⊃	3
⊂4⊃	$A \times $ ⊂3⊃	$^-15$
⊂5⊃	$B - $ ⊂4⊃	$^-2$

Notice that when A is zero, the value of $A \mid B$ is the same as the value of B.

The residue function is defined for fractional numbers as well as for integers. For instance, if B is 2.385 then

     $1 \mid B$ yields
0.385

which is the fractional part of the value of B, and

     $.1 \mid B$ yields
0.085

the part of the fraction which is less than 0.1.

APL also provides functions for computing exponentials and logarithms:

   $\star A$ computes e^A, the exponential function of A,
   $\circledast A$ computes ln A, the natural logarithm of A, the inverse of
      the exponential function (the symbol $\circledast$ is O overstruck on $\star$).
   $B \circledast A$ computes $\log_B A$, the base B logarithm of A.

There are other functions for:

   Factorials: $!A$ is equal to $1 \times 2 \times 3 \times 4 \times \ \ldots \ \times A$.
   Binomial coefficients: $A!B$ is equal to $(!B) \div (!A) \times !(B-A)$
      (the number of A-element subsets which there are in a set of
      B elements).

Trigonometric functions:

1○A is the sine of A,
2○A is the cosine of A, and
3○A is the tangent of A.

Notice that the trigonometric functions all are applications of the same dyadic "circle" (○) function. The monadic circle function computes the value of PI times its argument. For example, the area of a circle of radius R is ○$R×R$ and the value of PI (its first 10 digits, rounded) is

```
      ○1
3.141592654
```

There are a number of other applications of the circle function, including inverse and hyperbolic trigonometric functions. However, those are beyond the scope of this book; consult your APL reference manual for details.

There is no separate function for square roots. The expression $A*.5$ (A to the one-half power) computes the square root of A.

EXERCISES

4.1.1.   Using the general definition given for the residue function, compute by hand the values of the following expressions:

```
  3 |  ¯17
 ¯3 |  17
 ¯3 | ¯17
1.5 | 4.75
1.5 | ¯4.75
¯1.5 | 4.75
¯1.5 | ¯4.75
```

4.1.2.   Write a function ∇ $R←INTEGER$ N whose value will be 1 if the value of N is an integer (i.e., a positive, zero, or negative whole number), and 0 if the value of N is not an integer. You may assume that the value of N will be a scalar number.

4.1.3.   Write a function ∇ $R←WHOLEPART$ X whose value will be the integer part(s) of the value of X, as illustrated by the following expression:

```
    WHOLEPART 2.01 ¯2.01 6
2 ¯2 6
```

4.1.4.   Using the logarithm function and other functions, write a function ∇ $D←DIGITSIN$ N to compute the number of digits there are in a given integer (or the number of digits in each member of an array of integers). Assume that the number zero has one digit. For example,

```
    DIGITSIN 237 0 ¯35589 10 1 should yield
3 1 5 2 1
```

4.1.5. Modify the function ∇ *V←A THRU B* of Exercise 3.2 (Chapter 3) so that it will work when *A* is greater than *B*, as well as when *A* is less than or equal to *B*. For example,

    3 *THRU* ‾5 should produce the vector
3 2 1 0 ‾1 ‾2 ‾3 ‾4 ‾5

4.1.6. Write a function ∇ *R←D ROUND N* to round off a number *N* to *D* decimal places to the right of the decimal point, if *D* is ≥ 0. If *D* is negative, *N* should be rounded in the appropriate position to the left of the decimal point. The rounding should be symmetrical, in the sense that digits 5 or greater cause rounding up of the digit to the left, while digits 4 or less cause rounding down of the digit to the left, regardless of the sign of the number being rounded. *ROUND* should also work if *D* and/or *N* is an array. The following are some examples:

      2 *ROUND* 12.745 ‾.345 .345 6.2049
12.75 ‾0.35 0.35 6.2

      ‾1 ‾2 ‾3 ‾4 *ROUND* 1234567
1234570 1234600 1235000 1230000

      2 0 ‾2 *ROUND* 555.555 444.555 666.555
555.56 445 700

(As usual, APL drops trailing zeros from fractional parts of the numbers printed.)

4.2   Maximum (⌈) and Minimum (⌊)

A⌈*B* yields the maximum of the values of *A* and *B*. The maximum function and the similar minimum function (dyadic ⌊) can be applied only to numeric values. For example

      3 ⌈ 1 2 3 4 5 6 yields
3 3 3 4 5 6   and
      1 2 3 4 5 6 ⌊ 6 5 4 3 2 1 yields
1 2 3 3 2 1

Among other uses, maximum and minimum can be used to provide default values when parameters of a function are outside of a valid range. For example, the following function pads a character string on the right end with blanks to a specified *LENGTH*. However, if the string is already as long as or longer than the given *LENGTH*, the string is returned without being padded. The maximum function is used here to provide a default value of zero for use by reshape, in cases where *LENGTH* is less than the length of *STRING*:

```
      ∇   S←STRING PADTO LENGTH
[1]       S←STRING,(0⌈LENGTH-ρ,STRING)ρ' '
      ∇
```

The *QUOTE* function of Exercise 3.3 can be used to display results of testing the *PADTO* function:

```
      QUOTE 'ABCDE' PADTO 8
'ABCDE   '
      QUOTE 'ABCDE' PADTO 5
'ABCDE'
      QUOTE 'ABCDE' PADTO 3
'ABCDE'
      QUOTE 'ABCDE' PADTO ‾2
'ABCDE'
      QUOTE 'ABCDE' PADTO 0
'ABCDE'
      QUOTE 'A' PADTO 3
'A  '
      QUOTE 'A' PADTO 1
'A'
      QUOTE 'A' PADTO 0
'A'
```

EXERCISES

4.2.1.   Write a function ∇ *S←STRING CHOPTO LENGTH* to return the result of truncating a given *STRING* on the right to a specified *LENGTH*. If the *STRING* is not longer than the given *LENGTH*, the value of *STRING* should be returned unchanged.

4.2.2.   Suppose *M* is a rectangular matrix. Write a function ∇ *S←SQUAREMATRIX M* which will return the largest square submatrix of *M* which contains the element *M*[1;1]. That is, the result will be either the top square part of *M* or the left square part of *M*, depending on whether or not *M* has more rows than it has columns.

4.2.3.   Rewrite the function *INSERT* from Section 3.5 so that it will work even if part or all of the given *ELEMENT* is outside the *PICTURE*. In that case, only the part inside the *PICTURE* should be inserted, as the following example illustrates:

```
      PICTURE←7 10ρ' '
      BORDER SAILBOAT
```

```
SAILBOAT INSERT  ¯2  0  —partly outside at upper left
SAILBOAT INSERT  ¯1   7  —partly outside at upper right
SAILBOAT INSERT   5  ¯1  —partly outside at lower left
SAILBOAT INSERT   6   8  —partly outside at lower right
SAILBOAT INSERT   8  ¯4  —outside PICTURE altogether
SAILBOAT INSERT   3   4  —in the center of PICTURE
BORDER PICTURE
```

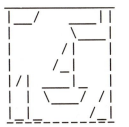

4.3 Logical Functions

Logical functions apply to the Boolean values 1 (true) and 0 (false). Their *truth table* definitions can be given by applying them to vectors which provide all of the possible combinations of arguments 1 and 0 for them:

```
    0  0  1  1  ∧  0  1  0  1  (and)
0  0  0  1
```

```
    0  0  1  1  ∨  0  1  0  1  (or)
0  1  1  1
```

```
    ~  0  1                    (not)
1  0
```

```
    0  0  1  1  ⊼  0  1  0  1  (nand - ⊼ is ~ over ∧)
1  1  1  0
```

```
    0  0  1  1  ⊽  0  1  0  1  (nor - ⊽ is ~ over ∨)
1  0  0  0
```

```
    0  0  1  1  ≠  0  1  0  1  (exclusive or, or inequivalence)
0  1  1  0
```

```
    0  0  1  1  =  0  1  0  1  (equivalence)
1  0  0  1
```

Notice that $A \mathbin{⊼} B$ is equivalent to $\sim(A \wedge B)$ and $A \mathbin{⊽} B$ is equivalent to $\sim(A \vee B)$.

The truth tables for the logical functions can be displayed in a clearer way by writing functions like the following function, which displays the truth table for the *and* function:

```
      ∇   ANDTABLE;A;B
[1]        '  '
[2]        '  A  B  A∧B'
[3]        A← 0  0  1  1
[4]        B← 0  1  0  1
[5]        A,B,[1.5]A∧B
      ∇

          ANDTABLE

A  B  A∧B
0  0  0
0  1  0
1  0  0
1  1  1
```

Logical functions are used, among other things, to combine the values of comparison functions. For example, the following is a revision of the *SUBSTRING* function from Section 3.6 so that it will yield an empty result in more cases in which incorrect values are given for the *POS* parameter. In particular, an empty string will result if the starting position for the substring is less than or equal to zero, if the length specified for the substring is less than (or equal to) zero, or if the substring would run off the end of the *STRING*:

```
      ∇   SUB←STRING SUBSTRING POS;OK
[1]        STRING←,STRING
[2]        OK←(POS[1]>0)∧(POS[2]≥0)∧(ρSTRING)≥POS[2]+POS[1]−1
[3]        POS←¯1+POS[1]+⍳POS[2]×OK
[4]        SUB←STRING[POS]
      ∇

          S←'EXAMPLE'

          S SUBSTRING 3   5
AMPLE

          S SUBSTRING 1   4
EXAM

          S SUBSTRING 0   2

          S SUBSTRING 3   6

          S SUBSTRING 4  ¯1

          ρ S SUBSTRING 4  ¯1
0
```

Since logical functions, like many other APL functions, can be applied to arrays, they can be used to combine Boolean patterns. For example, suppose *F* and *L* are two character matrices of the same shape which contain patterns represented by blanks and a single kind of nonblank character:

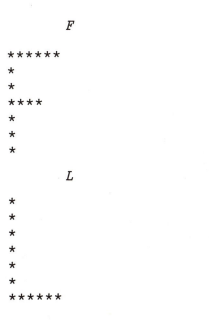

```
        F
* * * * * *
*
*
* * * *
*
*
*

        L
*
*
*
*
*
*
* * * * * *
```

Then their overlap (intersection) can be formed by the expression

$$' \star '[1+(F='\star')\wedge(L='\star')]$$

```
*
*
*
*
*
*
*
```

and their union can be formed by the expression

$$' \star '[1+(F='\star')\vee(L='\star')]$$

```
* * * * * *
*
*
* * * *
*
*
* * * * * *
```

EXERCISES

4.3.1. Write a function ∇ $R \leftarrow LEAPYEAR\ YEAR$ which tests whether a given $YEAR$ is a leap year. The result should be 1 for true or 0 for false, as is usual in APL. Note: Years divisible by 4 are leap years, except for the century years which are not divisible by 400. (That is, 2000 is a leap year, but 1800, 1900, and 2100 are not.)

4.3.2. Extend Exercise 2.13.5 by writing an expression to point to two different kinds of characters, $CH1$ and $CH2$, in a string ST. For example, if

```
ST←'CONSTANTINOPLE'
CH1←'N'
CH2←'O'
```

then the expression should produce the two-row matrix

```
CONSTANTINOPLE
 ↑↑    ↑   ↑↑
```

4.3.3. What other functions which we have seen yield the same values as ∧ and ∨ do when applied to Boolean arguments?

4.3.4. The logical function "implies" has the following truth table:

A	B	A IMPLIES B
0	0	1
0	1	1
1	0	0
1	1	1

Although APL does not have a primitive function specifically to implement *implies*, there is a primitive function that is equivalent to the *implies* function when it is applied to Boolean arguments. What is that primitive function?

4.3.5. Write a function ∇ $N←YEAR$ $DAYSIN$ $MONTH$ to return the number of days in a given $MONTH$ (specified by number) of a given $YEAR$. If $YEAR$ is not an integer ≥ 1700, or if $MONTH$ is not an integer between 1 and 12, the result should be zero. Use the $LEAPYEAR$ function above, and the $INTEGER$ function (Exercise 4.1.2.).

4.4 Reduction (/)

Reduction, represented by the slash symbol (/), is a different kind of function than we have seen until now. It is called an *operator*. Instead of taking an array as its left argument, it takes a dyadic function as its left argument.

The effect of a reduction applied to a vector is the same as if the function on the left of the reduction were inserted between all the values in the vector. For example, the sum reduction

```
+/ 1 2 3 4
```

yields the same value as the expression

```
1+2+3+4
```

namely, 10.

Not all functions can be used on the left of reduction. In order to be used with reduction a function must (1) be a dyadic function, and (2) yield a scalar value when it is applied to two scalars. Such a function is called a *dyadic scalar function*. Most of the primitive dyadic functions introduced so far in this book are dyadic scalar functions. The exceptions are reshape (ρ), catenate, and laminate (**,**).

When reduction is used with nonassociative functions like minus, it is important to bear in mind that it is applied in keeping with the right-to-left precedence rule. For instance,

$$-/\iota 4 \qquad \text{yields the same value as}$$

$$1-2-3-4 \qquad \text{or}$$

$$1-(2-(3-4)) \qquad \text{which yields } ^-2.$$

Reduction can be performed along any dimension of an array. The number of the dimension to be used is indicated in square brackets after the slash symbol, in the same way as for catenate and laminate. The examples following illustrate reduction on a matrix M whose value is

```
5   1   3
2   6   4
```

$$\lceil/[2]M \qquad \text{(the largest element in each row)}$$

```
5   6
```

$$\lfloor/[1]M \qquad \text{(the smallest element in each column)}$$

```
2   1   3
```

The operator is called *reduction* because, by combining values along one dimension of an array, it reduces the number of dimensions by one.

The slash symbol by itself, without a number in brackets, always indicates reduction along the last dimension of an array. There is also an overstruck reduction symbol ⌿ (– overstruck on /) which indicates reduction along the first dimension of an array. (That is, ⌿ is equivalent to /[1].)

One must be careful not to confuse dyadic reductions with monadic functions using similar symbols. For example, it is an easy mistake to write

$$\lceil \ 2.5 \ 0 \ ^-2.4 \qquad \text{and get the value}$$

```
3   0   ¯2
```

$$\qquad \text{(the ceiling of each element in the vector)}$$

when you mean to write

$$\lceil/2.5 \ 0 \ ^-2.4 \qquad \text{and get the value}$$

```
2.5
```

$$\qquad \text{(the maximum of the elements in the vector).}$$

Reduction with the logical functions $\wedge$ and $\vee$ yields functions which are called *quantifiers* in logic. $\wedge/$ represents the quantifier *all*, and $\vee/$ represents the quantifier *some*. That is, if B is a Boolean vector, then

$$\wedge/B \qquad \text{determines whether or not all values in } B \text{ are}$$
$$\qquad \qquad 1 \text{ (true)}$$

$\vee/B$ determines whether at least one value in B is 1.

For example, if S is a character vector, then

$\wedge/S='\ '$ determines whether all characters in S are blank,

and

$\vee/S='\ '$ determines whether some character(s) in S are blank.

To see how the expression $\vee/S='\ '$ works, consider the assignment

$S\leftarrow'ONE\ BLANK'$

Then the subexpression

$S='\ '$ yields the Boolean vector

0 0 0 1 0 0 0 0 0

Now if or-reduction is applied to the Boolean vector, the value is obtained as shown below:

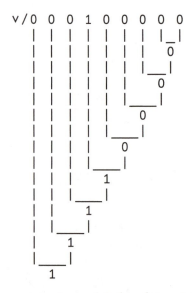

Reduction on empty vectors is useful for determining *identity elements* for dyadic scalar functions.* These are the initial values used when a reduction begins. For example,

$+/\iota 0$ yields

0   (the initial value for a sum reduction), and

$\times/\iota 0$ yields

1   (the initial value for a product reduction).

---

* For an associative function f (such as +, ×, $\lceil$, $\lfloor$, ∧, or ∨), reduction is defined in such a way that $f/A,B$ is equivalent to $(f/A)f(f/B)$ for arbitrary vectors A and B, including empty vectors. That determines the appropriate value for $f/\iota 0$.

Since a maximum reduction starts with the smallest possible number and increases it as the reduction proceeds, the expression

$\lceil / \iota 0$

will yield the smallest (i.e., most negative) number representable by whatever version of APL is being used. Likewise,

$\lfloor / \iota 0$

will yield the largest representable number.

When and-reduction is applied to an empty vector, the value produced is 1, but or-reduction applied to an empty vector yields 0. Those values are consistent with the usual definitions of logical *all* and *some* when they are applied to empty sets:

"All natives of the moon are green."

is considered true in logic, but

"Some natives of the moon are green."

is considered false (assuming there really are no natives of the moon). Thus in APL the expression

$\wedge / S = '$ $'$

applied to an empty string S yields 1 because all characters that there are (namely none) in an empty string are blank. However the expression

$\vee / S = '$ $'$

applied to the same empty string yields 0 because there are no characters, and hence no blank characters, in an empty string.

EXERCISES

4.4.1. Write an expression to count the number of blanks in a given $STRING$.

4.4.2. Write an expression to count the number of positive ($>$ 0) elements in a numeric $ARRAY$ of arbitrary rank and shape.

4.4.3. Write an expression to determine whether (1) or not (0) all numbers in a given numeric $VECTOR$ are integers (whole numbers).

4.4.4. Write an expression to determine whether (1) or not (0) the maximum value in a numeric $MATRIX$ occurs only once in the matrix.

4.4.5. Write a function ∇ $R \leftarrow TOTALS$ M to augment a given numeric matrix with row totals at the right, column totals at the bottom, and a grand total in the lower right corner. For example, if MAT is the matrix

```
 16   125    8
201    34   90
```

then *TOTALS MAT* should yield the matrix

```
 16   125    8   149
201    34   90   325
217   159   98   474
```

4.4.6. Write an expression to determine whether or not all values in a given *VECTOR* are equal to each other. Assume that the vector may contain either numeric or character data. Try to write an expression that will work even if *VECTOR* is empty; in that case the value of the expression should be 1.

4.4.7. Suppose *B* is a Boolean matrix, containing only ones and zeros. Write an expression to test whether each row and each column of *B* contains exactly one 1.

4.4.8. Write a function ∇ *V←MINIMAX M* to compute the "minimax" value of a matrix: the minimum of the maximum values in the columns. For example, if *A* is the matrix

```
 10   ‾100   20
‾20      5  100
  5     50   ‾5
```

then the value of *MINIMAX A* should be 10, since the maximum values in the columns are 10 50 100 and the minimum of those is 10. (The minimax value of a matrix is used in game theory.)

4.4.9. Given a matrix *GRADES* containing the following words:

EXCELLENT

VERY GOOD

GOOD

FAIR

POOR

and given a variable *SCORE* which is a number between 0 and 100, inclusive, write an expression to yield the word or phrase which corresponds to *SCORE*, according to the following specifications:

	SCORE < 60	*POOR*
60 ≤	*SCORE* < 70	*FAIR*
70 ≤	*SCORE* < 80	*GOOD*
80 ≤	*SCORE* < 90	*VERY GOOD*
90 ≤	*SCORE*	*EXCELLENT*

Note: It is all right for the word or phrase that results from the expression to have some trailing blanks.

4.5 Compression and Replication (/)

The compression function uses the same symbol (/) that is used for reduction. However, compression takes a Boolean vector as its left argument. It selects the values from its right argument which are in same positions as the 1's in its left argument. Thus,

      1 0 1 0 1 / *'STOPS'* yields

SOS

Compression can be thought of as eliminating the values from its right argument which are in the positions of the zeros in its left argument. That is, it *com-
presses* its right argument. Clearly, the Boolean vector on the left must have the
same length as the vector on the right.

The Boolean vector used on the left of compression often is the result of a
comparison function. By using a comparison with compression, one can select
from the right argument the values that pass a certain test. For example, the expression

$$(V>0)/V$$

will select from a vector V all values which are greater than zero.

Compression is frequently used with iota, the index generator, to convert a
Boolean vector into a vector of position numbers. For instance, if S is a character vector, then the expression

$$(S=' ')/\iota\rho S$$

will produce a vector consisting of the subscript numbers of the blanks in S.

A scalar 1 or 0 can be used as the left argument of compression. In that case,
the scalar is implicitly reshaped to fit the right argument, and the result of the
compression is either the entire right argument or an empty array, depending on
whether the left argument is 1 or 0. Compression by a scalar can be used, for
example, to create strings containing optional characters, as in the expression

$$'CHILD',(NUMBER\neq 1)/'REN'$$

which produces the word *CHILD* if *NUMBER* is equal to 1 and produces the
word *CHILDREN* if *NUMBER* is not equal to 1.

When compression is applied to a matrix or higher-dimensional array, it
selects rows, columns, planes, or hyperplanes of the right argument. The left argument is always a Boolean vector (or scalar). A number in square brackets is
used after the slash symbol to indicate the dimension along which the compression is to be performed. For example, suppose M is the following numeric matrix

```
  25   ¯1273      0
   0       0      0
 ¯17     982     34
   0      ¯3      0
   0       0      0
   0       0      0
   1      ¯9   9000
```

Then the following expression eliminates the rows that contain only zeros:

$$(\vee/M\neq 0)/[1]M$$

```
  25   ¯1273      0
 ¯17     982     34
   0      ¯3      0
   1      ¯9   9000
```

Notice how reduction is used to find the rows of *M* which contain at least one nonzero element. Then compression is used to select those rows.

Compression without a dimension number in brackets always results in compression along the last dimension of an array, the column dimension. Compression along the first dimension of an array can be indicated either by /[1] or by the overstruck symbol ⌿.

EXERCISES

4.5.1.   Write an assignment statement to remove all of the blanks from a given *STRING*.

4.5.2.   Write an expression that will select from a numeric vector *VEC* all elements that are between 10 and 60, inclusive.

4.5.3.   Given a character matrix *PAGE* representing a page of English text, write an expression to extract from *PAGE* the first line of each paragraph. That is, the result should be a new matrix containing those lines of *PAGE* which are blank in the first column but are not entirely blank.

4.5.4.   Given a numeric vector *VEC*, write an assignment statement to replace all negative elements of *VEC* by the smallest non-negative element in *VEC*. Thus, if *VEC* initially is the vector

   8 ‾6 3 ‾2 ‾1 5

then its value after the assignment should be

   8 3 3 3 3 5

You may assume that *VEC* has at least one non-negative element.

4.5.5.   Given a numeric vector *VEC*, write an expression to produce a new vector containing the same elements as *VEC*, but with all of the negative elements moved to the front. For example, if *VEC* is the vector in Exercise 4.5.4, the result should be

   ‾6 ‾2 ‾1 8 3 5

4.5.6.   Suppose *NAMES* is a matrix containing the names of marathon runners, such as

   BACHELER
   BEDANE
   FOSTER
   HILL
   KIMIHARA
   LISMONT
   MACGREGOR
   MOORE
   SHORTER
   WOLDE

and suppose $TIMES$ is a three-column numeric matrix containing a corresponding list of times for their runs (in hours, minutes, and seconds):

2	17	38.2
2	18	36.8
2	16	56.2
2	16	30.6
2	16	27
2	14	31.8
2	16	34.4
2	15	39.8
2	12	19.8
2	15	8.4

Suppose finally that $CUTOFF$ is a three-element numeric vector representing an elapsed time in hours, minutes, and seconds. Write an expression to create a matrix containing the names of the runners whose times are less than the $CUTOFF$ value.

4.5.7.   Write a function $\nabla R \leftarrow CH\ BLANKOUT\ S$ to return the result of replacing each copy of character CH in string S by a blank.

4.5.8.   Write a function

$\nabla\ R \leftarrow FOREGROUND\ OVERLAYON\ BACKROUND$

whose value is the result of replacing all blanks in a character vector $FOREGROUND$ by the corresponding a characters in a character vector $BACKGROUND$ which has the same length as $FOREGROUND$. For example,

      'THIS   THAT' OVERLAYON 'DAYS AND DAYS'
      should yield
THIS AND THAT

4.5.9.   Modify the solution to Exercise 4.5.7 so that the function $\nabla\ R \leftarrow CH\ BLANKOUT\ S$ will work for an array S of any rank and shape.

4.5.10. Modify the solution to Exercise 4.5.8 so that the $OVERLAYON$ function will work when $FOREGROUND$ and $BACKGROUND$ are any character arrays of the same rank and shape (or when $BACKGROUND$ is a scalar). This generalized version of $OVERLAYON$, along with the general version of $BLANKOUT$ from Exercise 4.5.9, can be used to combine separate character matrices into pictures. For example, suppose $SAILBOAT$ and $WATER$ are the following character matrices (displayed using the $BORDER$ function of Exercise 3.4):

BORDER SAILBOAT

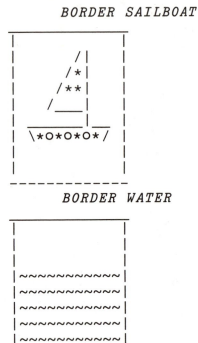

BORDER WATER

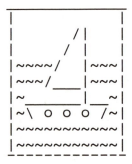

Then *SAILBOAT* and *WATER* can be combined into a single picture
as follows:

BORDER '' BLANKOUT SAILBOAT OVERLAYON WATER*

```
 _____
|              |
|        / |   |
|       /  |   |
|~~~~/     |~~~|
|~~~/____  |~~~|
|~_____|__~ |
|~\  o  o  o /~|
|~~~~~~~~~~~~~~|
|~~~~~~~~~~~~~~|
 --------------
```

In some versions of APL the compression function has been extended to accept a vector of non-negative integers as the left argument. The extended function is called the *replication* or *replicate* function. Each number in the left argument

indicates how many times the corresponding element (or row, column, or plane) of the right argument is to be repeated in forming the result. The following examples illustrate the use of replicate:

```
      1  1  0  2  1  1  1/'SEATING'
SETTING
      3/'-*-*-'
---**---**---
      3/[1] 2 1/2 2ρ⍳4
1  1  2
1  1  2
1  1  2
3  3  4
3  3  4
3  3  4
```

Notice that a scalar left argument is extended, as usual, to match the size of the appropriate dimension of the right argument.

As an example of an application of replication, suppose S is a character vector such as

```
      S←'THIS SHORT  TEST  STRING'
```

Then the following expression will replicate each blank in S N times:

```
      (1+(N-1)×S=' ')/S
```

If the value of N is 4, the result will be

```
THIS    SHORT      TEST      STRING
```

ion is useful for systematically distorting patterns that are represented
    character matrices. For instance, it is possible to form large letters of various
sizes and shapes from a single stored pattern, as shown by the following example:

```
      BIGF←4 3ρ'FFFF  FF F  '
      BIGF
FFF
F
FF
F
      2 2 2 3/[1]2/BIGF
FFFFFF
FFFFFF
FF
FF
FFFF
FFFF
FF
FF
FF
      2 3 2 4/[1]3 5 5/BIGF
FFFFFFFFFFFF
FFFFFFFFFFFF
FFF
FFF
FFF
FFFFFFF
FFFFFFF
FFF
FFF
FFF
FFF
```

EXERCISES

4.5.11.   Suppose *PAGE* is a character matrix. Write an expression to double
           each line of *PAGE* which is entirely blank.

4.5.12.   Let *TICTACTOE* be the matrix created by the following assignment:

```
      TICTACTOE←5 5ρ' | |  -+-+- | |  -+-+- | |  '
      TICTACTOE

   | |
  -+-+-
   | |
  -+-+-
   | |
```

Write expressions applying replication to *TICTACTOE* to produce the following patterns as character matrices:

a.   b.   c.

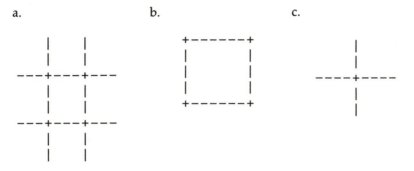

4.5.13.   Write a function

   ∇ *B←BOARDSIZE CHECKERBOARD SQUARESIZE*

which will produce a checkerboard pattern of "squares" made of `'×'` and blank characters. The right argument should indicate the shape of each square in the checkerboard, and the left argument should indicate the numbers of rows and columns of squares. For example:

        2 4 *CHECKERBOARD* 3 5

```
××××× 	 ×××××
××××× 	 ×××××
××××× 	 ×××××
        ×××××        ×××××
        ×××××        ×××××
        ×××××        ×××××
```

4.6 Membership (∈)

The dyadic *membership* function, represented by the Greek letter epsilon (∈), tests each element of its left argument to see whether it is an element of the right argument. Both arguments can be arrays of any rank and shape, not necessarily the same. The result is a Boolean array with the same rank and shape as the left argument.

For example, to test whether an array A contains any zeros, one can write simply

        0∈*A*

and the result will be a scalar 0 or 1. Similarly, the following expression can be used to test whether a character array C contains only digit characters:

        ∧/(,*C*)∈'0123456789'

Membership can be used with compression to extract the elements of a vector which are members of another array. For example, the expression

        (*STRING*∈'0123456789')/*STRING*

will produce a vector containing just the digit characters from a given character vector $STRING$.

The index generating function (ι) can be used with membership to convert a vector of small positive integers into a Boolean vector with 1's in the positions corresponding to the given integers. For instance, if VEC is the vector

8 3 10 2 1 5 12

then the expression

$$(\iota\lceil/VEC)\epsilon VEC$$

yields the Boolean vector

1 1 1 0 1 0 0 1 0 1 0 1

which has 1's in positions 8, 3, 10, 2, 1, 5, and 12.

EXERCISES

4.6.1. Using membership and other functions, write an expression that yields the result of deleting all commas, periods, and semicolons from a given $STRING$. The punctuation marks should be deleted, not replaced by blanks.

4.6.2. Suppose M is a numeric matrix. Write an assignment statement to set to zero all elements of M which are not integers between 1 and 10, inclusive. Use the membership function.

4.6.3. Write an expression to count the number of vowels (A E I O U) there are in a given $WORD$.

4.6.4. Redo Exercise 4.3.5 (the function ∇ $N\leftarrow YEAR$ $DAYSIN$ $MONTH$) using the membership function to test for validity of the $MONTH$ parameter.

4.6.5. Write a function ∇ $I\leftarrow S$ $INTERSECT$ T which will compute the set intersection of vectors S and T. That is, the result should be a vector containing all elements of S which are also in T. Assume that S and T each contain no repeated values.

4.6.6. Write a function ∇ $U\leftarrow S$ $UNION$ T which will compute the set union of vectors S and T: a vector that contains all elements that are in S or T or both. As in Exercise 4.6.5, assume that S and T each contain no repeated values. The result should also have no repeated values.

4.6.7. Modify the function ∇ $R\leftarrow CH$ $BLANKOUT$ S of Exercises 4.5.7 and 4.5.9 so that it will replace by blanks all characters in array S which are also in CH. The result should have the same rank and shape as S.

4.6.8. Suppose VEC is a vector of small positive integers, such as

2 5 7 2 12 6 20 9 7 2

Write an expression using the membership function and others to create a vector which contains one copy of each element from the original vector, and which has its elements in ascending order. The result for the example *VEC* should be

```
2  5  6  7  9  12  20
```

4.7   Index (ι)

The dyadic *index* function, represented by the Greek letter iota (ι), takes a vector (or scalar) as its left argument. Its right argument can be of any rank and shape, and the result has the same rank and shape as the right argument. Each element in the resulting array gives the position in the left argument of an item in the right argument, as the following examples illustrate:

```
        M
SAMPLE
MATRIX

        'ABCDEFGHIJKLMNOPQRSTUVWXYZ' ι M
19   1   13   16   12    5
13   1   20   18    9   24

        YEARS
1980  1976  1982  1981  1980  1982

        YEARS ι 1980 1981 1982
1  4  3
```

Notice that each element of the right argument is looked up separately in the left argument, and that the position of the first match is used if an item on the right occurs more than once on the left. If the left argument is a scalar, it is treated as if it were a one-element vector.

If an element is not found in the left argument, the result for that element is one more than the length of the left argument. Thus,

```
        'EXAMPLE' ι 'AEIOU' yields
3  1  8  8  8
```

and

```
        'AEIOU' ι 'EXAMPLE' yields
2  6  1  6  6  6  2
```

That fact can be exploited in various ways. For instance, the following expression will yield the result of blanking out all characters in a given array which are not in a specified *ALPHABET* vector:

```
        (ALPHABET,' ')[ALPHABETιARRAY]
```

EXERCISES

4.7.1.   Write an expression using the index function and subscripting to get the substring of a given *STRING* which consists of all characters up to, but not including, the first blank. If the given string contains no blanks, the result should be the entire string.

4.7.2.   Write an expression to find the position of the first vowel (A E I O or U) in a given $STRING$. If the string contains no vowels, the result should be zero. (This exercise can be solved in at least two different ways, one using the membership function.)

4.7.3.   Write a function ∇ $P \leftarrow STRING$ $VERIFY$ $ALPHABET$ to find the position of the first character in vector $STRING$ which is not in vector $ALPHABET$. If all characters in $STRING$ are in $ALPHABET$ the result should be zero. (This function is similar to a function in the PL/I programming language.)

4.7.4.   Write a function ∇ $B \leftarrow SETTEST$ V using the index function to test whether (1) or not (0) all elements of a given vector are different from one another (i.e., whether or not the vector forms a set).

4.7.5.   Write a function ∇ $R \leftarrow MAKESET$ V to make a given vector into a set by returning only one copy of each different element in the vector. For example,

> $MAKESET$ '$ABRACADABRA$' should yield the vector
> $ABRCD$

(Note: The solution here should be more general than that for Exercise 4.6.8. $MAKESET$ should apply to character data and to numbers of any size.)

4.7.6.   Write an expression to compute the row number of the first row in a given numeric matrix M which contains a zero. If M has no zeros, the result should be 1 + the number of rows in M.

4.7.7.   Write a function ∇ $D \leftarrow DIGITVECTOR$ S to take a string of digit characters and return the corresponding numeric vector of digits. For example,

> $DIGITVECTOR$ '1982' should yield the vector
> 1 9 8 2

4.7.8.   Suppose S is a character vector or scalar, and A is a two-row character matrix. Write a function ∇ $R \leftarrow S$ $REPLACE$ A to yield the result of replacing each character of S that occurs in row 1 of A by the character that occurs in the same column of row 2 of A. For example, if A is the 2-by-4 matrix

[]<>
()()

then

> '[<A+2>×B<3>]' $REPLACE$ A should yield
> ((A+2)×B(3))

4.7.9.   Suppose M is a character matrix containing arrows $\uparrow$ $\rightarrow$ $\downarrow$ $\leftarrow$ representing compass directions. Write a function ∇ $R \leftarrow DIRECTIONS$ M

to produce a corresponding numeric matrix giving the directions in positive degrees from north. For instance, if M is

→↑↓

↑←↓

then the result should be

```
90     0   180
 0   270   180
```

4.8   Take (↑) and Drop (↓)

The dyadic *take* function (↑) gets an initial part (prefix) or final part (suffix) from its right argument vector. The left argument tells how many elements are to be included in the prefix or suffix taken. A positive left argument indicates that the elements are to be taken from the beginning of the right argument; a negative left argument indicates that they are to be taken from the end. The following are some examples:

```
        S←'ABCDEF'
        3↑S
ABC
        ¯2↑S
EF
        ¯2↑4↑S
CD
```

Take also works with scalars: $1↑2$ has the same value as $,2$.

If the left argument of take specifies more items than the right argument contains, then zeros or blanks are supplied (depending on whether the right argument is a numeric or character array) to produce a vector of the indicated length. That feature is useful for padding character strings with blanks to a specified length, as the following examples show. (The $QUOTE$ function from Exercise 3.3 has been used to show where the strings begin and end.)

```
        QUOTE 6↑'ABC'
'ABC   '
        QUOTE ¯6↑'ABC'
'   ABC'
```

When take is applied to an empty vector, $1↑\iota 0$ yields a vector containing the number zero, while $1↑'$ $'$ yields a vector containing a single blank character. That fact, together with the fact that $0='$ $'$ yields the value 0, can be used to devise a test to distinguish numeric arrays from character arrays. (See Exercise 4.8.1.)

The dyadic *drop* function (↓) does essentially the opposite of take: It deletes a prefix or suffix of specified size from its right argument. For example,

```
        3↓\iota 6                yields
4  5  6
```

and

$$^-3\downarrow'WALKING'\qquad\text{yields}$$

WALK

If the left argument has an absolute value larger than the length of the right argument, the result is empty.

The index function can be used to compute a left argument for take or drop. For instance, if S is a string of words, each followed by a single blank, the following statements will remove the first word from S and assign it to the variable $WORD$:

$$P\leftarrow S\iota'\ '$$
$$WORD\leftarrow(P-1)\uparrow S$$
$$S\leftarrow P\downarrow S$$

The drop function is also useful for shifting a vector to the right or left. For example, to test whether the values in a numeric vector V are in ascending order, one can use the expression

$$\wedge/(^-1\downarrow V)\leq 1\downarrow V$$

which compares each element of the vector, except the last, with the element that follows it. Notice that the expression can be considered to be almost a phrase-by-phrase translation from English:

$\wedge/$	$(^-1\downarrow V)$	$\leq$	$1\downarrow V$
all	elements of V except the last	are less than or equal to	their successors in V

Take and drop can also be applied to matrices and higher-dimensional arrays. To take or drop elements from a matrix, a vector of two numbers is used as the left argument, the first for the number of rows to be taken or dropped, and the second for the number of columns. The following are some examples (using the $BORDER$ function from Exercise 3.4):

```
      BORDER M
 _____
|WHENEVER|
|SOMEONE |
|KNOWHOW |
|WHATEVER|
 -----------
```

        BORDER $^-$3 4$\uparrow$M   (taking the last three rows and first four columns)

```
 _____
|SOME|
|KNOW|
|WHAT|
 ------
```

        BORDER 2 4$\downarrow$M   (dropping the first two rows and first four columns)

```
 _____
|HOW |
|EVER|
 -----
```

```
          ¯4  ¯4  ↑  3  3ρι9
  0   0   0   0
  0 , 1   2   3
  0   4   5   6
  0   7   8   9
```

Notice how zeros have been supplied in the last case to make four rows and four columns.

EXERCISES

4.8.1.   Write a function ∇ *B←NUMERIC A* using the take function and others to determine whether (1) or not (0) a given array of arbitrary rank and shape contains numeric data (as opposed to character data). For instance, *NUMERIC* 1 2 3 should yield 1, but *NUMERIC* '123' should yield 0.

4.8.2.   Given—a—numeric—vector—*VEC*, write an expression to compute the differences between the successive elements in *VEC*. (If *VEC* is 8 12 20 23 the result should be 4 8 3.)

4.8.3.   Write an expression to find the position of the first value in a numeric vector *VEC* which is less than its predecessor. If *VEC* is in nondescending order, the value should be zero.

4.8.4.   Write a function ∇ *R←SQUEEZE S* to return the result of removing from a given string all initial and final blanks and all blanks that are followed by other blanks. For example (using the *QUOTE* function from Exercise 3.3)

         QUOTE   SQUEEZE ' A STRING OF   WORDS   '
should yield

'A STRING OF WORDS'

If the given string is all blank or empty, the result should be the empty vector.

4.8.5.   Suppose *A* is a scalar, vector, or matrix. Write an expression whose value is the result of reshaping the value of *A* into a matrix: with one row and one column if *A* is scalar; with one row and ρ*A* columns if *A* is a vector; or the same shape as *A* if *A* is a matrix.

4.8.6.   Suppose *PAGE* is a global variable whose value is a character matrix representing a page of text. Suppose *LINE* is a global variable whose value is a character vector representing a line to be added to the bottom of the page. Write a function ∇ *ADDLINE* (with no parameters) to pad *PAGE* or *LINE*, whichever is narrower, on the right with blanks and then catenate the value of *LINE* onto the bottom of *PAGE*.

4.8.7.   Suppose *A* and *B* are two character vectors that are treated as strings. Write a function ∇ *R←A LEXLESS B* to test whether (1) or not (0) string *A* is less than string *B* in lexicographic (dictionary) order. If *A* and *B* have different lengths, pad the shorter one on the right with blanks to make them the same length before performing the comparison. Some examples are

          'PLAIN' LEXLESS 'PLANE'
1

          'PLANE' LEXLESS 'PLAIN'
0

          'SOME' LEXLESS 'SOMETHING'
1

          'WORD' LEXLESS 'WORD   '
0

This exercise assumes that the version of APL which you are using allows comparisons like < to be applied to characters. If not, the exercise becomes slightly more complicated. In that case you can use the ordering of characters given by the system variable □*AV* (atomic vector), which is a vector of all valid APL characters.

4.9   Reverse and Rotate (ɸ)

The monadic function *reverse* (ɸ) reverses the order of elements of a vector. Thus,

          ɸι6   yields
6 5 4 3 2 1

and

          ɸ*'STOP'*   yields
POTS

The symbol ɸ is ○ (uppershift letter *O*) overstruck with |.

Reverse is particularly useful with functions like index and reshape which work from the beginning to the end of a vector. Reverse allows them to be applied, in effect, from the end to the beginning. For example, the expression

          1+(ρ,*STRING*)-(ɸ*STRING*)ι' '

finds the position of the last blank in a vector *STRING*. (The value is zero if there are no blanks.)

When reverse is applied to a matrix, it reverses each row. Reverse can also be modified by following it with a number in square brackets to make it apply along any dimension of an array. (This use of a number in square brackets should be familiar from functions discussed earlier.) For the case of reversal along the first dimension, φ[1], there is a special symbol, ⊖, which can also be used (○ overstruck with −). For example,

```
        ⊖ 3 3ρι9           yields
7   8   9
4   5   6
1   2   3
```

Of course, reverse can also be applied to three-dimensional and higher-dimensional arrays.

The same symbol φ used dyadically represents the *rotate* function. (The line can be thought of as representing an axis of rotation, and the circle as representing rotation about the axis.) The right argument is the array to be rotated, and the left argument specifies the amount and direction of rotation: Left rotation is indicated by positive numbers and right rotation by negative numbers. *Rotation* in this case means a process of shifting elements of the array up or down along the dimension of the rotation, putting elements that get shifted off the end of the array back into the array at the other end. For example,

```
     1φ'STOP'
```

causes each character to be shifted left one place and the first character (*S*) to be moved to the right end. The result is

TOPS

Negative rotation is similar, except that elements are shifted to the right and reappear at the left. Thus

```
       ¯3 φ ι9           yields
7 8 9 1 2 3 4 5 6
```

The amount of a rotation can be arbitrarily large. If the amount is greater than the size of the dimension along which the rotation is being done, the rotation is done modulo the size of the dimension. Thus, 1φ'*STOP*' and 5φ'*STOP*' both have the same value: *TOPS*.

Matrices can be rotated row by row (i.e., along the second dimension) or column by column (i.e., along the first dimension), and each row or column can be rotated by a different amount. The amount of rotation is specified by a scalar or by a vector with one element for each row or column of the matrix. For example, suppose *M* is the 3-by-4 matrix

STOP
TOPS
SPOT

the following rotations yield the values shown:

        1 ⌽ M   (rotating all rows left by one)
TOPS
OPST
POTS

        1 ‾1 0 ⌽ M   (rotating the rows by different amounts)
TOPS
STOP
SPOT

        0 1 2 ‾1 ⌽[1] M (rotating the columns)
SOOT
TPOP
STPS

The last example could also be written as

        0 1 2 ‾1 ⊖ M

Notice that positive rotation along columns is upward and negative rotation is downward. In all cases, positive rotation is in the direction of smaller subscripts, and negative rotation is in the direction of larger subscripts.

   As an example of an application of rotation to a matrix, suppose *LIST* is a matrix of words with one word in each row, each beginning in the first column:

        BORDER LIST

```
 _____
|A      |
|SHORT  |
|LIST   |
|OF     |
|WORDS  |
 ───────
```

(The words are said to be "left-justified" in the matrix.) Now suppose the words are to be shifted to the right, so that they all end in the last column (i.e., they are to be "right-justified"). Then the following use of rotation will do the job:

        BORDER (-+/LIST=' ')⌽LIST

```
 _____
|      A|
|SHORT  |
|  LIST |
|    OF |
|WORDS  |
 ───────
```

When rotation is applied to a three-dimensional array, the left argument can be a scalar or a matrix. For instance, suppose A is assigned the three-dimensional array

```
        A←2 3 4ρι24
        A
 1    2    3    4
 5    6    7    8
 9   10   11   12

13   14   15   16
17   18   19   20
21   22   23   24
```

and suppose the rows in the first plane are to be rotated left by 1, 2, and 3, respectively, and the rows in the second plane are to be rotated to the right by the same amounts. Then the appropriate left argument for the rotation is the matrix

```
        B
 1    2    3
¯1   ¯2   ¯3
```

and

```
        BφA              yields
 2    3    4 | 1
 7    8 | 5   6
12 | 9   10   11

16 | 13   14   15
19   20 | 17   18
22   23   24 | 21
```

(Lines have been added to show the old boundaries of the array, so the effect of the rotation can be seen clearly.)

EXERCISES

4.9.1.   Write an expression involving reverse and other functions to get the last word from a vector $STRING$ of words which are separated by single blanks (with no leading or trailing blanks). For example, if $STRING←$'THESE THREE WORDS' then the result should be the vector of five characters, $WORDS$.

4.9.2.   Given a character vector $STRING$ containing words separated by single blanks (with no leading or trailing blanks), write an expression to move the first word of the string to the end of the string. For instance, if $STRING$ is assigned

$STRING←$'THIS SHORT PHRASE'

then the expression should yield the vector
SHORT PHRASE THIS (with no leading or trailing blanks)
If *STRING* is empty or has only one word, the result should be the same as *STRING*.

4.9.3. Suppose *STRING* and *NEW* are character vectors, and suppose *POS* is a scalar integer between 0 and $\rho STRING$, inclusive. Write an expression to produce a new vector by inserting *NEW* into *STRING* right after position *POS*. If *POS* is zero, the insertion should be at the beginning of *STRING*. Solve this exercise in two ways: (1) using rotation, and (2) using take and drop.

4.9.4. Write an expression using the rotate function and others to test whether or not the elements in a given numeric *VECTOR* are in strictly increasing order (each greater than its predecessor).

4.9.5. Given a matrix *LIST* of words, with one word in each row, left-justified, write an expression to center each word in its row, with as many blanks to the left of it as to the right of it. If the total number of blanks in a row is odd, put the extra blank on the right side of the word in that row.

4.9.6. Write a function ∇ *M←WIDTH CENTER TEXT* using the rotate function and others to center a character matrix *TEXT* in a specified number of columns (*WIDTH*) by padding it on the left and right with appropriate numbers of blank columns. If an odd number of blank columns are added as padding, let the extra blank column be on the left side. If *WIDTH* is less than the number of columns in *TEXT*, return *TEXT* unchanged as the result.

4.9.7. Write a function ∇ *S←DIAGONALSUMS M* to compute a two-element vector containing the sums along the two main diagonals of a square matrix. *S[1]* should be the sum along the "northwest" to "southeast" diagonal, and *S[2]* should be the sum along the "northeast" to "southwest" diagonal.

Using the *DIAGONALSUMS* function and others from earlier exercises, write another function ∇ *R←MAGICTEST M* to test whether a given matrix *M* is a magic square. To be a magic square, *M* must be a square matrix filled with consecutive positive integers starting with 1, arranged in such a way that the sums of its rows, columns, and two main diagonals are all equal. The following function can be used to generate magic squares for testing the *MAGICTEST* function:

```
      ∇  R←MAGICSQUARE N
[1]      ⍝ GENERATES AN N-BY-N MAGIC SQUARE WHEN N IS ODD.
[2]        R←(N,N)⍴⍳N×N
[3]        N←(⍳N)-⌈0.5×N
[4]        R←(-N)⊖⊖N⌽R
      ∇
```

```
          MAGICSQUARE 5
    11   18   25    2    9
    10   12   19   21    3
     4    6   13   20   22
    23    5    7   14   16
    17   24    1    8   15
```

4.9.8.   Redo Exercise 4.5.10

(∇ *R←FOREGROUND OVERLAYON BACKGROUND*)

using lamination and rotation, among other functions.

4.10 Transpose (⍉)

The monadic *transpose* function (⍉) rearranges the elements of an array in such a way that the dimensions of the array are reversed. (That is, ρ⍉A is the reverse of ρA.) In the case of a matrix, it yields the usual matrix transpose, in which rows become columns and columns become rows. For example,

```
    ⍉ 2 3ρι6            yields
1 4
2 5
3 6
```

and if M is the 5-by-7 character matrix

```
    W
CROSSED
    R
    D
    S
```

then ⍉M yields the 7-by-5 matrix

```
    C
    R
WORDS
    S
    S
    E
    D
```

(The symbol ⍉, which is ○ overstruck with \, suggests rotation of a matrix about its main diagonal.)

When transpose is applied to a vector, the result is just the same vector. In the case of a three-dimensional array, monadic transpose causes the planes to become columns and the columns to become planes, as the following example illustrates:

```
        A
ABCD
EFGH
IJKL

MNOP
QRST
UVWX
        ρA
2  3  4
        ⍉A
AM
EQ
IU

BN
FR
JV

CO
GS
KW

DP
HT
LX
        ρ⍉A
4  3  2
```

Besides being useful for ordinary matrix mathematics, the transpose function is useful in combination with other functions like reshape and ravel which operate on matrices by rows. Transpose can be used, in effect, to reshape or ravel matrices by columns. For example, with reshape and the index geneator one can produce a matrix in which the first column contains all 1's, the second column all 2's, and so on:

```
        4  4ρ⍳4
1  2  3  4
1  2  3  4
1  2  3  4
1  2  3  4
```

With the help of the transpose function, a similar matrix can be generated in which each row is constant:

```
        ⍉4  4ρ⍳4
1  1  1  1
2  2  2  2
3  3  3  3
4  4  4  4
```

EXERCISES

4.10.1.   Given a vector *VEC* and a scalar number *N* write an expression, without using replication, to create a new vector by repeating each element of *VEC* *N* times. For example, if

VEC←'EXAMPLE'

N←3

then the result should be the 21-character vector

EEEXXXAAAMMMPPPLLLEEE

4.10.2.   Write a function ∇ *U←UPPER N* to generate the *N*-by-*N* "upper triangular" Boolean matrix which has ones on and above the main diagonal and zeros below it. For instance,

```
        UPPER 5     should yield the matrix
1 1 1 1 1
0 1 1 1 1
0 0 1 1 1
0 0 0 1 1
0 0 0 0 1
```

4.10.3.   Write a function ∇ *R←SYMMETRIC M* to test whether or not a given square matrix is symmetrical about its main diagonal. (You may assume that the function will be applied only to square matrices.)

4.10.4.   Write an expression to rotate a given matrix *M* clockwise by 90 degrees. For example, if *M* is the numeric matrix

```
1 2 3                 the result should be the matrix   4 1
4 5 6                                                    5 2
                                                         6 3
```

Write similar expressions to rotate *M* by 180 degrees and by 90 degrees counterclockwise.

4.10.5.   Given a positive integer *N*, write an expression, without using replication, to generate an *N*-by-*N*-by-*N* numeric array in which the first plane contains only 1's, the last plane contains only *N*'s, and in general the *J*th plane contains only *J*'s.

There is also a dyadic transpose function which uses the same symbol ⍉ that is used for monadic transpose. Whereas monadic transpose always reverses the dimensions of an array, dyadic transpose allows one to specify an arbitrary rearrangement of the dimensions. The left argument gives the particular transposition which is desired. For example, if *A* is the 2-by-3-by-4 character array

ABCD
EFGH
IJKL

MNOP
QRST
UVWX

then $1\ 3\ 2 \Phi A$ exchanges the second and third dimensions but leaves the first dimension alone, thus transposing each plane of A separately:

```
AEI
BFJ
CGK
DHL


MQU
NRV
OSW
PTX
```

In the case of a dyadic transpose $B \Phi A$ the left argument B must have one element for each dimension of the right argument A. (That is, ρB must equal $\rho \rho A$.) Element $B[J]$ of the left argument tells where the Jth dimension of A goes in the result. For example,

$$3\ \ 1\ \ 2\ \ \Phi\ \ A$$

indicates that the first dimension of A is to become the third dimension of the result, the second dimension is to become the first, and the third dimension is to become the second. This transposition can be represented by the following diagram:

```
Old dimension:    1    2    3
                  ↓    ↓    ↓
New dimension:    3    1    2
```

Thus, if A is the 2-by-3-by-4 array

```
ABCD
EFGH
IJKL


MNOP
QRST
UVWX
```

as before, and if the assignment

$$R \leftarrow 3\ \ 1\ \ 2\ \ \Phi\ \ A$$

is made, then element $A[J;K;L]$ of A will be

equal to element $R[K;L;J]$ of R, and R will be the 3-by-4-by-2 array

```
AM
BN
CO
DP

EQ
FR
GS
HT

IU
JV
KW
LX
```

Another way of looking at a dyadic transpose is to see where each dimension of the result comes from in the original array. In the preceding example, since the 1 in the left argument is in the second position, it indicates that the first dimension of the result comes from the second dimension of the right argument A.

If a number is repeated in the left argument, it means that a dimension of the result is derived from two or more dimensions of the right argument. For instance, if M is a matrix, the assignment

$$R \leftarrow 1 \ 1 \lozenge M$$

yields a vector R in which $R[J]$ is equal to $M[J;J]$ for each subscript J. That is, R is the main diagonal of M. Thus, if M is

```
1   2   3
4   5   6
```

R will be the vector

```
1   5
```

Notice that the left argument, B, of a dyadic transpose $B \lozenge A$ must contain consecutive integers starting with 1, possibly with repetitions, and that the largest integer in B gives the rank of the array which results from the transposition.

EXERCISES

4.10.6.   Rewrite the function $\nabla \ S \leftarrow DIAGONALSUMS \ M$ from Exercise 4.9.7, using dyadic transpose.

4.10.7.   Suppose A is the 2-by-3-by-4 character array

```
ABCD
EFGH
IJKL

MNOP
QRST
UVWX
```

Evaluate the following expressions by hand and find both the shapes and the values of the resulting arrays:

   $2 \ 3 \ 1 \lozenge A$

   $1 \ 2 \ 1 \lozenge A$

   $2 \ 1 \ 2 \lozenge A$

Check your answers on a computer.

4.10.8.   Suppose $WORDS$ is a matrix containing words, with one word in each row, left-justified. Write a function

   $\nabla \ M \leftarrow WORDS \ INCOLUMNS \ NCOLS$

to rearrange the words into a matrix containing *NCOLS* columns of words. The words should be put into the new matrix one column at a time, and the new matrix should contain only as many rows as necessary to contain all of the words. Any leftover space in the last column or columns should be filled with blanks. For example, if *WORDS* is the 7-by-7 matrix

```
TRY
THIS
SAMPLE
MATRIX
OF
VARIOUS
WORDS
```

then *WORDS INCOLUMNS* 3 should yield the 3-by-23 matrix

```
TRY      MATRIX   WORDS
THIS     OF
SAMPLE   VARIOUS
```

Notice that the columns of words are separated by columns of blank characters.

Chapter 5

More About User-Defined Functions

So far we have seen how to do many things in APL by using only one-line expressions and straight-line functions. This chapter will introduce some additional features of user-defined functions, including input and output operations and the branch operation.

5.1 Input and Output (□ and ▯)

Besides using parameters and nonlocal variables to communicate with its environment, a function can use the symbols *quad* (□) and *quote-quad* (▯) for input and output during execution.

We have already seen in Chapter 3 that function lines that are not assignment statements have their values printed as soon as they are evaluated. Printed output can also be produced by assignment to the quad symbol, □. This can be done in calculator mode as wel¹ as in user-defined functions. For example, the line

$$□←V← \text{ expression}$$

will assign a value to variable V and will also print the value.*

---

* In general, an assignment $A←$ expression can occur as a subexpression of a larger expression. Its value is the value of the expression on the right of the assignment arrow.

Quad output is useful for printing the values of subexpressions of complicated expressions. For example, it can be used to trace evaluation of the expression which was presented in Section 4.1 as the definition of the residue function:

```
        A←¯5
        B←¯17
        B−□←A×□←⌊□←B÷□←A+□←A=0
0
 ¯5
3.4
3
 ¯15
 ¯2
```

Notice that the right-to-left rule applies to the quad assignments just as it does to the other functions in the expression.

If a quad symbol appears anywhere except on the left side of an assignment arrow, it represents a niladic (no-argument) input function. When such a quad is encountered during evalution of an expression, its value is obtained as follows:

1.   The system types □: on a new line as a prompt and waits for a reply from the user.

2.   The user types any APL expression (often just a number or a vector of numbers) and presses the RETURN key.

3.   The system evaluates the expression typed by the user and uses its value as the value of the quad symbol in the original expression.

Quad input is often employed in functions that are to be used by persons not trained in APL, such as students using APL packages for computer-assisted instruction. For example, the following function will ask an addition problem and evaluate the answer:

```
      ∇    PROBLEM;ANSWER
[1]        'WHAT IS THE SUM OF 12 AND 39?'
[2]        ANSWER←□
[3]        (2 6 ρ'WRONG!RIGHT!') [1+ANSWER=51;]
      ∇
```

(Of course, much more general functions of the same kind can be written.) Notice, however, that a clever student can fool the function in the following way:

```
        PROBLEM
WHAT IS THE SUM OF 12 AND 39?
□:
        12+39
RIGHT!
```

The trick works because the quad input function will accept any APL expression. (To screen out undesirable input expressions, one can use the functions quote-quad and *execute* which will be described later.)

Quad input can also be used in calculator mode as a sort of "I'll tell you later" function, to postpone typing of subexpressions. The following is an example:

```
      □ρ□
□:
      ι6
□:
      2 3
1   2   3
4   5   6
```

Quad can be used in this way to enter a very long expression which cannot be typed in a single line:

```
      STRING←'THIS EXAMPLE ILLUSTRATES HOW QUAD INPUT CAN BE USED ',□
□:
      'TO ENTER A LONG CHARACTER VECTOR WHICH WHICH CANNOT BE TYPED ',□
□:
      'IN A SINGLE LINE.'
      ρSTRING
124
```

Since quad input accepts any APL expression, quad can be used in a function for timing the evaluation of expressions:

```
      ∇   TIMER;ΔTIME;Δ
[1]       ΔTIME←□AI[2]
[2]       Δ←□
[3]       □AI[2]-ΔTIME
      ∇
```

TIMER uses the *□AI* system function, whose value is a vector of accounting information. Line 1 gets the second element of the *□AI* vector, which is the number of milliseconds of central processing unit (CPU) time which have been used since the beginning of the session. Line 2 gets the expression that is to be timed, evaluates the expression, and assigns its value to a local variable (to avoid printing the value, in case the value is a large array). Line 3 then prints the CPU time that has elapsed since line 1. Since the time measured includes some overhead time for evaluating the *TIMER* function itself, *TIMER* should be used only for comparing relative execution times of expressions, not for measuring absolute execution times.

   As an example, $TIMER$ can be used to compare the expressions $1 \epsilon A$ and
$\vee / A$, which are equivalent for Boolean vectors A. For the timing comparison,
long Boolean vectors A and B are used so that the time differences between the
two expressions will show up clearly:

```
      A←(10000ρ0),1
      B←1,10000ρ0
      TIMER
□:
      1∈A
280
      TIMER
□:
      1∈A
274
      TIMER
□:
      ∨/A
73
      TIMER
□:
      ∨/A
65
      TIMER
□:
      1∈B
78
      TIMER
□:
      1∈B
72
      TIMER
□:
      ∨/B
60
      TIMER
□:
      ∨/B
72
```

Notice that when the Boolean vector has a single 1 at the end, as A does, or-
reduction seems to be clearly faster than membership, at least for the version of
APL which was used for the test. However, when there is a single 1 at the beginning of the vector, as in B, there seems to be no significant difference in the
timings of the two expressions. Notice also that there is some small variation in
time if the same expression is timed more than once.

   Like the quad function, the quote-quad function (⍞) accepts an input line
when the quote-quad is encountered during evaluation of an expression. However, quote-quad does not evaluate the line the user types. Instead, the line up

to but not including the carriage-return is taken as a character vector, and that vector becomes the value of the quote-quad. (The input line is treated as a normal line of APL; BACKSPACE can be used freely, for example, to create legal overstruck characters, and BACKSPACE and LINEFEED or INDEX can be used to correct errors in the line being typed.)

⍞ does not print a prompting symbol to indicate that the system is waiting for input. The system simply waits in column 1 for the user to begin typing input. Hence, any function that uses quote-quad should provide its own prompting.

The following example shows how quote-quad input can be used in a function for generating a form letter:

```
     ∇   CONGRATULATIONS;TO;EVENT;FROM;DUMMY
[1]      'NAME OF ADDRESSEE?'
[2]      TO←⍞
[3]      'OCCASION?'
[4]      EVENT←⍞
[5]      'YOUR NAME?'
[6]      FROM←⍞
[7]      'PRESS RETURN KEY TO PRINT THE LETTER'
[8]      DUMMY←⍞
[9]      'DEAR ',TO,','
[10]     ' '
[11]     '        CONGRATULATIONS ON YOUR ',EVENT,'!'
[12]     ' '
[13]     (25ρ' '),'YOURS SINCERELY,'
[14]     ' '
[15]     (30ρ' '),FROM
     ∇

        CONGRATULATIONS
NAME OF ADDRESSEE?
SUE AND BOB
OCCASION?
50TH WEDDING ANNIVERSARY
YOUR NAME?
DAD
PRESS RETURN KEY TO PRINT THE LETTER

DEAR SUE AND BOB,

        CONGRATULATIONS ON YOUR 50TH WEDDING ANNIVERSARY!

                         YOURS SINCERELY,

                              DAD
```

EXERCISES

5.1.1.   Suppose the following assignments are made:

$$A←(10000ρ0),1$$
$$\Delta TIME←(10000ρ0),1$$

Would you expect the sequence

    TIMER
□:
    $1 \epsilon A$

to yield a time close to that for the sequence

    TIMER
□:
    $1 \epsilon \Delta TIME$?

Explain.

5.1.2.   Write a function ∇ *R←QUESTION S* to ask a question by printing the value of its argument, and to accept an answer by using quote-quad. *QUESTION* should return the value

  1 if the answer begins with *'Y'*
  0 if the answer begins with *'N'*
  ⁻1 if the answer begins with anything other than *'Y'* or *'N'*

Have *QUESTION* ignore any leading blanks in the answer.

5.2 Semicolon (;) and Diamond (◊)

Two or more expressions can be put in a single line of a user-defined function if they are separated by semicolons. What happens when such a line is executed varies somewhat among different versions of APL. However, most implementations produce the same effect as long as there are no assignment statements in the line: They simply print the values of the expressions, in left-to-right order. The use of semicolon allows numeric and character output to be mixed in the same line. An example is the following function:

```
     ∇   MEASURE MATRIX
[1]      'THE NUMBER OF ROWS IS ';1↑ρMATRIX
[2]      'THE NUMBER OF COLUMNS IS ';⁻1↑ρMATRIX
     ∇

     MEASURE 2 3ρι6
THE NUMBER OF ROWS IS 2
THE NUMBER OF COLUMNS IS 3
```

If two-dimensional or higher-dimensional arrays are involved, they are printed beginning on separate lines, as in the following example evaluated in calculator mode:

```
     'IDENTITY MATRIX:';4 4ρ1 0 0 0 0
IDENTITY MATRIX:
 1 0 0 0
 0 1 0 0
 0 0 1 0
 0 0 0 1
```

If the expressions separated by semicolons are assignment statements, the assignments are made in right-to-left order. For example, one may write three assignment statements in one line to exchange the values of two variables A and B, using variable T to hold one of the values temporarily*:

```
        A
2
        B
3
        B←T ; A←B ; T←A
        A
3
        B
2
```

When semicolon is used to separate assignment statements, some versions of APL will print the values of some or all of the expressions, and other versions will not print anything. Because the use of semicolon as a statement separator is not standardized, it is recommended that semicolon be used only to separate output items and not to separate assignment statements.

Some newer versions of APL use the diamond symbol ◇ to separate statements in a line. Statements separated by diamonds are executed in left-to-right order. Hence, the exchange of values which was done above using semicolons as separators would be done differently using diamonds as separators:

```
        T←A  ◇  A←B  ◇  B←T
```

Unfortunately, the use of diamond as a statement separator is also not standard among different versions of APL. For instance, some may execute statements that are separated by diamonds in right-to-left order. Consult the reference manual for the particular version of APL you are using.

5.3   Branch (→) and Labels

Branch, symbolized by the right arrow (→), is a monadic operation whose argument must be a numeric scalar or vector. Execution of a branch in a user-defined function causes execution of the function to jump to the line which corresponds to the first number in the argument of the branch. Thus,

→8	will cause a branch to line 8, and
→2 4	will cause a branch to line 2.

A branch to zero or to a number greater than the last line number in a function causes exit from the function. If the argument of a branch is the empty vector, no branch occurs, and the function continues on to the next line in the usual way.

---

* This example is presented only to illustrate the order of execution of statements separated by semicolons. Use of several statements in a line in this way, particularly when the order of their execution is significant, is considered by many APL programmers to be bad practice.

A *label* in APL is an identifier, formed like a variable name and followed by a colon. It is written at the beginning of a function line, as in the example

> `[5] HERE: A←ι17`

A label is essentially a local variable, except that it need not be declared local in the header line of the function, and its value cannot be changed by assignment. The value of a label is the number of the line in which it appears. If a function is edited by insertion or deletion of lines, the values of the labels in it change accordingly; consequently it is recommended that labels, rather than absolute line numbers, be used with branch.

Labels are most commonly used as arguments of branch, but since their values are simply numbers, they can be used as arguments for other functions as well. For example, the following statement would cause a branch to the line after the one labeled *LOOPEND*:

> `→1+LOOPEND`

5.4 Conditional Branches

To write a conditional branch statement in APL, one constructs an argument expression for branch whose value will depend on the desired condition. The argument expression can involve any functions, as long as it yields a numerical scalar or vector as its value.

One-way Conditional Branches In another language one might write a conditional branch in a form something like

> if CONDITION then go to LABEL

In APL an equivalent expression can be written in various ways:

> `→ CONDITION/LABEL` (using compression)
>
> `→ CONDITION↑LABEL` (using take)
>
> `→ CONDITIONρLABEL` (using reshape)

In each of these expressions, the argument for the branch will be the value of *LABEL* if the value of *CONDITION* is 1, but it will be the empty vector of the value of *CONDITION* is 0. For example,

> `→(A>B)/LOOP`

will cause a branch to the line labeled *LOOP* if, and only if, the value of *A>B* is 1. (The parentheses are needed because of APL's right-to-left evaluation rule.)

Some people prefer to use a conditional of the form

> `→LABEL×ιCONDITION`   as in the example
>
> `→LOOP×ιA>B`

because it can be written without parentheses around the condition. However, that form will not work properly if the origin for index generation is changed from 1 to 0. (See Section 2.11.) The preferred form for the conditional seems to be the one that uses compression.

Two-way Branches A conditional like

if $CONDITION$ then
go to $TRUELABEL$
else
go to $FALSELABEL$

can be written in APL in the following forms, among others:

$\rightarrow(CONDITION,1)/TRUELABEL,FALSELABEL$ (using compression)

$\rightarrow CONDITION\phi FALSELABEL,TRUELABEL$ (using rotation)

$\rightarrow(FALSELABEL,TRUELABEL)[1+CONDITION]$ (using subscripting).

However, the form involving subscripting will not work correctly if the index origin is changed from 1 to 0. (Again, see Section 2.11.)

Multiway Branches A variable such as $CASE$ with a positive integer value can be used to select one of many label values from a vector, also by compression, by rotation, or by subscripting:

$\rightarrow(CASE=\iota 4)/LABEL1,LABEL2,LABEL3,LABEL4$

$\rightarrow(CASE-1)\phi LABEL1,LABEL2,LABEL3,LABEL4$

$\rightarrow(LABEL1,LABEL2,LABEL3,LABEL4)[CASE]$

Again, the form using subscripting depends on the value of the index origin.

As an example of the use of branch, the following function will accept one or more lines of input and catenate them together into a single long string, until it encounters a specified $BREAK$ character:

```
     ∇  S←INPUTSTRING BREAK;LINE;POS
[1]     S←''                        —Initialize result to empty,
[2]     READLOOP:LINE←,⎕           —Accept an input line,
[3]     POS←LINEιBREAK              —Look for break character in the line,
[4]     →(POS≤ρLINE)/LOOPEND        —If found, exit from the loop,
[5]     S←S,LINE                    —Catenate line onto result vector,
[6]     →READLOOP                   —Repeat the loop,
[7]     LOOPEND:S←S,(POS-1)↑LINE   Catenate the part of the last line before the
                                     break character onto the result.

     ∇
```

The following function is another example that uses branch. It performs a *binary search* in a given vector, beginning in the middle of the vector, and eliminating about half of the remaining portion of the vector after each comparison.

The function should be treated only as an illustration of branching, not as a useful utility function. The dyadic iota function is generally faster than the *BINARYSEARCH* function for searching all but very large vectors.

```
      ∇   POS←VECTOR BINARYSEARCH KEY;HIGH;TESTITEM
[1]    ⍝ SEARCHES FOR POSITION OF A GIVEN KEY VALUE IN A GIVEN VECTOR.
[2]    ⍝ ITEMS IN THE VECTOR MUST BE IN ASCENDING ORDER. THE RESULT IS
[3]    ⍝ ZERO IF THE KEY VALUE IS NOT FOUND IN THE VECTOR.
[4]    LOW←1                         —LOW and HIGH delimit the part of the
[5]    HIGH←ρVECTOR←,VECTOR            vector yet to be searched,
[6]    LOOP:→(LOW>HIGH)/ENDLOOP      —Search ends if no items remain
                                      between LOW and HIGH,
[7]    POS←⌊0.5×(LOW+HIGH)           —POS points to the item midway
                                      between LOW and HIGH,
[8]    TESTITEM←VECTOR[POS]          —item to be compared with given KEY
[9]    →((KEY=TESTITEM),KEY<TESTITEM)/0,LOWER —If TESTITEM matches KEY
                                                then exit
                                                else if KEY < TESTITEM
                                                then go to LOWER.
[10]   LOW←POS+1        —Since KEY>TESTITEM, eliminate items ≤ TESTITEM,
[11]   →LOOP
[12]   LOWER:HIGH←POS-1 —Eliminate items ≥ TESTITEM,
[13]   →LOOP
[14]   ENDLOOP:POS←0   —Set POS to indicate unsuccessful search.
      ∇
```

The following sequence shows some testing of the $BINARYSEARCH$ function:

```
      VEC
2 3 5 7 11 13 17 19 23 29
      VEC BINARYSEARCH 2      —first item
1
      VEC BINARYSEARCH 13     —an item in the middle
6
      VEC BINARYSEARCH 29     —last item
10
      VEC BINARYSEARCH 9      —missing value between two items
0
      VEC BINARYSEARCH 1      —value less than the first item
0
      VEC BINARYSEARCH 30     —value greater than the last item
0
      VEC BINARYSEARCH 3      —values at other positions
2
      VEC BINARYSEARCH 4
0
      VEC BINARYSEARCH 5
3
      VEC BINARYSEARCH 6
0
      VEC BINARYSEARCH 7
4
      VEC BINARYSEARCH 11
5
      VEC BINARYSEARCH 12
0
      VEC BINARYSEARCH 14
0
      VEC BINARYSEARCH 17
7
      VEC BINARYSEARCH 18
0
      VEC BINARYSEARCH 19
8
      VEC BINARYSEARCH 20
0
      VEC BINARYSEARCH 23
9
      VEC BINARYSEARCH 28
0
```

EXERCISES

5.4.1.   What will happen if the expression
         $\rightarrow LABEL \times \iota CONDITION$

is executed in a user-defined function when the index origin is zero, and:

a. *CONDITION* is 1?

b. *CONDITION* is 0?

5.4.2.   Write a two-way conditional branch statement involving *CONDITION*, *FALSELABEL*, and *TRUELABEL* and using the drop function. If *CONDITION* is 1, the branch should go to *TRUELABEL*; if *CONDITION* is 0, it should go to *FALSELABEL*.

5.4.3.   Write a branch statement to branch to one of the following three labels, depending on the value of variable X:

POSITIVE if $X > 0$

ZERO if $X = 0$

NEGATIVE if $X < 0$

5.4.4.   Write a function ∇ *B←X IDENTICAL Y* to determine whether (1) or not (0) any two given values X and Y are identical in all respects: having the same type of data (character or numeric), the same rank, the same shape, and the same values for their elements. Some examples are:

```
      1 2 3 IDENTICAL ι3
1
      (0ρ0) IDENTICAL ι0
1
      'TOPS' IDENTICAL 1φ'STOP'
1
      2 IDENTICAL ,2
0
      2 IDENTICAL 1 1ρ2
0
      8 IDENTICAL '8'
0
      '' IDENTICAL ι0
0
```

5.4.5.   Consider the following two functions:

```
      ∇  TEST1
[1]  TEST2
[2]  'SECOND'
[3]  LABEL:'THIRD'
      ∇

      ∇  TEST2
[1]  →LABEL
[2]  'TWO'
[3]  'THREE'
      ∇
```

What will be printed if $TEST1$ is executed in calculator mode? Explain.

5.4.6.   Use the $TIMER$ function from Section 5.1 to compare the execution times of $BINARYSEARCH$ and dyadic iota for searching vectors of various sizes.

5.5   Interrupting Execution, and the State Indicator Stack

When branch is used to code explicit loops in a function, it is possible for an unending loop to be coded, perhaps accidentally. In that case some way is needed to interrupt the execution of a function, so an unending loop can be terminated. The exact method of interrupting an executing function differs from one version of APL to another, but it generally involves pressing some key on the keyboard, such as the BREAK key or the ATTN (attention) key. You should consult your APL reference manual for the exact method for your computer.

If an unending loop contains a quad or quote-quad function that requests input, one can escape from the loop and interrupt the function by typing the branch symbol (→) in response to a quad, or by overstriking the letters O U T as $\textbf{U}$ in response to a quote-quad.

Execution of a user-defined function is also interrupted if an error is encountered by the system during execution of the function. When a function is interrupted by an error, APL prints the name of the function, the number of the line in which it was interrupted, and the reason for the interruption.

Upon interruption, the function becomes *suspended,* and the system reverts to calculator mode. At that point, information about the suspended function and about any functions that have called it is available in a structure called the *state indicator stack.* The system command

```
)SI
```

causes the contents of the state indicator stack to be listed, in the reverse of the order in which functions were invoked. For example,

```
)SI
INPUT[3]  *
EDIT[5]
USE[2]
```

indicates that a function called $INPUT$ is suspended at line [3], that a function called $EDIT$ has called $INPUT$ from line [5] and is awaiting a return from $INPUT$, and that a function called USE has called $EDIT$ from line [2] and is awaiting a return. USE, at the bottom of the stack, was invoked from calculator mode. The structure is called a *stack* because functions are put onto the top of the list when they are called and are taken off the top of the list when they return.

Suspended functions in the state indicator stack are marked by asterisks. Functions like *EDIT* and *USE* which are not suspended, but are simply awaiting returns from other functions, are called *pendent* functions. They are not marked with asterisks.

There is another system command,)*SIV* or)*SINL* (the name is not yet standard), which lists the state indicator stack. It also lists the names of the local variables for each function in the stack. When a function has been suspended, the values of its local variables can be printed from calculator mode.

Unless some action is taken to empty, or clear, the state indicator stack after interruption of a function, the information in it will remain in the active workspace indefinitely and will even be saved if the workspace is saved in the library. Accumulated information in the state indicator stack can crowd and ultimately fill a workspace. So it is important to check the state indicator from time to time, especially before saving workspaces, and to keep it as empty as possible.

The simplest way to clear the state indicator stack is to type a branch symbol (→) with no argument at all. That will clear off the top suspended function and any pendent functions that have called it, directly or indirectly. However, if the state indicator has not been cleared recently, there may be other suspended functions and related pendent functions below the top one. In that case, branch may have to be typed several times to clear the entire stack.

Another way to clear a suspended function and its associated pendent functions from the state indicator stack is to resume execution of the suspended function. That is done by typing a branch to the line number at which execution of the function is to be resumed. Of course, one should be careful not to resume an unending loop or to resume at a line that contained an error.

Some example functions will illustrate interrupting a function, examining the state indicator stack, resuming the function, and clearing the stack. The function *LOOPER*1 contains a simple unending loop which involves only computation. *LOOPER*2 and *LOOPER*3 contain unending loops which request input; one involves quad and the other uses quote-quad:

```
     ∇   TEST
[1]      'CALLING FIRST LOOPER:'
[2]      LOOPER1
[3]      'PAST FIRST LOOPER.'
[4]      'CALLING SECOND LOOPER:'
[5]      LOOPER2
[6]      'PAST SECOND LOOPER'
[7]      'CALLING THIRD LOOPER:'
[8]      LOOPER3
[9]      'PAST THIRD LOOPER'
     ∇
```

```
      ∇   LOOPER1;N
[1]       N←1
[2]       N←N+1
[3]       →2
[4]       'VALUE OF N:';N
      ∇

      ∇   LOOPER2;I
[1]       I←⎕
[2]       →1
[3]       'INPUT VALUE:';I
      ∇

      ∇   LOOPER3;S
[1]       S←⍞
[2]       →1
[3]       'INPUT STRING:';S
      ∇
```

```
        TEST
CALLING FIRST LOOPER:
ATTENTION SIGNALED          —interruption from the keyboard
LOOPER1[3]  →2              —the line at which interruption occurred
          ∧
        )SIV                —displaying the state indicator stack
LOOPER1[3]  *      N        —suspended in line 3; N is local
TEST[2]                     —pendent in line 2
        N                  —printing the value of local variable N
133
        →4                 —resuming LOOPER1 at line 4
VALUE OF N:133
PAST FIRST LOOPER.
CALLING SECOND LOOPER:
☐:
        1981               —typing input for quad
☐:
        1982
☐:
        →                  —interrupting at quad in LOOPER2
        )SIV
LOOPER2[1]  *      I
TEST[5]
        I
1982
        →3                 —resuming LOOPER2 at line 3
INPUT VALUE:1982
PAST SECOND LOOPER
CALLING THIRD LOOPER:
FIRST STRING               —typing input for quote-quad
SECOND STRING
☑                          —interrupting at quote-quad in LOOPER3
        )SIV
LOOPER3[1]  *      S
TEST[8]
        S
SECOND STRING
        →                  —clearing the state indicator stack
        )SIV               —checking that the stack is empty
```

EXERCISES

5.5.1.   Write a function

```
    ∇ POS← STRING MATCHFIRST SUBBSTRING
```

to find the position of the first character of the first occurrence of a given substring in a given string. The result should be zero if the substring is empty or does not occur in the string. For example,

```
    'SINGING' MATCHFIRST 'ING' should yield
```

2

5.5.2.   Define a function ∇ *POS← STRING MATCHALL SUBSTRING* which yields a vector of the positions of the first characters of all occurrences of a given substring in a given string. In this case the result should be the empty vector if the substring is empty or does not occur in the string. For example,

         'MISSISSIPPI' MATCHALL 'ISSI' should yield

2 5

5.5.3.   Write a function ∇*M←STRING CUTAT CHAR* to create a character matrix by cutting a given *STRING* into its substrings which are separated by a given character *CHAR*. Each substring should be put in a separate row of the matrix, and the matrix should be just as wide as the longest substring. Short substrings should be padded on the right with blanks to the width of the matrix. The characters of *STRING* which are equal to *CHAR* should not appear in the matrix. As an example,

         'THIS/LIST/OF/WORDS' CUTAT '/'

should yield the 4-by-5 matrix

```
THIS
LIST
OF
WORDS
```

Note: If *STRING* is empty, the result should be a matrix with 1 row and 0 columns.

    You may use branch in writing the *CUTAT* function. However, if your version of APL has the replication function, it is possible to use replication to define *CUTAT* without any branching.

5.5.4.   Use the *CUTAT* function of Exercise 5.5.3 to write a function ∇ *M←WORDLIST S* which will take a string of words separated by blanks (with one or more blanks between words) and will return a matrix with each of the words in a row by itself, left-justified. The width of the matrix should be equal to the length of the longest word. For example,

WORDLIST '   THE QUICK BROWN FOX   '

should produce the 4-by-5 matrix

```
THE
QUICK
BROWN
FOX
```

(This function may use the *SQUEEZE* function from Exercise 4.8.4.)

5.6   User-defined Control Functions

Branch is the only operation which APL provides for writing explicit loops and conditional logic in user-defined functions. APL does not have the kinds of "if ... then ... else" and "do ... while" statements that some other programming languages have. One can argue that APL does not need such statements, since it is rarely necessary to write complicated nested loops and conditionals in APL, because of the power of its array operations. However, various utility functions can be defined in APL to make the coding of conditional and looping logic easier and clearer, if desired. Such functions can be useful during development of applications in APL. Once development of a system has been completed, calls to the control functions can be replaced by more efficient expressions if execution time needs to be reduced.

The first control function we will consider is a function for handling error conditions. It is an adaptation of a function suggested by Geller and Freedman in their book *Structured Programming in APL*. It evaluates a given Boolean condition, and if the condition is true (1) it prints a given message and then clears the state indicator stack, thus aborting the function that called it. If the condition is false (0), it simply returns to the function that called it:

```
      ∇   MESSAGE ERROR CONDITION
[1]       →(~CONDITION)/0
[2]       MESSAGE
[3]       →
      ∇
```

A modification of the *MAGICSQUARE* function from Exercise 4.9.7 provides an example of the use of the *ERROR* function:

```
      ∇   R←MAGICSQUARE N
[1]       ⍝ GENERATES AN N-BY-N MAGIC SQUARE WHEN N IS ODD.
[2]       'ERROR: ARGUMENT FOR MAGICSQUARE MUST BE ODD' ERROR~2|N
[3]       R←(N,N)⍴⍳N×N
[4]       N←(⍳N)-⌈0.5×N
[5]       R←(-N)⊖⊖N⌽R
      ∇
      MAGICSQUARE 3
4  9  2
3  5  7
8  1  6
      MAGICSQUARE 4
ERROR: ARGUMENT FOR MAGICSQUARE MUST BE ODD
      )SI
```

Notice that the state indicator stack is empty, which means that the *ERROR* function has correctly aborted *MAGICSQUARE* 4.

Another useful function is the following one, which allows conditional branches to be written more clearly:

```
     ∇ R←LABEL IF CONDITION
[1]    R←CONDITION/LABEL
     ∇
```

This allows one to write conditional branch statements like

```
     →EXIT IF A>B
```

in other functions. Notice how the *IF* function uses the fact that the value of a label is just a number.

Most versions of APL have a niladic system function $\Box LC$ whose value is a vector containing the current line numbers of the functions in the state indicator stack. The line number of the topmost function on the stack is $\Box LC[1]$; the second function from the top of the stack has current line number $\Box LC[2]$, and so on. The $\Box LC$ vector can be used in writing some additional control functions. For instance, the following function allows one to write one-line conditional statements without using labels:

```
     ∇ R←WHEN CONDITION
[1]    R←(~CONDITION)/1+□LC[2]
     ∇
```

When the *WHEN* function is used in a function line of the form

```
     →WHEN test ◇ statement
```

or

```
     statement ;→WHEN test
```

(depending on whether the diamond symbol or the semicolon is used as statement separator), it causes the given statement to be executed only when the given test is true. If the test is false, the *WHEN* function returns the number of the line following the *WHEN*, and the branch causes the statement to be skipped.

Further control functions can be written using the $\Box LC$ vector, which will permit one to write nested loops of the following form: (The brackets at left show the scopes of the loops.)

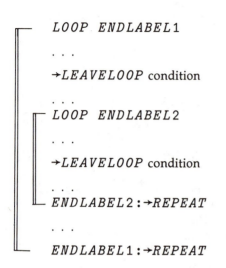

```
    LOOP ENDLABEL1

    . . .

    →LEAVELOOP condition

    . . .

    LOOP ENDLABEL2

    . . .

    →LEAVELOOP condition

    . . .

    ENDLABEL2:→REPEAT

    . . .

    ENDLABEL1:→REPEAT
```

For example, the *BINARYSEARCH* function of Section 5.3 can be rewritten as follows, provided that the appropriate control functions have been defined:

```
        ∇ POS←VECTOR BINARYSEARCH KEY;LOW:HIGH;TESTITEM
[1]       LOW←1
[2]       HIGH←ρVECTOR←,VECTOR
[3]       LOOP PROBE
[4]       →LEAVELOOP LOW>HIGH
[5]       POS←⌊0.5×(LOW+HIGH)
[6]       TESTITEM←VECTOR[POS]
[7]       →LEAVELOOP KEY=TESTITEM
[8]       →WHEN KEY>TESTITEM ◊ LOW←POS+1
[9]       →WHEN KEY<TESTITEM ◊ HIGH←POS-1
[10]    PROBE:→REPEAT
[11]      →WHEN LOW>HIGH ◊ POS←0
        ∇
```

The functions for loop control require two global variables to keep track of the line numbers for beginnings and ends of loops:

   REPEAT will be used to keep track of loop beginnings, and

   ΔEND will be used to keep track of loop ends.

The values of *REPEAT* and *ΔEND* will be vectors, which will be used as stacks (i.e., last-in–first-out lists) of line numbers. They should be initialized as empty vectors in any workspace which is to use the loop control functions.

The job of the *LOOP* function is to save on the *REPEAT* stack the number of the line which begins the loop body, and to save on the *ΔEND* stack the number of the line following the end of the loop:

```
     ∇    LOOP LABEL
[1]       REPEAT←(1+□LC[2]),REPEAT
[2]       ΔEND←(1+LABEL),ΔEND
     ∇
```

At the end of each loop there must be a →*REPEAT* statement preceded by the label that is used in the corresponding *LOOP* statement. The branch to *REPEAT* sends execution back to the beginning of the loop that was most recently entered.

Exit from a loop is accomplished by means of the following *LEAVELOOP* function, which removes the top items from the *REPEAT* and ΔEND stacks and returns the number of the line just after the loop when the *CONDITION* is 1:

```
     ∇    R←LEAVELOOP CONDITION
[1]       R←ι0
[2]       →(~CONDITION)/0
[3]       R←1↑ΔEND
[4]       ΔEND←1↓ΔEND
[5]       REPEAT←1↓REPEAT
     ∇
```

A number of variations of the foregoing control functions have appeared in APL literature. However, it should be noted that such functions (particularly ones like *LOOP* and *LEAVELOOP* which involve global variables) are controversial among APL programmers. Many consider their use inadvisable because they are not standard and because they may leave "garbage" data in the active workspace when function execution is interrupted.

EXERCISES

5.6.1.   What should be added to the *ERROR* function if it is to be used in the same workspaces as the functions *LOOP* and *LEAVELOOP*?

5.6.2.   Write functions *SOME* and *ALL* for use in expressions like the following ones:

→*NOGOOD IF SOME STRING*ϵ*'0123456789'*

→*POSTIVE IF ALL MATRIX*>0

5.6.3.   Write a function ∇ R←*ESCAPE N* to terminate the *N* innermost loops (coded with *LOOP* and *REPEAT*) in which the *ESCAPE* occurs. For instance, the *ESCAPE* in the following loop structure should cause an escape to the line just after the one labeled *A* when *CONDITION* is 1:

```
LOOP A

. . .

LOOP B

. . .

→ESCAPE 2 IF CONDITION

. . .

B:→REPEAT

. . .

A:→REPEAT
```

If N is zero or empty, $\rightarrow ESCAPE\ N$ should do nothing. (Notice that for a Boolean $CONDITION$, $\rightarrow ESCAPE\ CONDITION$ will be equivalent to $\rightarrow LEAVELOOP\ CONDITION$.)

5.6.4.   Using the control functions $IF, WHEN, LOOP, LEAVELOOP,$ and/or $ESCAPE$, rewrite the solutions to Exercises 5.5.1, 5.5.2, and 5.5.3.

5.7   Recursive Programming

A function which calls itself, either directly or indirectly, is called *recursive*. APL permits recursive functions. Of course, if one is not careful, a function that calls itself may keep on calling itself indefinitely. For recursive functions to work, the recursive calls must ultimately "bottom out," with an invocation of the function that returns to its caller without itself generating another recursive call. For that to happen, each recursive call must operate on data that are in some way "smaller" than the data provided to the previous call.

The most commonly used example of recursion is the factorial function, which may be defined as follows:

```
     ∇   R←FACTORIAL N
[1]      R←1
[2]      →(N≤1)/0
[3]      R←N×FACTORIAL N-1
     ∇
```

It computes the product $N \times (N-1) \times (N-2) \times \ldots \times 1$, which has the same value as the expression $!N$. Notice how the function reduces the lem $FACTORIAL\ N$ to a problem of exactly the same kind but one step smaller ($FACTORIAL\ N-1$), and notice how exit occurs without a recursive call when N becomes less than or equal to one.

Unfortunately, the $FACTORIAL$ function is not a very good illustration of the usefulness of recursion, since the same function can be defined almost as easily without recursion:

```
     ∇   R←FACTORIAL N
[1]      R←1
[2]      LOOP:→(N≤1)/0
[3]      R←R×N
[4]      N←N-1
[5]      →LOOP
     ∇
```

(And of course the primitive function $!$ makes it unnecessary to define the factorial function at all.)

More interesting and sophisticated applications of recursion result from combing recursion with catenation, to generate arrays recursively. For example, suppose it is desired to construct a matrix M containing all of the subsets of K

numbers chosen from the integers 1 , 2 , 3 up to a given number N. Each row of M is to contain one subset. That is, if N is 4 and K is 3, the matrix should be

```
1   2   3
1   2   4
1   3   4
2   3   4
```

One can define a function ∇ $M \leftarrow K$ *SUBSETS* N to generate such a matrix recursively, by recognizing that the desired subsets fall into two distinct classes:

A. those subsets that do not contain the number N

B. those subsets that do contain N

That means that the problem can be reduced to two subproblems of exactly the same kind as the original problem, but smaller:

A. the problem of generating a matrix of all K-element subsets of the integers from 1 up to $N-1$

B. the problem of generating a matrix of all $(K-1)$-element subsets of the integers from 1 up to $N-1$

Then the results can be combined by catenation to yield a solution to the original problem in the manner indicated by the following diagram:

```
|                     |
|          A          |
|                     |
| _____  |
|                  |N |
|                  | .|
|          B       | .|
|                  | .|
| _____|N |
```

A column of N-values is catenated onto submatrix B so that the bottom submatrix will contain all K-element subsets of the numbers 1 through N which do contain the number N. For example, the lines in the following diagram show the catenation used to construct the matrix for 3 *SUBSETS* 4:

```
| 1   2   3 |
|-----------|
| 1   2| 4 |
| 1   3| 4 |
| 2   3| 4 |
```

When the special cases have been considered which stop the process of recursive reduction of the problem, the result is a function definition like the following one (the *IF* function used is from Section 5.6.):

```
      ∇  M←K SUBSETS N;A;B
[1]       →CASE2 IF(K>0)∧K≤N
[2]      ⍝ THERE ARE NO SUBSETS IF K≤0 OR K>N:
[3]       M← 0 0 ρ0
[4]       →0
[5]      CASE2:→CASE3 IF K>1
[6]      ⍝ EACH ELEMENT IS IN A SUBSET BY ITSELF WHEN K=1:
[7]       M←(N,1)ριN
[8]       →0
[9]      CASE3:→CASE4 IF K<N
[10]     ⍝ ALL ELEMENTS TOGETHER FORM THE ONLY SUBSET WHEN K=N:
[11]      M←(1,N)ριN
[12]      →0
[13]     CASE4:
[14]     ⍝ A←THE K-ELEMENT SUBSETS THAT DO NOT CONTAIN N:
[15]      A←K SUBSETS N-1
[16]     ⍝ B←THE K-ELEMENT SUBSETS THAT DO CONTAIN N:
[17]      B←(K-1)SUBSETS N-1
[18]      B←B,N
[19]     ⍝ THE FINAL MATRIX:
[20]      M←A,[1]B
      ∇
```

(The case in lines 6 through 8 is not really necessary, but is included to make the function execute faster than it would otherwise.)

If the diamond symbol is used to separate several statements in a single line, and if the *WHEN* function from Section 5.6 is used, the *SUBSETS* function (without comment lines) can be shortened to the following definition:

```
      ∇  M←K SUBSETS N
[1]      →WHEN (K≤0)∨K>N ◇ M←0 0ρ0 ◇ →0
[2]      →WHEN K=1 ◇ M←(N,1)ριN ◇ →0
[3]      →WHEN K=N ◇ M←(1,N)ριN ◇ →0
[4]      M←(K SUBSETS N-1),[1]((K-1) SUBSETS N-1),N
      ∇
```

Certain non-numerical patterns can also be formed recursively, as the following example illustrates:

```
      ∇  M←A SPIRAL B
[1]      →(A>1)/CASE2
[2]      M← 1 2 ρ'∘'
[3]      →0
[4]      CASE2:M←(B-A)SPIRAL A
[5]      M←⍉⌽M
[6]      M←M,(A,A)ρ'∘',Aρ' '
      ∇
         3 SPIRAL 5
 ∘∘
∘  ∘
∘∘  ∘
```

8 *SPIRAL* 13

34 *SPIRAL* 55

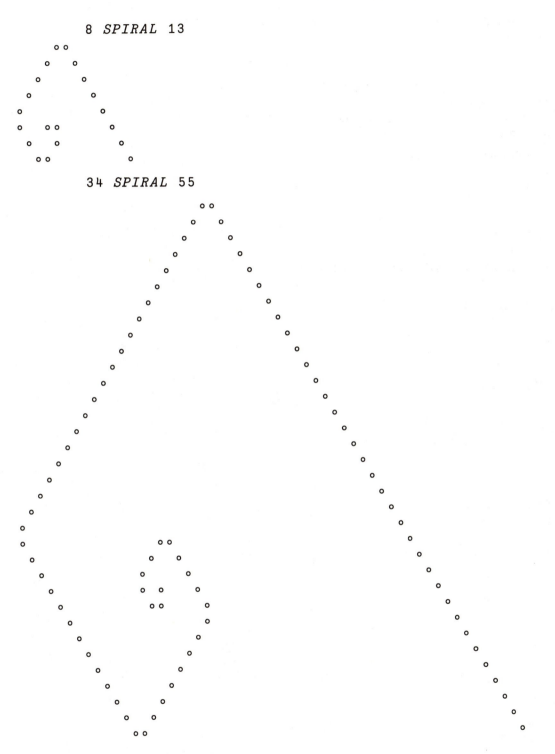

The arguments A and B of $SPIRAL$ must be consecutive numbers in the so-called "Fibonacci" sequence

$$1 \quad 2 \quad 3 \quad 5 \quad 8 \quad 13 \quad 21 \quad 34 \quad 55 \quad 89 \quad \ldots$$

in which each number is the sum of the two preceding numbers. The shape of the resulting matrix is always A,B.

Another recursive character matrix is generated by the following $CRISSCROSS$ function.

```
      ∇ M←CRISSCROSS N;A;B
[1]      →(N>1)/CASE2
[2]      M← 1 1 ρ'×'
[3]      →0
[4]   CASE2:A←CRISSCROSS N-1
[5]      B←3*(N-2)
[6]      B←(B,B)ρ' '
[7]      M←(A,B,A),[1](B,A,B),[1]A,B,A
      ∇

      CRISSCROSS 1
×



      CRISSCROSS 2
×  ×
 ×
×  ×



      CRISSCROSS 3
×  ×    ×  ×
 ×       ×
×  ×    ×  ×
    ×  ×
     ×
    ×  ×
×  ×    ×  ×
 ×       ×
×  ×    ×  ×
```

CRISSCROSS 4

EXERCISES

5.7.1. Revise the function ∇ *M←K SUBSETS N* so that it will generate the *K*-subsets of the numbers 1 through *N* in "lexicographic" order: that is, in increasing order if the numbers in each row of the matrix are considered as digits in a single number. For example, 3 *SUBSETS* 5 should generate the following numeric matrix (without the lines, which have been added to suggest the manner of recursive construction of the matrix):

```
 _____
| 1| 2   3 |
| 1| 2   4 |
| 1| 2   5 |
| 1| 3   4 |
| 1| 3   5 |
| 1| 4   5 |
|------------|
| 2   3   4 |
| 2   3   5 |
| 2   4   5 |
| 3   4   5 |
 --------------
```

5.7.2.   Use the *SUBSETS* function to generate all 4-letter subsets of the letters *ABCDEF*.

5.7.3.   Write a function ∇ *M←K SELECTIONS N* which uses the *SUBSETS* function to generate a matrix containing all of the ways of selecting *K* numbers, possibly with repetitions, from the integers 1 through *N*. For example, 3 *SELECTIONS* 3 should yield

```
1   1   1
1   1   2
1   1   3
1   2   2
1   2   3
1   3   3
2   2   2
2   2   3
2   3   3
3   3   3
```

5.7.4.   Write a recursive function ∇ *M←TREE N* to generate a matrix containing a tree pattern, as shown by the following examples:

TREE 0

```
/\
```

TREE 1

```
  /\
 /  \
/\  /\
```

TREE 2

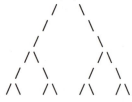

TREE 3

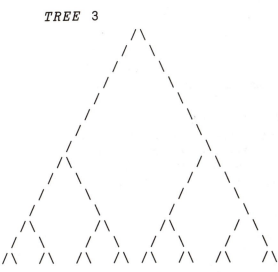

5.7.5.   Redefine the functions *SPIRAL*, *CRISSCROSS*, and *SUBSETS* without using recursion. How do the new versions compare with the recursive ones in length and complexity?

5.7.6.   Write a recursive function ∇ *M←K SUMSTO N* to generate a matrix with *K* columns, whose rows are all of the *K*−element vectors of non-negative integers which add up to the non-negative integer *N*. The rows of the matrix should be in lexicographic order. For example, 3 *SUMSTO* 5 should yield the following matrix:

```
0   0   5
0   1   4
0   2   3
0   3   2
0   4   1
0   5   0
1   0   4
1   1   3
1   2   2
1   3   1
1   4   0
2   0   3
2   1   2
2   2   1
2   3   0
3   0   2
3   1   1
3   2   0
4   0   1
4   1   0
5   0   0
```

Notice how, when N is 9 or less, the matrix represents all integers with K or fewer digits whose digits add up to N.

5.7.7.   A "partition" of a positive integer N is a collection of positive integers, possibly with repetitions, which add up to N. For example, (3, 1, 1, 1) is a partition of 6 into four "parts." Some other partitions of 6 are (4, 2), (2, 2, 1, 1), and (6). Only the members of a partition are significant, not their order as in Exercise 5.7.6.

Write a recursive function ∇ *M←N PARTITIONS K* to generate a matrix containing all partitions of positive integer N into at most K parts. Each row of the matrix should contain one partition, with its members in descending order across the row and with zeros used to fill out the row to width K. For example, 6 *PARTITIONS* 3 should yield the matrix:

```
6  0  0
5  1  0
4  2  0
3  3  0
4  1  1
3  2  1
2  2  2
```

The desired function is related to the following recurrence relation which can be used to calculate the number, $P(N, K)$, of such partitions:

$$P(N, K) = \qquad P(N, K - 1) \qquad + \qquad P(N - K, K)$$

the number of partitions of N into at most $K - 1$ parts.	the number of partitions of N into exactly K parts. (Since, given a partition of N into exactly K parts, substracting 1 from each part yields a unique corresponding partition of $N - K$ into at most K parts, and vice versa, $P(N - K, K)$ is the number of partitions of N into exactly K parts.)

The recurrence is valid for $N > K > 1$. There are also the following special cases:

When $K = 1$, $P(N, K) = 1$. (There is only one partition into at most one part.)

When $N \leq K$, $P(N, K) = P(N, N) = P(N, N - 1) + 1$. (There is only one partition of N into exactly N parts.)

5.7.8.   Write a recursive function ∇ *M←AMOUNT CHANGE COINS* to display in the rows of a matrix the different ways in which a specified

AMOUNT of money can be made up of coins whose denominations are given by a vector *COINS*. (*COINS* should have no repeated values.) The following are some examples:

```
      25  CHANGE  25  10  5
25     0     0     0   0
10    10     5     0   0
10     5     5     5   0
 5     5     5     5   5

      52  CHANGE  25  10  5

      55  CHANGE  25  10  5
25    25     5     0   0   0   0   0   0   0   0
25    10    10    10   0   0   0   0   0   0   0
25    10    10     5   5   0   0   0   0   0   0
25    10     5     5   5   5   0   0   0   0   0
25     5     5     5   5   5   5   0   0   0   0
10    10    10    10  10   5   0   0   0   0   0
10    10    10    10   5   5   5   0   0   0   0
10    10    10     5   5   5   5   5   0   0   0
10    10     5     5   5   5   5   5   5   0   0
10     5     5     5   5   5   5   5   5   5   0
 5     5     5     5   5   5   5   5   5   5   5
```

5.7.9. Write a recursive function ∇ *M←AMOUNT CHANGE2 COINS*, like the function in Exercise 5.7.8, but yielding the results in a different form. Each column of the result should correspond to an element in the *COINS* vector, and the numbers in a row should indicate how many coins of each denomination are used:

```
    55  CHANGE2  25  10  5
2    0    1
1    3    0
1    2    2
1    1    4
1    0    6
0    5    1
0    4    3
0    3    5
0    2    7
0    1    9
0    0   11
```

Chapter 6

Advanced and Specialized Functions and Operators

In this chapter most of the remaining APL primitive functions and operators will be introduced. The functions in this chapter are somewhat more specialized than those in earlier chapters. However, each does something which is not so easy to do without it.

6.1 Scan (\)

The *scan* operator, represented by the backslash symbol \, extends the power of the reduction operator (Section 4.4) by computing all initial partial reductions of a given array by a given scalar dyadic function. For instance, the scan

        $+\backslash VECTOR$

computes all of the partial sums from the beginning of a given $VECTOR$. That is, $(+\backslash VECTOR)[POSITION]$ has the same value as $+/POSITION\uparrow VECTOR$ for each $POSITION$ in the $VECTOR$. Thus,

        +\1 2 3 4 5   yields
1 3 6 10 15

For example, the following function uses a sum scan to compute the running balance for a bank account after each transaction in a vector of transactions (where deposits are positive and withdrawals are negative):

```
      ∇   BALANCE BANKBOOK TRANSACTIONS;W;D
[1]       ' '
[2]       'WITHDRAWAL        DEPOSIT         BALANCE'
[3]       W←0,|TRANSACTIONS×TRANSACTIONS<0
[4]       D←0,TRANSACTIONS×TRANSACTIONS≥0
[5]       BALANCE←+\BALANCE,TRANSACTIONS
[6]       W,D,[1.5]BALANCE
      ∇
```

```
     2174.32 BANKBOOK 500 ‾23.75 50 ‾175.23 ‾219 125.42
```

WITHDRAWAL	DEPOSIT	BALANCE
0	0	2174.32
0	500	2674.32
23.75	0	2650.57
0	50	2700.57
175.23	0	2525.34
219	0	2306.34
0	125.42	2431.76

As another application of scan, consider the problem of checking whether a string of characters has "balanced" parentheses. For parentheses to be balanced, each left parenthesis must be followed by a corresponding right parenthesis, and each right parenthesis must be preceded by a corresponding left parenthesis. Thus, the first of the following four strings is balanced, but the last three are not:

```
'A + (B × (C ÷ D)) × (E + F)'
'A + (B × (C ÷ D) × (E + F)'
'A + (B × C ÷ D)) × (E + F)'
'A + (B × C ÷ D)) × ((E + F)'
```

As the last string shows, it is not enough that the total numbers of left and right parentheses are the same. Balancing also requires that as a string is scanned from left to right the number of right parentheses encountered up to each point never exceeds the number of left parentheses encountered up to the same point.

Since the scan $+\backslash STRING = '('$ counts the number of left parentheses up to each point in a $STRING$, one can define a function to test for balanced parentheses as follows:

```
     ∇  R←BALANCED STRING;EXCESS
[1]     STRING←,STRING
[2]     EXCESS←(+\STRING='(')-+\STRING=')'
[3]     R←(∧/EXCESS≥0)∧0=‾1↑EXCESS
     ∇
```

That is, $STRING$ is balanced if the $EXCESS$ of left parentheses over right parentheses is never negative and if it is zero at the end of the $STRING$. (Note: If $STRING$ is empty, $BALANCED$ will yield the value 1. Why?)

When scan is applied to matrices or higher-dimensional arrays, the dimension along which the scan is to be performed is indicated by giving the dimension number in square brackets, in the same way as for reduction. Scan without a dimension number is always done along the last dimension, and the overstruck symbol $⍀$ is equivalent to $\backslash[1]$, which indicates scan along the first dimension. Thus, if M is a matrix, $+\backslash[1]M$ or $+⍀M$ will compute the sum scan down the columns, and $+\backslash[2]M$ or $+\backslash M$ will compute the sum scan across the rows.

Although scan with the plus function is perhaps the most common scan, scans with other functions can also be useful. For example, the following product scan was used in the second example session of Section 1.2 to generate powers of 2:

```
     ×\16ρ2
2  4  8  16  32  64  128  256  512  1024  2048  4096  8192  16384  32768  65536
```

Also, various useful scans can be applied to Boolean vectors. For instance, if B is a Boolean vector such as

```
1  1  1  1  0  0  1  0  1  1  1  0  0  1  0
```

then $\wedge\backslash B$

```
1  1  1  1  0  0  0  0  0  0  0  0  0  0  0
```

sets all 1's after the first zero to zeros. That can be used to left-justify the rows of a character matrix as in the example below:

```
     BORDER M
```

```
 _____
|     FIRST LINE         |
|        SECOND LINE     |
| THIRD      LINE        |
 ------------------------
```

```
     BORDER  (+/∧\M=' ')φM
```

```
 _____
|FIRST LINE              |
|SECOND LINE             |
|THIRD       LINE        |
 ------------------------
```

The following are some other useful scans on Boolean vectors:

```
         ∨\0  0  0  1  1  0  1  0  0  1  1  1  0  1  1  0  0
0  0  0  1  1  1  1  1  1  1  1  1  1  1  1  1  1
```

Or-scan sets all zeros after the first 1 to 1's.

```
         ≠\1  1  1  1  0  0  1  0  1  1  1  0  0  1  0  0  0
1  0  1  0  0  0  1  1  0  1  0  0  0  1  1  1  1
```

In this case a 1 occurs at a position in the result if and only if there are an odd number of 1's up to and including that position in the argument vector.

```
         ≤\1  1  1  1  0  0  1  0  1  1  1  0  0  1  0  0  0
1  1  1  1  0  1  1  1  1  1  1  1  1  1  1  1  1
```

The scan $\leq\backslash$ sets all zeros after the first zero to 1's. A few other useful scans appear in the exercises for this section.

As scan is defined, in terms of reduction, a scan on an N-element vector involves

$$1 + 2 + 3 + \ldots + (N - 1) = N \times (N - 1) \div 2$$

applications of the function used with the scan. For example,

```
      -\5  4  3  2  1
5  1  4  2  3
```

is equivalent to

```
      5,(5-4),(5-(4-3)),(5-(4-(3-2))),(5-(4-(3-(2-1))))
5  1  4  2  3
```

which involves 10 subtractions.

In some cases the number of operations involved in a scan can be reduced considerably by changing the order in which the function is applied to the elements of the vector being scanned. Those cases involve "associative" functions like the maximum function ($\lceil$), for which $(A\lceil B)\lceil C$ always has the same value as $A\lceil(B\lceil C)$ regardless of the values of the arguments A, B, and C. Associativity means that a scan like

```
      \lceil\2  ¯1  3  9  5
2  2  3  9  9
```

which is strictly defined as equivalent to

```
      2,(2\lceil¯1),(2\lceil(¯1\lceil3)),  (2\lceil(¯1\lceil(3\lceil9))),  (2\lceil(¯1\lceil(3\lceil(9\lceil5))))
2  2  3  9  9
```

and involves 10 applications of maximum, can be computed instead from left to right as the catenation of

```
2
(2\lceil¯1)
((2\lceil¯1)\lceil3)
(((2\lceil¯1)\lceil3)\lceil9)  and
((((2\lceil¯1)\lceil3)\lceil9)\lceil5)
```

After the rearrangement, each element of the result can be computed from the previous element by a single application of the maximum function. Hence only four applications of maximum are needed altogether. Thus, in general, a scan with an associative function on an N-element vector requires only $(N-1)$ applications of the function used in the scan. Most good implementations of APL optimize the evaluation of scans in this way.

The plus function, probably the most commonly used with scan, is associative in ordinary arithmetic. That is, $(A+B)+C$ is always equal to $A+(B+C)$. However, in computer arithmetic plus is not strictly associative. It is possible for the value of $(A+B)+C$ to be slightly different from the value of $A+(B+C)$ because numbers are represented to only a finite number of decimal places in a computer. Nevertheless, many versions of APL treat plus as associative when it is used with scan, so that plus scans can be computed as efficiently as possible. The following example using VAX-11 APL shows the discrepancy that can occur:

```
VEC←1E10,100ρ1E¯7
□PP←16                  —setting the number of digits of precision to
                         be displayed to the maximum internal
                         precision used

      ¯1↑+\VEC
10000000000
      +/VEC
10000000000.00001
```

VEC contains one very large number followed by 100 very small numbers. When it is summed from left to right, according to the optimized method for computing the sum scan, each of the small numbers is so small compared with the large number as to be insignificant. The 16 digits of precision with which the computer represents numbers are not enough to hold all of the digits of the sum of the large number and one of the small numbers. So the small numbers are effectively ignored. However, when the vector is summed from right to left in computing the sum reduction, the small numbers are added together first, and their sum is large enough to be significant when added, finally, to the large number at the beginning of the vector.

EXERCISES

6.1.1.   Write an expression using scan and other functions to yield the result of removing all leading blanks from a given character vector, $STRING$.

6.1.2.   Determine which of the following functions are associative when applied to Boolean arguments:

= ≠ < ≤ ≥ > ⍲ ⍱

(*Hint*: Try all possible combinations of arguments 0 and 1.)

6.1.3.   Compute the value of each of the following expressions, and describe in English what the scan in each expression does in general:

=\0 0 0 1 1 1 0 1 1 0 0 0 1 0 1

<\0 0 0 1 1 1 0 1 1 0 0 0 1 0 1

≥\0 0 0 0 0 1 1 1 0 0 0 0 1 0 1

>\1 1 1 1 1 0 0 1 1 0 0 0 1 0 1

6.1.4.   Write an expression using scan and other functions to yield the result of deleting the first occurrence of a given $ELEMENT$ from a given $VECTOR$. If the given $ELEMENT$ does not occur in the $VECTOR$, the result should be the given $VECTOR$.

6.1.5. Write a function ∇ *NEWSTRING←SHRINKQUOTES STRING*, using scan but not branch, to reduce all quoted substrings in a given character vector to single quotation marks. For instance, if *S* is the string

THIS 'STRING' CONTAINS 'QUOTED SUBSTRINGS'

then *SHRINKQUOTES S* should yield

THIS ' CONTAINS '

(Such a function could be used with the *BALANCED* function, to avoid counting quoted parentheses when determining whether a string has balanced parentheses.)

6.1.6. If *B* is a nonempty Boolean vector which is treated as a binary number, the 2's-complement of *B* is defined to be another Boolean vector *C* of the same length as *B* such that when *B* and *C* are added together as binary numbers and any carry off the left end is ignored, the result is an all-zero vector. For example, the 2's-complement of

0 1 0 1 1 0 1 0 0   is

1 0 1 0 0 1 1 0 0

Negative numbers are often represented in 2's-complement form in computers.

Using the scan operator and other functions, but not branch, write a function ∇ *C←COMPLEMENT2 B* to compute the 2's-complement of a given Boolean vector. Notice that in the 2's-complement of *B* the rightmost 1 and the zeros after it are the same as in *B*, but all of the elements to the left of the rightmost 1 are changed from what they were in *B*: 1's have become 0's and 0's have become 1's.

6.1.7. Suppose *SALES* is a matrix representing sales volumes at each location in a retail store chain for each month of a year. Each row represents one location, and each column represents a month. Write expressions using scan and other functions to find:

a. For each month, which location had the maximum sales volume.

b. For each location, which month had the highest sales volume.

For example, if *SALES* is the following matrix,

```
3835 7117 9040 6488 7030 6634  666 4392 5628 8096 5286 6004
4953 9250 2302 3868 1159 8798 7908 1935 4284 9974 3769 2320
4541 8856 9494 1356 8581 2515 6910 1378 3812 7833 8100 7585
5421 4391 7858 3933 5591 3018 2684 7421 7455 3190 1630 1789
 696 4670 6273 8484 3737 9324 3281 7473 9837 9322 8004  777
8946 3915 7227 4330 7530 4782 5146 1593 8636 7436 5878 2525
6824 4443 7730  900 7113  734 8178 8586 8000 4044 3934 4319
```

then (a) should yield 6 2 3 5 3 5 7 7 5 2 3 3 and (b) should yield 3 10 3 3 9 1 8. If a maximum value occurs twice in the same row or column, report the position of the first occurrence.

6.1.8.   The effect of some scans can be reversed. That is, it is possible to go from the result of the scan back to the original vector scanned. Write expressions to compute such "inverses" of $+\backslash$ on arbitrary numeric vectors and of $\neq\backslash$ on Boolean vectors. (Note: The expressions for the inverses need not use the scan operator.)

6.1.9.   (For versions of APL which do not have the replication function.) Write a function $\nabla R \leftarrow NUMBER\ COPIES\ VECTOR$ to take a given $VECTOR$ and produce a new vector in which each element $VECTOR[J]$ of the old vector occurs $NUMBER[J]$ times. For example,

$$3\ \ 0\ \ 1\ \ 2\ \ 4\ \ COPIES\ \ 'ABCDE'$$

should produce the vector

$$AAACDDEEEE$$

Note: If $NUMBER$ is a scalar, it should be applied to each element of the given $VECTOR$. Forward branches may be used in this function (e.g., in connection with error checking or handling of special cases), but backward branches (to create explicit loops) should not be used.

6.2   Grade up (⍋) and Grade down (⍒)

The functions *grade up* (or *upgrade*) and *grade down* (or *downgrade*) perform sorting. They are represented by the overstruck characters ⍋ and ⍒, respectively. Actually, instead of sorting its argument directly, grade up or grade down yields a vector of position numbers which corresponds to the sorted order of its argument. For example,

```
      ⍋25  16  3  8  37  16 yields
3  4  2  6  1  5
```

since the third item in the argument vector is the smallest, the fourth item is the second smallest, the second item is the third smallest, and so on up to the fifth item, which is the largest. Notice that the given order of equal items (the two 16's in the example) is preserved.

   Grade down operates similarly to grade up, but in descending order. For instance,

```
      ⍒'AARDVARK'       yields
5  3  7  8  4  1  2  6
```

(However, not all versions of APL allow grade up and grade down to be applied to character data.)

   When the result of grade up or grade down is used to subscript the vector that was graded, it actually sorts the elements of that vector into ascending or descending order, producing a new vector:

```
      VECTOR←25  16  3  8  37  16
      VECTOR[⍋VECTOR]
3  8  16  16  25  37
```

The advantage of having grade up and grade down produce vectors of subscripts, rather than sorting their arguments directly, is that that allows elements of one array to be sorted according to values in another array. For example, suppose *YEARS* is a vector of year numbers and *SNOW* is a vector of snowfall amounts for those years:

```
    YEARS
1972 1973 1974 1975 1976 1977 1978 1979 1980 1981 1982
    SNOW
240 276 160 274 162 203 227 164 255 195 286
```

Then the following expression lists the years and amounts of snow in descending order of snowfall amounts:

```
    (YEARS,[.5]SNOW)[;⍒SNOW]
1982 1973 1975 1980 1972 1978 1977 1981 1979 1976 1974
 286  276  274  255  240  227  203  195  164  162  160
```

The process of sorting an array can be looked at in two ways:

1. from the point of view of the original array: asking where each element goes into the sorted array
2. from the point of view of the sorted array: asking where each element comes from in the original array

A single grade up or grade down describes sorting from the second point of view. That is, (⍋*VECTOR*)[*J*] tells where the *J*th element of the sorted vector comes from in the original *VECTOR*. This can be shown by a diagram like the following example:

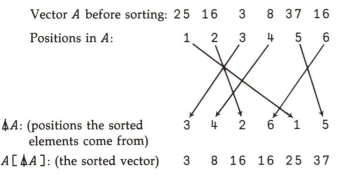

Vector *A* before sorting: 25 16 3 8 37 16

Positions in *A*:   1 2 3 4 5 6

⍋*A*: (positions the sorted   3 4 2 6 1 5
elements come from)

A[⍋*A*]: (the sorted vector)   3 8 16 16 25 37

Now consider what happens if grade up is applied twice. In the foregoing example,

```
    ⍋⍋A                 yields the vector
5 3 1 2 6 4
```

which gives the positions that the elements of vector *A* go to when they are sorted. That is, two grade ups describe a sort from the first of the two points of view mentioned above, as the following diagram shows:

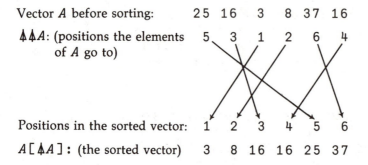

Vector *A* before sorting: 25 16   3   8 37 16

⍋⍋*A*: (positions the elements
      of *A* go to)   5   3   1   2   6   4

Positions in the sorted vector: 1   2   3   4   5   6

A[⍋*A*] : (the sorted vector)   3   8   16 16 25 37

Hence, if a vector *A* is to be sorted so that the sorted vector becomes the new value of *A*, this can be done either by the assignment

$$A \leftarrow A[\triangle A]$$

or by the assignment

$$A[\triangle\triangle A] \leftarrow A$$

Furthermore, double grade up can be used to undo a sort, as in the following example:

```
      A
25 16 3 8 37 16        —the original vector

      S←⍋A

      B←A[S]
      B
3 8 16 16 25 37        —the vector sorted

      B[⍋S]
25 16 3 8 37 16        —the original vector restored
```

In some versions of APL grade up and grade down can be applied to matrices as well as to vectors. In that case each row of the matrix is treated as a string, whose components are the individual numbers or characters in the row, and the sorting is done in lexicographic order. For instance, if *M* is the matrix

```
SUCH
WORDS
SORTS
GRADE UP
SIMPLY
```

(and if the version of APL allows grade up to be done on character data) then the value of *M*[⍋*M*;] will be the matrix

```
GRADE UP
SIMPLY
SORTS
SUCH
WORDS
```

Similarly, if *DATES* is a numeric matrix like

1979	12	1
1980	3	5
1979	8	2
1979	12	31
1980	1	1
1980	3	1

then ⍋*DATES* yields 3 1 4 5 6 2 and *DATES*[⍋*DATES*;] yields

1979	8	2
1979	12	1
1979	12	31
1980	1	1
1980	3	1
1980	3	5

EXERCISES

6.2.1.   Under what circumstances will the value of ⍋*VECTOR* be the same as the value of ⌽⍒*VECTOR*?

6.2.2.   Give a simpler expression that always has the same value as the expression ⍋⍋⍋*A*.

6.2.3.   Suppose *NAMES* is a matrix containing the names of marathon runners in alphabetical order, and *TIMES* is another matrix containing a corresponding list of the times for their runs, as in Exercise 4.5.6. Write an expression to list the names of the runners in order of increasing times.

6.2.4.   Given 10-row matrices like those in Exercise 6.2.3 (and 4.5.6), and given another matrix, *ORDINALS*, containing the words

FIRST
SECOND
THIRD
FOURTH
FIFTH
SIXTH
SEVENTH
EIGHTH
NINTH
TENTH

write an expression to produce a matrix containing the alphabetical list of names, and alongside each name that person's order of finish, as in the example

```
BACHELER   NINTH
BEDANE     TENTH
FOSTER     EIGHTH
HILL       SIXTH
KIMIHARA   FIFTH
LISMONT    SECOND
MACGREGOR  SEVENTH
MOORE      FOURTH
SHORTER    FIRST
WOLDE      THIRD
```

6.2.5. Suppose *WORDS* is a matrix of words with one word in each row. Write an expression to sort the words in order of increasing lengths.

6.2.6. If *A* is a vector of numbers, which of the following assignments sorts *A* into descending order?

$A[\Psi\Psi A]\leftarrow A$

$A[\blacktriangle\Psi A]\leftarrow A$

6.2.7. Write a function ∇ *R*←*K LARGEST VECTOR* to return the *K* largest elements from a given numeric *VECTOR*. The elements in the result should be in the same sequence as in the given vector. You may assume that the given vector will contain no duplicate values. For example, if *VECTOR* is

```
39 26 15 8 57 2 5 45 12
```

then

```
     4 LARGEST VECTOR should yield
39 26 57 45
```

Note: If *K* is greater than ρ*VECTOR*, the result should be the same as the given *VECTOR*. Do not use branch in this problem.

6.2.8. Given an array *A* of arbitrary rank, write an expression to perform a dyadic transpose on *A* in such a way that the new array will have its dimensions in ascending order of size. For example, if

```
A←4 2 3 2ρι48
```

then the transposed result should be the array

```
 1   13   25   37
 3   15   27   39
 5   17   29   41

 2   14   26   38
 4   16   28   40
 6   18   30   42

 7   19   31   43
 9   21   33   45
11   23   35   47

 8   20   32   44
10   22   34   46
12   24   36   48
```

which has shape 2 2 3 4.

6.3 Expansion (\)

The *expansion* function, represented by the backslash symbol \, is a kind of inverse of the compression function. It inserts blanks or zeros into an array, depending on whether the array contains characters or numbers. Expand takes a vector, matrix, or higher-dimensional array as its right argument, and a Boolean vector as its left argument. Ones in the left argument correspond to the elements, rows, columns, or planes along one dimension of the right argument, and zeros in the left argument indicate the places where the new blanks or zeros are to be inserted. For example, if S is assigned the character vector

        S←'*THESEARESTORES*'

then the following applications of expansion yield the values shown:

        1 1 1 0 1 1 1 0 1 1 1 1 1 1 1 1\S
THE SEA RESTORES
        1 1 1 1 1 0 1 1 1 0 1 1 1 1 1 1 1\S
THESE ARE STORES

Another example illustrates application of expand to a numeric vector:

        (28ρ1 0 0)\ι10
1 0 0 2 0 0 3 0 0 4 0 0 5 0 0 6 0 0 7 0 0 8 0 0 9 0 0 10

The Boolean left argument must contain as many 1's as there are elements in the right argument along the dimension being expanded.

Expansion of matrices will be illustrated by use of the following 9-by-7 character matrix:

```
      DATES
79JAN16
79MAR05
79JUL31
80FEB29
80DEC01
81JAN22
82APR04
82JUN30
82NOV15
```

The pair of assignment statements

```
NEW←1 1 0 1 1 1 0 1 1\DATES
NEW[;3 7]←'-'
```

inserts columns of hyphens into the matrix. (Notice the use of assignment with subscripting to replace the inserted blanks by hypens.)

```
      NEW
79-JAN-16
79-MAR-05
79-JUL-31
80-FEB-29
80-DEC-01
81-JAN-22
82-APR-04
82-JUN-30
82-NOV-15
```

Next, the expression

```
1 1 1 0 1 1 0 1 0 1 1 1\[1]NEW
```

can be used to insert some blank rows, producing the 12-by-9 matrix

```
79-JAN-16
79-MAR-05
79-JUL-31

80-FEB-29
80-DEC-01

81-JAN-22

82-APR-04
82-JUN-30
82-NOV-15
```

The expansion \[1] along the first dimension could be specified, alternatively, by the overstruck symbol ⍀.

If the right argument of expand is a scalar, it is replicated (in the usual way in APL) to become a vector of the same length as the left argument. For example,

$\quad\quad$ ((⍳64)∊1,×\6ρ2)\'*' yields the vector

** *   *   ·*   *   *

which has asterisks in positions corresponding to powers of 2.

Often when expand is used, the appropriate Boolean vector for the left argument must be computed from some other array. For example, the following function accepts a vector, *POSITIONS*, of position numbers in a given *VECTOR* and inserts blanks or zeros after those positions. It does so by converting *POSITIONS* into an appropriate Boolean vector for use with expansion. The numbers in the *POSITIONS* vector must be greater than or equal to zero and arranged in nondecreasing order. A zero position indicates insertion at the beginning of the given *VECTOR*.

```
      ∇   R←VECTOR EXPANDAFTER POSITIONS
[1]       R←((ρ,VECTOR)+ρ,POSITIONS)ρ1
[2]       R[POSITIONS+⍳ρ,POSITIONS]←0
[3]       R←R\,VECTOR
      ∇

      'NOWISHALLOWNIT' EXPANDAFTER 3 3 4 4 9 12
NOW  I   SHALL OWN IT

      (⍳8) EXPANDAFTER 0 0 3 5 5 5 8
0 0 1 2 3 0 4 5 0 0 0 6 7 8 0
```

If the positions for insertion are not in nondecreasing order, they must first be sorted, or, alternatively, a different version of the function can be defined as follows:

```
      ∇   R←VECTOR EXPANDAFTER2 POSITIONS
[1]       R←⍋(⍳ρ,VECTOR),POSITIONS
[2]       R←(R≤ρ,VECTOR)\,VECTOR
      ∇

      'NOWISHALLOWNIT' EXPANDAFTER2 9 12 3 4 4 3
NOW  I   SHALL OWN IT

      (⍳8) EXPANDAFTER2 5 0 8 5 3 0 5
0 0 1 2 3 0 4 5 0 0 0 6 7 8 0
```

EXERCISES

6.3.1. Write a function ∇ *R←SPACEOUT STRING* to insert a blank after every character in a given *STRING* except the last. If *STRING* is the empty vector, the result should also be empty. (This is similar to Exercise 2.12.3, but this time it is to be done with the expansion function.)

6.3.2. Write a function ∇ *R←DOUBLESPACE PAGE* to insert a blank line after each line in a given character matrix *PAGE*, except the last.

6.3.3. Redo Exercise 4.8.1 using expand instead of take to define a function ∇ *B←NUMERIC A* which will determine whether or not its argument array is numeric.

6.3.4. Given a numeric matrix *M*, write an expression that will yield a matrix of the same shape in which each row that contained any zeros at all has been replaced by an all-zero row.

6.3.5. Write a function ∇ *R←VECTOR INSERT QUANTITIES* to insert blanks or zeros into a given *VECTOR* according to the values given in a vector *QUANTITIES*. *QUANTITIES* will have one more element than *VECTOR*, and *QUANTITIES[J]* will specify how many blanks or zeros are to be inserted before *VECTOR[J]*. For example,

         6 7 8 *INSERT* 3 0 1 2 should yield
0 0 0 6 7 0 8 0 0

Do not use branch in this function.

6.3.6. Redo Exercise 5.5.3, using expansion to define the function ∇ *M←STRING CUTAT CHAR* without using branch.

6.3.7. Suppose *STRING* is a character vector. Write an expression that will create a two-row matrix in which *STRING* occupies the first row, and the second row consists of blanks and raised negative symbols (⁻), so that the nonblank characters in the first row are, in effect, underlined. For example, if *STRING* is

THIS STRING OF WORDS then the result should be

THIS STRING OF WORDS
‾‾‾‾ ‾‾‾‾‾‾ ‾‾ ‾‾‾‾‾

6.3.8. Write a function ∇ *R←JUSTIFY LINE* which will right-justify a *LINE* of English text by removing all blanks from the end of the *LINE* and distributing them as uniformly as possible in the gaps between the words in the *LINE*. The resulting string should have the same length as the given *LINE*. If the line is all blank or contains only one word, the result should be the same as the given *LINE*. Any string of consecutive nonblank characters can be considered to be a "word."

JUSTIFY may use the function *EXPANDAFTER* or *EXPANDAFTER*2, which were presented as examples. It may also involve use of branch, but only forward branches (to handle special cases), not backward branches for explicit looping. When testing *JUSTIFY*, use the *QUOTE* function from Exercise 3.3 to display the *LINE* before and after right-justification, so that one can see clearly that the length of the line and the number of initial blanks have not changed, and that no blanks remain at the end. For example, if *QUOTE LINE* is

'   *SUDDENLY, THERE APPEARED AT THE DOOR A*   '

the result (*QUOTED*) should be

'   *SUDDENLY,   THERE   APPEARED   AT   THE   DOOR   A*'

Note: If your version of APL has the replication function, *JUSTIFY* can be written using replication instead of expansion.

6.3.9. Write a function ∇ *R←EDIT STRING* which will edit a given character vector interactively, in a manner similar to the way the APL function-line editor works. (See Section 3.7.) Specifically, *EDIT* should display the given string and then wait on the next line for the user to type editing characters. Slash (/) should be used to indicate deletions, and digits or letters should be used to indicate insertions of spaces, exactly as for the APL line editor.

On the second pass, *EDIT* should print the modified line and then wait on the next line for new characters to be typed for the line. The new characters typed on this pass (except blanks) should replace the corresponding characters in the line. New characters should also be accepted at the end of the line, extending its length. The value of *EDIT* should be the final edited string. The following is an example of how *EDIT* should work:

```
      NEW←EDIT 'THIS SHORT TEST STRING'
THIS SHORT TEST STRING
    6//////      B3
THIS          TEST              STRING
  AT WAS A        OF EDITING A          OF CHARACTERS


        NEW
THAT WAS A TEST OF EDITING A STRING OF CHARACTERS
```

EDIT may use functions such as *INSERT* (Exercise 6.3.5) and *OVERLAYON* (Exercise 4.5.8). It should not use branch.

6.4 Outer Product (°. Function)

The *outer product* operator is represented by the pair of symbols °. followed by any dyadic scalar function symbol such as + or ×. If the arguments of the outer product are two vectors, it creates a matrix by applying the dyadic scalar function to all pairs of elements in the two vectors. For example,

        2 3 4 5°.*1 2 3 4 5 yields the matrix

```
2  4   8   16    32
3  9  27   81   243
4 16  64  256  1024
5 25 125  625  3125
```

Each element of the left-argument vector corresponds to a row of the result, and each element of the right-argument vector corresponds to a column of the result.

When outer products are written by hand, it helps to write the elements of the arguments beside the corresponding rows and above the corresponding columns, as in the following example, which shows the outer product $(\iota 5)\circ.=(\iota 5)$:

```
= | 1   2   3   4   5
--+-----------------
1 | 1   0   0   0   0
2 | 0   1   0   0   0
3 | 0   0   1   0   0
4 | 0   0   0   1   0
5 | 0   0   0   0   1
```

Outer products can be applied to character data as well as to numeric data, as in the example

```
        'AEIOU'∘.='AMELIORATE'
1 0 0 0 0 0 0 0 1 0 0
0 0 1 0 0 0 0 0 0 0 1
0 0 0 0 1 0 0 0 0 0 0
0 0 0 0 0 1 0 0 0 0 0
0 0 0 0 0 0 0 0 0 0 0
```

Of course, the dyadic scalar function used must be one which is applicable to character data.

Various patterns can be produced as character matrices by use of outer product combined with subscripting. For example, the expression

```
    ' □'[1+(10ρ1 0 0)∘.∨10ρ1 0 0]
```

yields the pattern

```
□□□□□□□□□□
□   □   □   □
□   □   □   □
□□□□□□□□□□
□   □   □   □
□   □   □   □
□□□□□□□□□□
□   □   □   □
□   □   □   □
□□□□□□□□□□
```

The arguments of an outer product need not be vectors. They can be arrays of any rank, and the shape of the result will be the catenation of their shapes. That is, $\rho(A\circ.+B)$ will be the same as $(\rho A),(\rho B)$.

As an example, suppose *GRID* is a numeric matrix whose elements represent physical measurements such as heights, temperatures, or pressures in a rectangular grid. (Assume that the original values have been converted to integers 0, 1, 2, 3, and 4 by an appropriate scaling computation.)

```
        GRID
0 0 0 0 1 1 0 0 0 0
0 0 0 1 2 2 1 0 0 0
0 1 1 2 3 3 2 1 0 0
1 1 2 3 3 4 3 2 1 0
1 2 3 3 4 4 4 3 2 1
1 2 2 2 3 3 3 2 1 0
0 1 1 2 2 2 2 1 0 0
0 0 0 1 1 1 1 1 0 0
```

Now suppose contours of equal nonzero values in the grid are to be displayed graphically. The following expression plots each contour separately by taking the outer product of the vector $\iota 4$ with the matrix *GRID*, creating a three-dimensional array. (The function *BORDER2* is a modification of the *BORDER* function of Exercise 3.4 which puts a border around each plane of the three-dimensional array.)

$$BORDER2 \quad ' \quad *'[1+(\iota 4)\circ.=GRID]$$

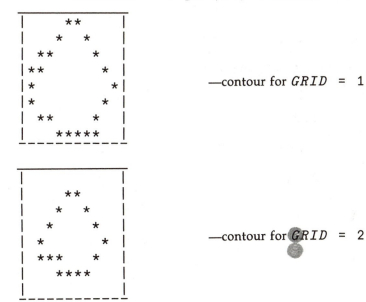

—contour for *GRID* = 1

—contour for *GRID* = 2

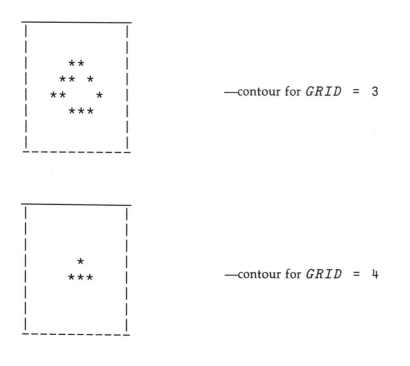

—contour for $GRID = 3$

—contour for $GRID = 4$

Outer product can be used to perform substring matching, as shown in the following function, which is adapted from a similar function in the book *APL \ 360 Reference Manual* by Sandra Pakin. The function computes a vector of the beginning positions of all occurrences of a given nonempty *SUBSTRING* in a given *STRING*. (It solves Exercise 5.5.2 without using branch.)

```
      ∇   POSITIONS←STRING MATCH SUBSTRING
[1]       SUBSTRING←,SUBSTRING
[2]       POSITIONS←∧/[1] (¯1+ιρSUBSTRING)⌽SUBSTRING∘.=,STRING
[3]       POSITIONS ←(1-ρSUBSTRING)↓POSITIONS∧0<ρSUBSTRING
[4]       POSITIONS←POSITIONS/ιρPOSITIONS
      ∇

      'MISSISSIPPI' MATCH 'ISSI'
2 5

      'MISSISSIPPI' MATCH 'PIM'

      'MISSISSIPPI' MATCH 'I'
2 5 8 11

      'SASSAFRAS' MATCH 'SSA'
3

      'NONEMPTY' MATCH ''

      'A' MATCH 'A'
1
```

```
    'AA' MATCH 'AA'
1

    'A' MATCH 'AA'

    '' MATCH 'ABC'

    '' MATCH ''
```

To see how the *MATCH* function works, consider

```
    'SASSAFRAS' MATCH 'SSA'
```

Line 1 simply ravels the *SUBSTRING* argument, in case it is a single character. In line 2 the outer product $SUBSTRING\circ.=,STRING$ yields the Boolean matrix

```
= | S A S S A F R A S
--+------------------
S | 1 0 1 1 0 0 0 0 1
S | 1 0 1 1 0 0 0 0 1
A | 0 1 0 0 1 0 0 1 0
```

in which the marked diagonal corresponds to a match of the given *SUBSTRING*. The rotation in line 2 then shifts each row of the matrix left by one-less-than its row number, converting the diagonals to columns. That is, the expression

$$({}^{-}1+\iota\rho SUBSTRING)\phi SUBSTRING\circ.=,STRING$$

yields the Boolean matrix

```
  S A S S A F R A S
  -----------------
| 1 0 1 1 0 0 0 0 1
| 0 1 1 0 0 0 0 1 1
| 0 0 1 0 0 1 0 0 1
```

Notice that the last column contains only ones; it corresponds to a false match of the substring *'SSA'* around the end of the *STRING*.

The and-reduction down the columns (still in line 2) yields ones in the positions where the substring matches begin. In the example there is one correct match in addition to the erroneous match at the end:

```
S A S S A F R A S

0 0 1 0 0 0 0 0 1
```

Line 3 of the function drops all elements of the *POSITIONS* vector from line 2 which are less than ρ*SUBSTRING* positions from the end of the *STRING*. (Any of those elements that are 1 correspond to false matches.) Also, if

SUBSTRING is empty, line 3 sets all elements of *POSITIONS* to zero. Finally, line 4 uses compression to convert the Boolean *POSITIONS* vector to a vector of corresponding line numbers.

The version of *MATCH* which has just been presented is not good for very long strings, since in such cases the generation of the outer product matrix requires considerable space (and time). A better version of *MATCH* is given in Exercise 6.5.5 in the next section.

EXERCISES

6.4.1.   Using outer product, write a function ∇ *M←DIAMOND SIZE* to produce a diamond-shaped pattern of asterisks in a matrix with *SIZE* characters on a side. Examples are:

```
        DIAMOND 5
      *
     ***
    *****
     ***
      *


        DIAMOND 6
      **
     ****
    ******
    ******
     ****
      **
```

6.4.2.   Using outer product, write a function ∇ *P←BARPLOT VECTOR* to create a character matrix that is a bar graph, or histogram, of the values in a given *VECTOR* of non-negative integers. The following is an example:

```
        BARPLOT 6 9 0 1 4 3 6
```

The height of each column of □'s should be equal to the corresponding number in the given vector, and the overall height of the matrix should be equal to the maximum of the given values.

6.4.3.   Write a function ∇ $N \leftarrow ITEMS\ NUMBERIN\ ARRAY$ to return a vector N of the same length as vector $ITEMS$, so that element $N[J]$ gives the number of occurrences of element $ITEMS[J]$ in an $ARRAY$ of any rank and shape. For example,

   $'AEIOU'\ NUMBERIN\ 'THE\ QUICK\ BROWN\ FOX'$
should yield   0 1 1 2 1

Use outer product; do not use branch.

6.4.4.   Suppose A and B are vectors containing the coefficients for two polynomials involving a variable x. Let $A[J]$ be the coefficient of the x raised to the $J-1$ power in the first polynomial, and let $B[J]$ be the coefficient of x to the $J-1$ power in the second polynomial. For instance, if the first polynomial is $1 - 2x + x^2$ and the second polynomial is $6x - x^2 + 3x^4$, then the vectors A and B should be

   $A \leftarrow 1\ \ ^-2\ \ 1$

   $B \leftarrow 0\ \ 6\ \ ^-1\ \ 0\ \ 3$

Write a function ∇ $P \leftarrow A\ POLYMULTIPLY\ B$ to produce the vector of coefficients resulting if two such polynomials are multiplied. In the case of the example polynomials A and B the result should be the vector

0 6 $^-$13 8 2 $^-$6 3

which corresponds to the product polynomial
$6x - 13x^2 + 8x^3 + 2x^4 - 6x^5 + 3x^6$
Use outer product, but do not use branch.

6.4.5.   Write a function ∇ $R \leftarrow UNIQUE\ A$ to return a vector containing those elements of vector A which occur only once in A. For example, if the value of A is 38 16 45 29 16 16 45 the result should be the vector 38 29. Use outer product; do not use branch.

6.4.6.   Suppose the grades for the students in a class are given as numbers in a vector $GRADES$. Write an expression to compute a vector of corresponding rank numbers, so that the first place ranking goes to the student or students with the highest grade, and the last place ranking goes to the student or students with the lowest grade. For example, if $GRADES$ is the vector

76 93 81 68 93 62 76 65 76 72 91 88 66 62

then the corresponding vector of rankings should be

6 1 5 10 1 13 6 12 6 9 3 4 11 13

(Notice how some rank numbers are omitted when other rank numbers appear more than once because of equal values in $GRADES$.)

6.4.7.   Suppose $US\Delta EXCHANGE$ is a vector giving the value of various currencies in terms of US dollars. For example, if the currencies are Canadian dollars, UK pounds, Japanese yen, German marks, and French francs, then the vector might be

$US\Delta EXCHANGE$
1 0.8086 1.801 0.00418 0.431 0.1666

(The 1 at the beginning is for the exchange of US dollars to US dollars; it acts simply as a place holder in the vector.) Write an assignment statement involving $US\Delta EXCHANGE$ to create a matrix $EXCHANGE$ such that $EXCHANGE[J;K]$ gives the result of converting one unit of country J's currency to country K's. For the example $US\Delta EXCHANGE$ vector above, the result (displayed with print precision of four digits by setting $\Box PP\leftarrow 4$) should be

$EXCHANGE$

1	1.237	0.5552	239.2	2.32	6.002
0.8086	1	0.449	193.4	1.876	4.854
1.801	2.227	1	430.9	4.179	10.81
0.00418	0.005169	0.002321	1	0.009698	0.02509
0.431	0.533	0.2393	103.1	1	2.587
0.1666	0.206	0.0925	39.86	0.3865	1

6.5   Inner Product (f.g)

Inner product is an operator that uses any two dyadic scalar functions to perform generalized vector or matrix multiplication. It is symbolized by a period, surrounded by the two dyadic scalar functions being used. For instance, if A and B are two vectors of the same length, then the inner product

$A+.\times B$

computes the sum of the products of corresponding elements of A and B:

$(A[1]\times B[1]) + (A[2]\times B[2]) + . . . + (A[\rho A]\times B[\rho B])$

That is, for vector arguments A and B, $A+.\times B$ has the same value as $+/A\times B$.

If inner product were restricted to vectors, it would be redundant. However, the effect of inner product with matrix or higher-dimensional arguments cannot be achieved easily by other means. An expression of the form

$VECTOR+.\times MATRIX$

computes the inner product of the given $VECTOR$ with every column of the given $MATRIX$, producing as the result a vector with as many elements as there are columns in the $MATRIX$. For each subscript A, the value of $(VECTOR+.\times MATRIX)[J]$ is the same as the value of $VECTOR+.\times MATRIX[;J]$. For example, if

$VECTOR\leftarrow 2$ 3 5
$MATRIX\leftarrow 3$ 4$\rho\iota 12$

then

$VECTOR+.\times MATRIX$ is computed as

```
2×1    2×2    2×3    2×4
 +      +      +      +
3×5    3×6    3×7    3×8
 +      +      +      +
5×9   5×10   5×11   5×12  producing the four-element vector
---   ----   ----   ----
62     72     82     92
```

Clearly, for the inner product $VECTOR+.\times MATRIX$ to be applicable, the given $VECTOR$ must have as many elements as there are rows in the given $MATRIX$.

If a matrix is used as the left argument of an inner product, with a vector as the right argument:

$MATRIX+.\times VECTOR$

then the vector must have as many elements as there are columns in the matrix, and the inner product is formed by taking the inner product of the $VECTOR$ with each row of the $MATRIX$. That is, $(MATRIX+.\times VECTOR)[J]$ is the same as $MATRIX[J;]+.\times VECTOR$ for each subscript J. Thus, if

$VECTOR\leftarrow 2\ \ 3\ \ 5$
$MATRIX\leftarrow 2\ \ 3\rho\iota 6$

the inner product $MATRIX+.\times VECTOR$ is formed as

```
(1×2) + (2×3) + (3×5)
(4×2) + (5×3) + (6×5)
```

producing the two-element vector $23\ \ 53$.

For an example application of inner product of a vector with a matrix, consider a retail chain such as a chain of fast-food outlets (see Exercise 2.13.11). Suppose $MONTHLY\Delta SALES$ is a matrix giving the quantities of items sold in a particular month, where row subscripts represent food item numbers and column subscripts represent store locations. Suppose also that $PRICES$ is a vector of prices for the food items during that month, and that subscripts in the $PRICES$ vector correspond to row subscripts of the $MONTHLY\Delta SALES$ matrix. Then the inner product

$PRICES+.\times MONTHLY\Delta SALES$

will yield a vector that gives the total dollar volume of sales for the month at each location. In particular, suppose the chain has three locations and eight food items (a low number for simplicity), and suppose $MONTHLY\triangle SALES$ is the matrix

```
        MONTHLYΔSALES
6744    7559    5446
8485    6468    9504
7969    9182    5324
9102    5376    7549
9275    6834    9422
8297    8257    7912
7194    8770    6005
9722    7997    6813
```

Then if $PRICES$ is the vector

```
     PRICES
1.89  2.25  2.75  0.75  0.95  0.4  0.5  0.6
```

the inner product is

```
     PRICES+.×MONTHLYΔSALES
82138.91  77100.31  71185.69
```

For an inner product of two matrices,

$$MATRIX1+.\times MATRIX2$$

the left matrix must have as many columns as the right matrix has rows, and in the resulting matrix the value of element

$$(MATRIX1+.\times MATRIX2)[ROW;COLUMN]$$

will be the same as the value of the vector inner product

$$MATRIX1[ROW;]+.\times MATRIX2[;COLUMN]$$

Thus, the inner product $+.\times$ on two matrices performs ordinary matrix multiplication.

In general, for arbitrary arrays, inner product combines the last dimension of the left argument with the first dimension of the right argument. (Consequently, those two dimensions must have the same length.) The shape $\rho(A+.\times B)$ of the result will be the same as $(^-1\downarrow\rho A),1\downarrow\rho B$.

Continuing the preceding example, suppose $SALES$ is a three-dimensional array, as in Exercise 2.13.11, which gives the quantities of items sold, subscripted by store location, item number, and month number:

$SALES$

```
6744  6772  7579  8038  7343  7590  9445  7157  9142  5417  8111  6316
8485  8161  9269  7575  6772  6806  7015  5318  9712  8321  9248  6491
7969  6165  8519  9595  8898  6149  7445  8583  6772  6997  9279  8091
9102  9025  5319  7291  9986  6415  8650  9034  7764  8084  5351  6215
9275  8468  5549  6755  7126  5102  8328  6921  5451  9881  5715  8612
8297  6017  9968  8151  5450  9202  5210  5426  8572  9931  6574  9269
7194  9301  5233  5087  8373  6463  9041  5845  9923  8665  8856  7005
9722  9040  8805  8998  8859  9643  6865  8292  8923  9212  7788  9909

7559  7961  7785  5502  9605  7047  6797  9761  6328  7770  7771  5320
6468  7680  5291  7505  5346  7679  8699  9131  7381  6916  6083  6660
9182  9381  7448  5148  5754  8642  5574  9909  9992  7973  5307  6184
5376  9195  7265  7699  6720  5594  7830  7908  7778  7389  5478  6896
6834  6347  8784  8482  9398  7194  7075  8611  8806  9658  6460  8096
8257  6181  5072  8436  9253  6703  8480  9936  6312  9310  9247  9043
8770  9101  8329  7048  5462  8670  9255  8431  6984  7283  7583  9890
7997  8590  8280  7519  9000  8949  6807  9557  6965  8947  6358  6410

5446  7128  6798  5633  5948  8872  8540  9064  5523  5231  5527  9335
9504  6354  8472  9564  9367  6325  7253  5257  7130  6501  8974  5507
5324  6521  6092  7396  6991  8660  9282  7778  8403  9614  9785  5998
7549  5388  5245  7585  5957  5678  6065  7485  9447  6004  9711  5385
9422  6784  9616  9495  9733  8038  8805  6324  5121  8711  7986  5514
7912  9294  7791  8228  6060  9644  5122  5174  7881  6966  9646  8347
6005  6451  9402  7698  6742  9914  8947  5519  5300  5711  8646  9404
6813  7970  8070  7896  8728  5145  7010  6882  9114  6868  8323  8307
```

(The $MONTHLY\Delta SALES$ matrix given earlier is the same as $SALES[;;1]$.)

Now suppose a matrix $DOLLAR\Delta VOLUME$ is to be computed from the $SALES$ array and the $PRICES$ vector to give the dollar volume of sales by month and by location. Since $DOLLAR\Delta VOLUME$ is to have shape 12 3, and since it is to be computed by taking an inner product which combines the $PRICES$ vector with the second dimension of the $SALES$ array, a dyadic transpose is applied to the $SALES$ array before taking the inner product:

$$DOLLAR\Delta VOLUME \leftarrow PRICES + . \times 3 \ 1 \ 2 \lozenge SALES$$

The transposed *SALES* array has shape 8 12 3 and the matrix resulting from the inner product is

DOLLAR∆VOLUME

```
82138.91    77100.31    71185.69
75409.73    83226.84    67912.07
79754.31    72055.25    74391.57
81710.02    66683.98    79091.17
79525.87    71805.75    76288.62
68924.6     77777.48    78610.53
79231.15    72445.03    81627.15
72514.03    94278.34    70928.56
82498.93    80440.17    72810.22
77484.18    79622.6     73493.49
82827.94    64518.79    85591.43
74790.39    67317.2     68830.45
```

The foregoing discussion of inner product has involved only inner products of the form +.×, which is the usual inner product in mathematics. However, other dyadic scalar functions can also be used in inner products. One inner product that is useful with Boolean arguments is ∨.∧. For example, the "directed graph"

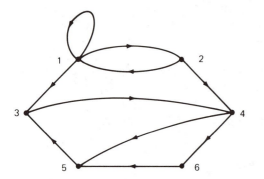

can be represented by the following "adjacency matrix," *A*, in which element *A*[*J*;*K*] has value 1 if and only if there is an edge (arrow) from node (point) *J* to node *K* in the graph:

```
   | 1   2   3   4   5   6
 --+------------------
 1 | 1   1   1   0   0   0
 2 | 1   0   0   1   0   0
 3 | 0   0   0   1   0   0
 4 | 0   0   0   0   1   1
 5 | 0   0   1   0   0   0
 6 | 0   0   0   0   1   0
```

Then the Boolean inner product of the adjacency matrix with itself finds all of the two-edge paths in the graph:

$$A \vee . \wedge A$$

```
1 1 1 1 0 0
1 1 1 0 1 1
0 0 0 0 1 1
0 0 1 0 1 0
0 0 0 1 0 0
0 0 1 0 0 0
```

That is, the value of $(A \vee . \wedge A)[J;K]$ is 1 if and only if there is at least one path of exactly two edges from node J to node K in the graph.

As an example application of such an inner product on Boolean matrices, suppose a matrix $DIRECTFLIGHT$ represents all direct flights (i.e., flights without changing planes) which an airline makes between various cities. (The row and column subscripts represent the cities, and $DIRECTFLIGHT[J;K]$ is 1 if there is a direct flight from city J to city K.) Then the expression

$$DIRECTFLIGHT \vee DIRECTFLIGHT \vee . \wedge DIRECTFLIGHT$$

will produce a matrix that indicates all pairs of the cities which one can travel between via that airline with at most one change of plane.

EXERCISES

6.5.1.   Suppose $COEFFS$ is a vector of coefficients for a polynomial, as described in Exercise 6.4.4, and X is the variable in the polynomial. ($COEFFS[J]$ is the coefficient of X to the $J-1$ power.) Write a function $\nabla \; V \leftarrow X \; POLYVALUE \; COEFFS$ using inner product and other functions to compute the value of the polynomial for a given value of X. Do not use branch.

6.5.2.   The example fast-food restaurant described earlier has a number of persons employed at its various locations. Suppose $LOCATION$ is a vector giving the location at which each employee works. (Employee J works at $LOCATION[J]$.) Let $SKILLS \Delta EMPLOYEE$ be a Boolean matrix that indicates for each employee the job skills for which that employee has been trained; that is, $SKILLS \Delta EMPLOYEE[S;E]$ is 1 if and only if employee E has skill S. Write an assignment statement to produce a matrix $LOCATIONS \Delta SKILLS$ which indicates, for each location and skill, how many employees at that location have that skill. For example, if $LOCATION$ is

```
1 1 3 2 1 1 1 1 2 3 2 3 3 1 1 2 1 2 1 1 2 2 3 1 3 2 3 2 3 3 3 2 1 2 2 3
```

and if $SKILLS \Delta EMPLOYEE$ is

```
1 1 0 0 0 1 1 0 1 1 1 0 1 0 1 1 0 1 0 0 1 0 1 0 1 0 1 0 1 0 0 1 1 1 0
1 1 0 1 0 1 1 1 0 1 1 0 0 0 0 0 0 0 1 0 1 1 1 0 1 0 0 1 0 1 0 1 1 0 0
0 1 0 1 0 1 0 0 1 0 1 0 1 0 1 1 1 1 1 0 1 1 0 1 1 1 1 0 1 0 1 0 1 1 1
0 1 0 0 0 0 1 1 1 1 1 1 0 0 1 1 1 1 1 0 1 0 1 1 0 0 0 1 0 1 0 0 0 0 1
0 0 1 1 1 0 0 0 1 1 0 1 1 1 0 1 1 0 0 1 0 0 0 1 1 1 1 1 0 0 0 0 1 1 0
```

then the result of the assignment should be the matrix

$$LOCATIONS \triangle SKILLS$$

6	7	7	7	5
7	6	10	6	7
6	4	6	5	6

6.5.3. Suppose *EXCHANGE* is a matrix of currency exchange rates, as in Exercise 6.4.7, and *CASH* is a vector representing an amount of money in mixed currencies. For example,

$$CASH \leftarrow 125\ 200\ 50\ 20000\ 500\ 1500$$

represents 125 US dollars, 200 Canadian dollars, 50 UK pounds, 20000 Japanese yen, 500 German marks, and 1500 French francs. Write an expression to compute the total value in the *CASH* vector as expressed in each of the six currencies. For the given example *CASH* vector and the *EXCHANGE* matrix from Exercise 6.4.7, the result should be the vector

```
925.77 1144.855 514.02 221465 2147.86 5556.85
```

6.5.4. Suppose *LIST* is a matrix containing a list of words, one word per row, left-justified, and suppose *WORD* is a vector containing a single word with no leading blanks. Write an expression that will give the numbers of all rows in the *LIST* matrix which contain the specified *WORD*. Thus, if *LIST* is the 7-by-7 matrix

```
CANADA
ENGLAND
USA
USSR
FRANCE
CANADA
USA
```

and *WORD* is `'CANADA'`, then the value of the expression should be the vector 1 6. Make sure that the expression will not match a word like `'ENGLANDER'` which is wider than the given *LIST* and whose first part matches a word in the *LIST*.

6.5.5. The following function for substring matching is adapted from the article "String Searching" by D.J. Keenan listed in the Bibliography:

```
     ∇  P←STRING MATCH SUB;LSUB;LAST
[1]     LAST←0⌈(ρ,STRING)+1-LSUB←ρ,SUB
[2]     P←((LSUB>0)∧((LAST↑STRING)=1↑SUB)∧((-LAST)↑STRING)=¯1↑SUB)/ιLAST
[3]     P←((,STRING)[P∘.+(ι0⌈LSUB-2)]∧.=1↓¯1↓SUB)/P
     ∇
```

Trace the function by hand for

`'ABRICABRACBRICK' MATCH 'BRIC'`

and explain how it works. Why does it work correctly when the length of *SUB* is 1 or 2?

6.5.6. Suppose *LIST* is a matrix containing words as in Exercise 6.5.4. Write an expression whose value will be 1 if all of the words in *LIST* are different but will be 0 if two or more words in *LIST* are the same.

6.5.7. Suppose *DISTANCE* is a square matrix of air flight distances between cities by the most direct routes. That is, *DISTANCE[CITYA;CITYB]* and *DISTANCE[CITYB;CITYA]* both give the shortest air distance between *CITYA* and *CITYB*. Write an expression whose value will be 1 if and only if such a *DISTANCE* matrix satisfies the constraint that for all *J*, *K*, and *M*

DISTANCE[J;K] ≤ DISTANCE[J;M] + DISTANCE[M;K]

(i.e., that the direct route is always the shortest). If the matrix does not satisfy the constraint, the value of the expression should be zero.

6.6 Roll and Deal (?)

The monadic function *roll* is represented by a question mark. When applied to a positive integer, it generates a random integer between 1 and that integer, inclusive. Each number in the set of possibilities is (as nearly as possible) equally likely to be generated. Since such numbers are actually generated by a deterministic, repeatable algorithm, they are technically called *pseudorandom* numbers.

Pseudorandom numbers are frequently used to simulate random processes. For example, the expression *?* 6 simulates the rolling of an ordinary cubical die:

```
        ?6
3
        ?6
4
        ?6
1
        ?6
4
```

Similarly, the following function prints the word *'HEADS'* or *'TAILS'* to simulate the tossing of a coin:

```
      ∇  TOSS
[1]    (2 5 ρ'TAILSHEADS')[?2;]
      ∇
        TOSS
TAILS
        TOSS
HEADS
        TOSS
TAILS
        TOSS
TAILS
```

If the argument of the roll function is an array, a pseudorandom number is generated separately for each element of the array, and the result has the same shape as the argument array. For instance, the rolling of a pair of dice can be simulated by the expression $?6\ 6$:

```
      ?6  6
6 5
      ?6  6
1 3
      ?6  6
6 3
      ?6  6
2 3
      ?6  6
6 6
```

The dyadic function *deal*, also represented by a question mark, generates a vector of pseudorandom numbers, but without repetition. That is, an expression of the form

```
      NUMBER  ?  RANGE
```

where $RANGE \geq 1$ and $0 \leq NUMBER \leq RANGE$ generates a vector of NUMBER different integers between 1 and RANGE, inclusive. Thus, if a deck of cards is represented by the integers 1 through 52, then

```
      5?52
41  19  28  14  12
```

simulates random choice of five cards from the deck, and the assignment

```
      SHUFFLE←52?52
```

produces a random permutation of the numbers 1 through 52, representing a shuffle of the entire deck.

It is very important to be aware of the difference between an expression like $?6\rho6$, which uses roll, and the similar expression $6?6$ which uses deal. In vectors produced by roll some values may be repeated:

```
      ?6ρ6
1 6 4 3 1 1
      ?6ρ6
1 3 5 4 6 5
```

but in vectors produced by deal the elements are always different:

```
      6?6
3 5 6 4 1 2
      6?6
5 2 6 3 1 4
```

Fractional pseudorandom numbers can be produced in APL by generating pseudorandom integers chosen from a large set and then dividing by an appropriate value. For instance, to generate eight numbers strictly between zero and 1 and having six fractional digits, one could use the expression $(?8\rho999999)\div1000000$ or

```
      (?8ρ1E6-1)÷1E6
0.348936 0.089324 0.293619 0.593913 0.064872 0.075363 0.855173 0.884407
      (?8ρ1E6-1)÷1E6
0.651497 0.438938 0.201008 0.59954 0.354555 0.425771 0.53603 0.233104
```

The algorithm for generating pseudorandom numbers depends on a "seed" value, which changes after each number is generated. The current value of the seed is saved whenever a workspace is saved. The system variable $\Box RL$ (for *random link*) gives the current value of the seed, and a previous seed value can be reassigned to $\Box RL$ to cause a sequence of pseudorandom numbers to be regenerated, as the following example shows:

```
      )CLEAR
CLEAR WS
      □RL                    —initial value of □RL in a clear workspace,
695197565                    in VAX-11 APL
      ?10ρ6
5 5 3 2 6 2 5 2 1 3
      □RL
1636171147
      ?10ρ6
6 5 4 5 6 5 1 2 1 4
      □RL
¯2109678199
      □RL←695197565          —resetting the random link to its initial value
      ?10ρ6
5 5 3 2 6 2 5 2 1 3          —same as the first "roll" after the )CLEAR
```

Valid values, and initial values, of $\Box RL$ vary from one version of APL to another. Consult your reference manual for details.

The ability to set the value of the random link to an arbitrary value (within its valid range) can be used to define functions like the following ones for encryption of character data. A number used as the encryption key is assigned to $\Box RL$ before encoding a string, and the same value is assigned to $\Box RL$ to decode the encrypted string.

```
     ∇   C←KEY ENCRYPT STRING;ALPHA
[1]      ALPHA←'ABCDEFGHIJKLMNOPQRSTUVWXYZ0123456789'
[2]      □RL←KEY
[3]      C←¯1+ALPHAι,STRING
[4]      C←1+(1+ρALPHA)|C+?(ρ,STRING)ρρALPHA
[5]      C←(ALPHA,'*')[C]
     ∇
```

```
     ∇  T←KEY DECRYPT STRING;ALPHA
[1]      ALPHA←'ABCDEFGHIJKLMNOPQRSTUVWXYZ0123456789'
[2]      □RL←KEY
[3]      T←¯1+ALPHA⍳,STRING
[4]      T←1+(1+ρALPHA)|T-?(ρ,STRING)ρρALPHA
[5]      T←(ALPHA,' ')[T]
     ∇
```

```
     CODE←6672479 ENCRYPT 'SENSITIVE DATA: DESTROY AFTER JULY 31.'
     CODE
V1UAE9UR86B6GQ3J3D56I4WXSMC6EPH9IH94RS
     123456 DECRYPT CODE
P2ELP0EFEY60VM0K4 KPQVF444M2NL7YB1LM P
     6672479 DECRYPT CODE
SENSITIVE DATA  DESTROY AFTER JULY 31
```

(Notice that attempting to decrypt with an invalid key yields nonsense.)

The functions $ENCRYPT$ and $DECRYPT$ work by character substitution: Each character in a given string is "looked up" in the vector $ALPHA$, and the positions at which the characters are found are adjusted by pseudorandom amounts. The adjusted position numbers are then used as subscripts back into the $ALPHA$ vector, to select the code characters. The asterisk in line 5 of $ENCRYPT$ and the corresponding blank in line 5 of $DECRYPT$ are to handle characters, such as punctuation marks, which are not in the $ALPHA$ vector. Notice that such characters are replaced by blanks when a string is encrypted and then decrypted.

EXERCISES

6.6.1.   Write a function ∇ $TOTAL←DICE$ N to simulate the total number of spots appearing when N dice are rolled.

6.6.2.   Write a function ∇ $BRIDGEDEAL$ to simulate the shuffling of a deck of 52 cards and dealing of four bridge hands: $NORTH$, $EAST$, $SOUTH$, and $WEST$, each of 13 cards. Let the cards be represented by the numbers 1 through 52.

6.6.3.   Write a function ∇ $R←RANDOMSELECTION$ $VECTOR$ to choose elements randomly from a given $VECTOR$. Each element of the $VECTOR$ should have a 50% probability of being chosen, and the chosen elements should appear in the result in the same order as they appear in the given $VECTOR$. Some examples are:

```
     RANDOMSELECTION 'ABCDEFGH'
ADEFG
     RANDOMSELECTION 'ABCDEFGH'
AEF
     RANDOMSELECTION 'ABCDEFGH'
BEFH
```

6.6.4.   Write a function ∇ $R←K$ $RANDOMSUBSET$ SET to choose randomly a K-element subset from a given SET vector (which is assumed to have no duplicate elements). All *K*-element subsets should be equally likely to be chosen. The chosen elements should appear in the result in the same order as they appear in the given *SET* vector. Examples are

```
        4 RANDOMSUBSET 'ABCDEFGH'
BEGH
        4 RANDOMSUBSET 'ABCDEFGH'
ABCF
        4 RANDOMSUBSET 'ABCDEFGH'
ADFH
```

6.6.5. The functions *ENCRYPT* and *DECRYPT* work by character substitution. Another way to encrypt a string is by character permutation, or transposition.   Write   a   pair   of   functions ∇ *CODE←KEY SCRAMBLE STRING*   and ∇ *STRING←KEY UNSCRAMBLE CODE* to perform encryption and decryption by a pseudorandom permutation of the characters in a string. The value of *KEY* should be a positive integer which is assigned to □*RL*, as in *ENCRYPT* and *DECRYPT*. An example is

```
CODE←6672479 SCRAMBLE 'SENSITIVE DATA: DESTROY AFTER JULY 31.'
      CODE
SR3SEI:TY1 AJ.TLETROA EDDVSNI YFUA TE
      123456 UNSCRAMBLE CODE
VEJYTIA:L.YETAUEDNST      3TRFAROESID1  S
      6672479 UNSCRAMBLE CODE
SENSITIVE DATA: DESTROY AFTER JULY 31.
```

6.6.6. A classical problem of probability is the problem of "derangements," also called the "hat-check problem." It may be stated as follows: Suppose *N* children attend a party having a gift exchange. Each child brings a gift; the gifts are collected and then given back to the children at random. What is the probability that no child gets his or her own gift back?

Write a function ∇ *P←E DERANGEMENTS N* to estimate that probability by simulating *E* gift exchanges involving *N* children. (Count the number of cases in which no child get his/her own gift, and divide that number by *E* to obtain the probability estimate.) You may use branch in this function.

6.6.7. The "birthday problem" is another classical problem in probability: In a group of *N* persons, what is the probability that at least two of them have the same birthday (month and day)? How large does *N* have to be for there to be a better than 50% chance that at least two of them have the same birthday?

Write a function ∇ *P←N BIRTHDAY T* to estimate, using *T* pseudorandom simulation trials, the probability that for *N* persons at least two have the same birthday. Assume that there are 365 possible birthdays, all equally likely. You may use branch in this problem.

6.7 Format (⍕)

The monadic *format* function, represented by the overstruck symbol ⍕, converts the value of its argument to a value of character type. If the argument is already a character array, the result is the same as the argument. However, if the argument is a numeric array, the result is a character array in the format in which numeric values are normally displayed by the APL system in calculator mode. The exact result of applying monadic format depends on the particular version of APL being used. (Differences are mainly in the number of blanks inserted and in the way numbers in scaled or exponential form are displayed.) The following examples are from VAX-11 APL. (*QUOTE* and *BORDER* are functions from Exercises 3.3 and 3.4.)

```
      QUOTE ⍕1
'1'
      QUOTE ⍕¯123.45
'¯123.45'
      QUOTE ⍕⍳3
'1 2 3'
      BORDER ⍕2 3⍴1
```

```
 _____
|1  1  1|
|1  1  1|
 -------
```

```
      BORDER ⍕2 3⍴2
```

```
 _____
|2   2  2|
|2   2  2|
 --------
```

```
      BORDER ⍕2 3⍴1.75
```

```
 _____
|1.75  1.75  1.75|
|1.75  1.75  1.75|
 ---------------
```

```
      QUOTE ⍕¯.234E16
'¯2.34E15 '
      QUOTE ⍕¯.234E¯16
'¯2.34E¯17'
```

For three-dimensional and higher-dimensional arrays, the result of monadic format has the same rank as the argument, as the following example shows:

```
      A←⍕2 3 4⍴⍳24
      A
 1  2  3  4
 5  6  7  8
 9 10 11 12

13 14 15 16
17 18 19 20
21 22 23 24
      ⍴A
2 3 11
```

Numbers in APL may be displayed in two different forms: (1) in ordinary, or decimal, form, or (2) in exponential, or scaled, form. The following are some examples; numbers in the same row are equivalent:

Ordinary	Scaled
1234567890	1.234567890E9
0.00000123456789	1.234567890E ̄6
12.34	1.234000000E1
1	1.000000000E0
̄0.2	̄2.000000000E ̄1

The following function uses the monadic format function to test whether or not the formatted representation of a given number will be in scaled form:

```
      ∇  R←SCALED NUMBER
[1]      R←'E'∈⍕NUMBER
      ∇
```

EXERCISES

6.7.1.   Suppose N is a number such that ⍕N is in ordinary, not scaled, form. Write a function ∇ $R←INTEGER$ N using the monadic format function to determine whether or not N is an integer. (Compare with Exercise 4.1.2.)

6.7.2.   Suppose N is an integer (positive, negative, or zero) such that ⍕N is in ordinary form. Write a function ∇ $D←DIGITSIN$ N using ⍕ to determine the number of digits in N. If the value of N is zero, the result should be 1. (Compare with Exercise 4.1.4.)

6.7.3.   Suppose N is an integer such that ⍕N is in ordinary, not scaled, form. Write a function ∇ $S←WIDTH$ $ZEROPAD$ N to pad the string representation of N with leading zeros to a specified $WIDTH$. If the representation of N is already as wide or wider than the specified $WIDTH$, the representation of N should be returned unchanged. Examples are:

```
      11 ZEROPAD  ̄25689
 ̄0000025689
      4 ZEROPAD 123
0123
      2 ZEROPAD 123
123
```

6.7.4.   Write a function ∇ *S←COMMAFORM N* which will take a positive integer and return its value as a string with commas inserted between groups of three digits, as in the following examples:

```
        COMMAFORM 999
999
        COMMAFORM 1234
1,234
        COMMAFORM 123456
123,456
        COMMAFORM 2147483647
2,147,483,647
```

More control over formatting of numeric arrays can be obtained by use of the dyadic format function, which is also represented by the symbol ⍕*. (Dyadic format does not apply to character data.) In its simplest use the left argument is a single integer which specifies the number of digits of precision desired in the result. A positive or zero left argument indicates that the values in the right argument are to be converted to ordinary form (not scaled), and the value of the left argument gives the number of fractional digits to be included in the character representation. The following are some examples:

```
    V←1 2.2 3.33 4.444 5.5555 ¯1 ¯2.2 ¯3.33 ¯4.444 ¯5.5555 0
    QUOTE 2⍕V
'1.00 2.20 3.33 4.44 5.56 ¯1.00 ¯2.20 ¯3.33 ¯4.44 ¯5.56 0.00'
    QUOTE 0⍕V
'1 2 3 4 6 ¯1 ¯2 ¯3 ¯4 ¯6 0'
```

Notice that the values are rounded to the number of digits specified.

To obtain more control over the number of blanks inserted in the result, a pair of numbers can be used as the left argument of the dyadic format function. The first number in the pair specifies the width (i.e., the number of characters) in which each number in the right argument is to be formatted, and the second number on the left specifies the precision desired, as above. Examples are:

```
    QUOTE 1 0⍕⍳9
'123456789'
    QUOTE 8 1⍕¯3+⍳5
'    ¯2.0    ¯1.0    0.0    1.0    2.0'
```

Notice that unscaled numbers formatted with dyadic format are right-justified in fields of the specified width.

Matrices (and higher-dimensional arrays) can also be formatted by the dyadic format function, as the following examples illustrate. The *BORDER* function is used again to show the resulting character matrices clearly.

---

* Versions of APL differ slightly in the way that they apply dyadic format. Check your reference manual or experiment with your computer to see exactly how your version formats numbers.

```
      BORDER 10 2⍕3 3ρ ¯5+⍳9
```

```
┌─────────────────────────────────────┐
│      ¯4.00        ¯3.00        ¯2.00│
│      ¯1.00         0.00         1.00│
│       2.00         3.00         4.00│
└─────────────────────────────────────┘
```

```
      BORDER 1 0⍕3 3ρ⍳9
```

```
┌───┐
│123│
│456│
│789│
└───┘
```

A negative number specifying precision in the left argument indicates that the result is to be displayed in scaled, or exponential, form. The absolute value of the precision number indicates the number of digits to be displayed:

```
      QUOTE ¯4⍕55555
'  5.556E4  '
      QUOTE 9 ¯4⍕55555
'5.556E4  '
      QUOTE ¯2⍕0
'0.0E0  '
      QUOTE 5 ¯1⍕0
'0E0  '
```

Finally, each column of a matrix can be formatted differently from the others if one includes a separate width-precision number pair for each column, as shown below:

```
      M←⍉3 5ρ100+⍳5
      M
101  101  101
102  102  102
103  103  103
104  104  104
105  105  105
      BORDER 3 0 7 2 9 ¯3⍕M
```

```
┌────────────────────────┐
│101 101.00 1.01E2      │
│102 102.00 1.02E2      │
│103 103.00 1.03E2      │
│104 104.00 1.04E2      │
│105 105.00 1.05E2      │
└────────────────────────┘
```

The first column has been formatted with width 3 and with no fractional digits; the second column has been formatted with width 7 and with 2 fractional digits; and the third column has been formatted in scaled form with width 9 and with 3 digits of precision.

Many versions of APL also have another, more powerful (and more complicated) format function, represented by a dollar sign, or by $\Box FMT$ or ΔFMT or some other name. However, that function is not standard and is beyond the scope of this book.

EXERCISES

6.7.5.   Given matrices *NAMES* and *TIMES* as in Exercise 4.5.6, write a function ∇ *NAMES DISPLAY TIMES* to display the names of the marathon runners beside their times, with headings and spacing as shown below:

```
      NAMES DISPLAY TIMES

   RUNNER     HOURS MINUTES SECONDS

   BACHELER     2      17     38.2
   BEDANE       2      18     36.8
   FOSTER       2      16     56.2
   HILL         2      16     30.6
   KIMIHARA     2      16     27.0
   LISMONT      2      14     31.8
   MACGREGOR    2      16     34.4
   MOORE        2      15     39.8
   SHORTER      2      12     19.8
   WOLDE        2      15      8.4
```

The seconds column should include one fractional digit, as shown. Do not use branch in this problem.

6.7.6.   Write a function ∇ *S←SPELLDATES M* to convert a three-column numeric matrix of dates, with one date per row in the form year month-number day-number, like

```
1980      3      1
1981     12     15
1982      3     27
1982      9      1
```

to a character matrix like

```
MAR.   1,  1980
DEC.  15,  1981
MAR.  27,  1982
SEP.   1,  1982
```

Use the first three letters of the name of each month. Assume that the given dates are all valid ones. Do not use branch.

6.7.7.   Suppose *V* is a vector of positive integers which are all less than 1000. Write an expression to format *V* as a three-column character matrix with one element of *V* in each row and with leading zeros supplied. For example, if the value of *V* is

1 16 89 246 999

then the value of the expression should be the matrix

```
001
016
089
246
999
```

6.7.8. Modify the function ∇ *P←BARPLOT VECTOR* of Exercise 6.4.2 so that it will include the numbers from the given vector below the corresponding columns of quad symbols. The columns of quads should be spaced apart evenly, so that there is a blank in front of the largest of the numbers printed at the bottom, and one or more blanks in front of each of the other numbers. Examples are

<pre>
          BARPLOT 1 0 4 2 3 2

      □
      □   □
      □ □ □ □
   □   □ □ □ □
   1 0 4 2 3 2
</pre>

<pre>
          BARPLOT 3 10 5 8 7 5 10

      □   □
      □   □
      □   □   □
      □   □ □ □
      □   □ □ □
      □ □ □ □ □ □
      □ □ □ □ □ □
   □ □ □ □ □ □ □
   □ □ □ □ □ □ □
   □ □ □ □ □ □ □
   3 10 5 8 7 5 10
</pre>

6.7.9. Write a function ∇ *M←FIRST CALENDAR LENGTH* to create a character matrix representing a calendar for a month, where *FIRST* is the day of the week (1 for Sunday, 2 for Monday, etc.) on which the month begins, and *LENGTH* is the number of days in the month. The result should be in the format shown in the following example (using the *BORDER* function to show its shape clearly):

BORDER 7 CALENDAR 31

```
|                                                      1 |
|     2     3     4     5     6     7     8 |
|     9    10    11    12    13    14    15 |
|    16    17    18    19    20    21    22 |
|    23    24    25    26    27    28    29 |
|    30    31                               |
---------------------------------------------
```

(The result is similar to the result of Exercise 2.11.2, except that in this case the zeros are suppressed and the result is a character matrix instead of a numeric matrix.)

6.8   Execute (⍎)

The monadic function *execute* is represented by the overstruck symbol ⍎, and sometimes also by monadic ⊥ or ∊. It normally takes a character string (scalar or vector) as its argument. Some versions of APL allow the argument to be numeric; in that case the result is the same as the argument.

Execute treats a character-string argument as an APL expression and evaluates it. Execute is sometimes called *unquote* because it, in effect, removes the quotation marks from a character string. The value of the execute function is the value of the executed expression.

One important use of the execute function is to undo the work of the format function: that is, to convert strings to numbers. For example, if V is a vector of numbers such as

1 2.2 3.33 4.444 5.5555 ¯1 ¯2.2 ¯3.33 ¯4.444 ¯5.5555 0

then the assignment $S \leftarrow 2 \bar{\top} V$ converts V to a character string S in which each of the numbers has been rounded to two decimal places. Now if the execute function is applied to S, the result is a numeric vector containing the rounded numbers:

```
      □←R←⍎S
1  2.2  3.33  4.44  5.56  ¯1  ¯2.2  ¯3.33  ¯4.44  ¯5.56  0
      ρR
11
```

Execute and format can be used to write a general rounding function similar to, but not quite the same as, the one in Exercise 4.1.6:

```
      ∇   R←D ROUND N
[1]       R←⍎D⊤N
      ∇
```

If D is zero or positive, this rounds the elements of N to D decimal places. If D is negative, it rounds each element of N to $|D$ significant digits (i.e., from the highest-order nonzero digit):

```
      2 ROUND 12.745 ¯12.745
12.75 ¯12.75
      ¯2 ROUND 125394 2391 ¯865419320
130000 2400 ¯870000000
```

In Section 5.1 there is a function, *PROBLEM*, which asks an addition problem and uses quad input to obtain a response. As you will recall, the disadvantage of using quad for input was that the *PROBLEM* function could be tricked by simply typing the problem expression as an answer to the problem. To overcome that drawback, one can use quote-quad for input of the answer, check the answer to make sure it is a valid number, and then use execute to obtain its value. For generality, the following function can be defined to ask an arbitrary question requiring a non-negative integer for an answer. It accepts a string as answer, checks that it is a non-negative integer, and repeats the question if the answer is unacceptable. When it gets an acceptable answer, it unquotes it to get its numeric value. (The function *GETANUMBER* uses the *SQUEEZE* function from Exercise 4.8.4 to eliminate any leading or trailing blanks from the input response.)

```
      ∇   N←GETANUMBER QUESTION
[1]     AGAIN:QUESTION
[2]     N←SQUEEZE,⎕
[3]     →((0<ρ,N)∧∧/N∈'0123456789')/OK
[4]     'PLEASE ANSWER WITH A POSITIVE WHOLE NUMBER.'
[5]     →AGAIN
[6]     OK:N←⍎N
      ∇
```

GETANUMBER can be used to define a better version of the *PROBLEM* function. This version also uses the roll function, to generate the addition problem randomly:

```
      ∇   PROBLEM;ANSWER;A;B
[1]     A←?99
[2]     B←?99
[3]     ANSWER←GETANUMBER 'WHAT IS THE SUM OF ',(⍕A),' AND ',(⍕B),'?'
[4]     (2 6 ρ'WRONG!RIGHT!')[1+ANSWER=A+B;]
      ∇

      PROBLEM
WHAT IS THE SUM OF 35 AND 51?
35+51
PLEASE ANSWER WITH A POSITIVE WHOLE NUMBER.
WHAT IS THE SUM OF 35 AND 51?
86
RIGHT!
```

Another important use of the execute function is for writing user-defined functions with *call-by-name* parameters. As discussed in Section 3.6, changes that a function makes to its input parameters are not made to the corresponding arguments of the function call. However, if one passes the names of variables, rather than their values, to a user-defined function, the function can change the values of those variables by using the execute function. For example, the following function uses call-by-name to sort the elements of a given vector variable:

```
      ∇   SORT ΔV
[1]      ⍎ΔV,'←',ΔV,'[⍋',ΔV,']'
      ∇
```

To see how it works, consider what happens if an expression like *SORT 'VEC'* is executed. The catenations inside the *SORT* function produce the string *'VEC←VEC[⍋VEC]'* and the execute function unquotes that string and executes the expression *VEC←VEC[⍋VEC]*, which sorts the value of the variable *VEC*. The following is an example use of *SORT*:

```
      VECTOR←2 3 1 5 4 6
      VECTOR
2 3 1 5 4 6
      SORT 'VECTOR'
      VECTOR
1 2 3 4 5 6
```

It should be noted that a function that uses call-by-name will not work for all arguments. For instance, the following sequence can occur with the *SORT* function:

```
      ΔV←2 3 1 5 4 6
      SORT 'ΔV'
      ΔV
2 3 1 5 4 6
```

You should be able to explain why the vector ΔV is not sorted in this case.

Still another use of the execute function is to include system commands within user-defined functions. Normally if a system command like *)SAVE* is typed during function definition, it is executed immediately. To postpone its execution until the user-defined function is executed, one quotes the system command and precedes it by the execute function ⍎*')SAVE'*. Use of the *)SAVE* command in this way allows the creation of *self-starting* workspaces.* This is illustrated by the following more elaborate version of the *PROBLEM* function, which asks a series of addition problems:

---

* The "latent expression" system variable ($\Box LX$) described in Appendix B provides another way to create self-starting workspaces.

```
      ∇   PROBLEMS;ANSWER;A;B
[1]      ⍎')SAVE'
[2]      'I WILL ASK YOU A SERIES OF ADDITION PROBLEMS.'
[3]   LOOP:' '
[4]      A←?99
[5]      B←?99
[6]      ANSWER←GETANUMBER 'WHAT IS THE SUM OF ',(⍕A),' AND ',(⍕B),'?'
[7]      (2 6 ρ'WRONG!RIGHT!')[1+ANSWER=A+B;]
[8]      'DO YOU WANT ANOTHER PROBLEM? (ANSWER Y OR N)'
[9]      →('Y'=1↑SQUEEZE,⎕)/LOOP
      ∇
```

When *PROBLEMS* is first executed, a copy of the workspace, including the
state-indicator stack, is saved as soon as line 1 has been executed. Thereafter,
whenever the workspace is loaded, the *PROBLEMS* function will begin executing immediately, at line 2, as in the following example run: (The)*WSID* is
MATH.)

```
      )LOAD MATH
SAVED 15:55:33 3-JUN-84 3K
I WILL ASK YOU A SERIES OF ADDITION PROBLEMS.

WHAT IS THE SUM OF 30 AND 90?
120
RIGHT!
DO YOU WANT ANOTHER PROBLEM? (ANSWER Y OR N)
Y

WHAT IS THE SUM OF 59 AND 83?
132
WRONG!
DO YOU WANT ANOTHER PROBLEM? (ANSWER Y OR N)
Y

WHAT IS THE SUM OF 7 AND 82?
89
RIGHT!
DO YOU WANT ANOTHER PROBLEM? (ANSWER Y OR N)
N
```

Self-starting workspaces are useful for applications that are to be run by persons who have little or no training in APL. The function that starts when a
workspace is loaded acts as the *main program* for the application. It can display
instructions and can prompt the user for input, as in the foregoing example.
The user can be restricted to data-entry operations only, if desired. The function can even sign the user off from the system automatically; in the
PROBLEMS function that could be done by adding the line

```
[10] ⍎')OFF'
```

to the function definition.

In addition to $)SAVE$ and $)OFF$, another system command that can be usefully included in user-defined functions by quoting it and applying execute is $)LOAD$. It allows workspaces to be loaded dynamically, under program control. That way a very large program, which will not fit in a single workspace, can be segmented into several workspaces that load each other as required.

Other system commands like $)ERASE$ and $)COPY$ might also be executed from within a user-defined function by using the execute function. It should be noted, however, that not all versions of APL will allow system commands to be executed in this way. In newer implementations of APL the trend has been to provide system functions and system variables such as $\Box EX$, $\Box IO$, $\Box LX$, $\Box NL$, $\Box PP$, and $\Box PW$ which can be used in user-defined functions without the execute function and which perform the same tasks as system commands. See Appendix B for details.

EXERCISES

6.8.1.   Write a function ∇ $N \leftarrow UNCOMMAFORM$ S to compute the inverse of the $COMMAFORM$ function of Exercise 6.7.4. That is, $UNCOMMAFORM$ should take a character string containing digit characters with commas between groups of three digits (counting from the right end) and produce the corresponding integer number, as in these examples:

        $UNCOMMAFORM$ '999'
999
        $UNCOMMAFORM$ '1,234'
1234
        $UNCOMMAFORM$ '023,456'
23456
        $UNCOMMAFORM$ '2,147,483,647'
2147483647

6.8.2.   Given matrices $NAMES$ and $TIMES$ as in Exercise 4.5.6 (and 6.7.5), write a single expression to assign to the names, as variables, the corresponding three-element time vectors. After the expression has been

executed using the example matrices, the following variables should
have the values shown:

```
        BACHELER
2  17  38.2
        BEDANE
2  18  36.8
        FOSTER
2  16  56.2
        HILL
2  16  30.6
        KIMIHARA
2  16  27
        LISMONT
2  14  31.8
        MACGREGOR
2  16  34.4
        MOORE
2  15  39.8
        SHORTER
2  12  19.8
        WOLDE
2  15  8.4
```

6.8.3.   Write a function *MATH* to ask randomly chosen arithmetic problems,
as shown in the following example dialog. Lines typed by the student
have been underlined for clarity. Try to make the *MATH* function as
"foolproof" as possible. You may use the function *GETANUMBER*
which was defined in this section, as well as other functions which
have been defined earlier. You may also define other functions to be
used by the main *MATH* function. Notice that the student gets up to
three tries at each problem, but a correct answer is counted in the
score only if it is given on the first try at a problem.

```
        MATH
I WILL ASK YOU SOME ARITHMETIC PROBLEMS.
HOW MANY PROBLEMS DO YOU WANT TO TRY?
4

CHOOSE ADDITION (+), SUBTRACTION (-),
        MULTIPLICATION (×), OR DIVISION (÷).
+
WHAT IS 51 + 4 ?
55
RIGHT!

CHOOSE ADDITION (+), SUBTRACTION (-),
```

```
          MULTIPLICATION (×), OR DIVISION (÷).
×
WHAT IS 70 × 1 ?
71
WRONG.
PLEASE TRY AGAIN.
WHAT IS 70 × 1 ?
70
RIGHT!

CHOOSE ADDITION (+), SUBTRACTION (-),
          MULTIPLICATION (×), OR DIVISION (÷).
-
WHAT IS 93 - 8 ?
85
RIGHT!

CHOOSE ADDITION (+), SUBTRACTION (-),
          MULTIPLICATION (×), OR DIVISION (÷).
÷
WHAT IS 498 ÷ 6 ?
75
WRONG.
PLEASE TRY AGAIN.
WHAT IS 498 ÷ 6 ?
84
WRONG.
PLEASE TRY AGAIN.
WHAT IS 498 ÷ 6 ?
82
WRONG.
THE CORRECT ANSWER IS 83.

YOUR SCORE IS 2 PROBLEMS CORRECT OUT OF 4.

DO YOU WISH TO TRY MORE PROBLEMS?
Y
HOW MANY PROBLEMS DO YOU WANT TO TRY?
1

CHOOSE ADDITION (+), SUBTRACTION (-),
          MULTIPLICATION (×), OR DIVISION (÷).
÷
WHAT IS 82 ÷ 2 ?
41
RIGHT!

YOUR SCORE IS 1 PROBLEM CORRECT OUT OF 1.

DO YOU WISH TO TRY MORE PROBLEMS?
NO
```

6.8.4.   Write a function ∇ *MATRIX←SHAPE MCREATE INITIAL* which will take a numeric or character scalar, *INITIAL*, and a two-element numeric vector, *SHAPE*, and will produce a *MATRIX* in the following manner: First, make *MATRIX* a matrix of specified *SHAPE*, with all of its elements equal to *INITIAL*. Then accept lines of input in which each line begins with a row number for *MATRIX*, followed by a colon, followed by the values to be put into the specified row of *MATRIX*. Input lines should be accepted and rows of the matrix assigned, until an input line with an illegal row number (e.g., zero) is encountered. The following are examples of how the *MCREATE* function should work:

```
      M←4 25 MCREATE '*'
3:THIS IS THE THIRD LINE
1:THIS IS THE FIRST LINE
0

      BORDER M
```

```
 _____
|THIS IS THE FIRST LINE***|
|*************************|
|THIS IS THE THIRD LINE***|
|*************************|
 ------------------------------
```

```
      A←3 4 MCREATE 10
1:4ρ1
2:ι6
2:8 8
0
        A
  1   1   1   1
  8   8   3   4
 10  10  10  10
```

Notice that input lines that are shorter than the width specified for the matrix are left-justified in the matrix. Input lines that are too long are truncated on the right. In the case of a numeric matrix, an input line may be specified by any expression that yields a numeric scalar or vector value.

6.8.5.   Using execute, but not branch, write a function ∇ *M←N ANAGRAMS WORD* to generate an *N*-row matrix of the same width as vector *WORD*, containing *N* random permutations of the elements of *WORD*, one permutation in each row of the matrix. Each permutation should be generated separately, but the permutations need not all be different.

6.9 Encode (⊤) and Decode (⊥)

The dyadic function *encode* (⊤) converts a decimal number to a representation in some other base, or radix. The result is a vector whose elements each represent a *digit* of the number in the new radix. For example, to convert the decimal number 25 to a 6-bit binary number, represented by a 6-element vector, one can write

```
      2 2 2 2 2 2⊤25  which yields
0 1 1 0 0 1
```

Similarly, an expression such as

```
      (4ρ10)⊤2830
2 8 3 0
```

can be used to break up a decimal number into a vector of separate digits.

Mixed-radix numbers can also be formed, as in the expression

```
      0 24 60 60⊤1759324
20 8 42 4
```

which converts 1759324 seconds to 20 days, 8 hours, 42 minutes, and 4 seconds.

Fractional digits in the right argument of encode are not converted separately, but appear as fractional digits of the rightmost element of the result. For instance,

```
      10 10 10 10⊤28.35  will produce the vector
0 0 2 8.35
```

(Notice that there are always as many elements in the result as there are in the left-argument vector.)

For a vector *BASE* and a scalar *NUMBER*, the value of the expression

```
      BASE ⊤ NUMBER
```

is the same as the value computed by the following function:

```
     ∇   RESULT←BASE ENCODE NUMBER;DIVISOR;REMAINDER
[1]       RESULT←ι0                  —begin with an empty result vector
[2]     LOOP:→(0=ρ,BASE)/0           —loop until the base vector is empty:
[3]       DIVISOR←¯1↑BASE            remove the next divisor from the end
[4]       BASE←¯1↓BASE               of the base vector;
[5]       REMAINDER←DIVISOR|NUMBER   put the remainder of dividing the
                                     current NUMBER by the divisor
[6]       RESULT←REMAINDER,RESULT    onto the front of the result vector
[7]       NUMBER←((NUMBER-REMAINDER)÷DIVISOR)-DIVISOR=0
                                     —divide the current NUMBER
                                     by the divisor and keep the
                                     floor of the result as the new
                                     NUMBER;
[8]       →LOOP
     ∇
```

The *ENCODE* function depends on the fact that in APL the expression $0 \mid NUMBER$ has the same value as *NUMBER*, and the fact that the expression $0 \div 0$ equals 1. *ENCODE* will work even if the *BASE* vector contains zeros. Line 7 contains the expression $(NUMBER-REMAINDER) \div DIVISOR$ rather than $\lfloor NUMBER \div DIVISOR$ so that the division will not fail if the *DIVISOR* is zero. For in that case line 5 will guarantee that $(NUMBER-REMAINDER)$ is also zero. Subtracting the value of $DIVISOR=0$ at the end of line 7 will set *NUMBER* to zero if the *DIVISOR* is ever zero, and consequently all items in the *RESULT* to the left of the first (i.e., rightmost) zero *DIVISOR* will be set to zero.

As you can see, the operation of the encode function is fairly complicated and somewhat hard to understand at first. It helps to compute its value by hand a few times by tracing the execution of the *ENCODE* function shown above. If this is done with the expression

$$0 \ 24 \ 60 \top 29322 \quad \text{or} \quad 0 \ 24 \ 60 \ ENCODE \ 29322$$

(to convert 29322 minutes to days, hours, and minutes), the result is the trace shown below.

			Value
		BASE:	0 24 60
		NUMBER:	29322
[1]	*RESULT*←ι0	*RESULT*:	empty
[3]	*DIVISOR*←¯1↑*BASE*	*DIVISOR*:	60
[4]	*BASE*←¯1↓*BASE*	*BASE*:	0 24
[5]	*REMAINDER*←60|29322	*REMAINDER*:	42
[6]	*RESULT*←*REMAINDER*,*RESULT*	*RESULT*:	42
[7]	*NUMBER*←((29322−42)÷60)−(60=0)	*NUMBER*:	488
[3]	*DIVISOR*←¯1↑*BASE*	*DIVISOR*:	24
[4]	*BASE*←¯1↓*BASE*	*BASE*:	0
[5]	*REMAINDER*←24|488	*REMAINDER*:	8
[6]	*RESULT*←*REMAINDER*,*RESULT*	*RESULT*:	8 42
[7]	*NUMBER*←((488−8)÷24)−(24=0)	*NUMBER*:	20
[3]	*DIVISOR*←¯1↑*BASE*	*DIVISOR*:	0
[4]	*BASE*←¯1↓*BASE*	*BASE*:	empty
[5]	*REMAINDER*←0|20	*REMAINDER*:	20
[6]	*RESULT*←*REMAINDER*,*RESULT*	*RESULT*:	20 8 42
[7]	*NUMBER*←((20−20)÷0)−(0=0)	*NUMBER*:	0

The final result is 20 8 42. The encoding can be summarized by a diagram:

number to be encoded
↓

Quotients:	20 ← 488 ← 29322
	÷ ÷ ÷
Encoding vector:	0 24 60
	↓ ↓ ↓
Remainders:	20 8 42

The following are some more examples of the use of the encode function, which you might verify by hand tracing:

```
      2 2 2 2 2 2T¯25
1 0 0 1 1 1
```

(The result is the 2's-complement of 25 in 6 bits— see Exercise 6.1.6.)

```
      0 1T123.456
123 0.456
      0 1T¯123.456
¯124 0.544
      0 ¯1T123.456
¯124 ¯0.544
      0 ¯1T¯123.456
123 ¯0.456
```

(For scalars A and B, $(0,A)TB$ yields the same value as $(\lfloor B \div A \rfloor),(A|B)$ provided A is not zero.)

The encode function can also be applied with a vector or higher-dimensional array as its right argument. In the case of a vector right argument, each element of the vector is encoded separately (using the left argument) to produce a column in the resulting matrix. The following is an example:

```
    2 2 2 T 0 1 2 3 4 5 6 7
0 0 0 0 1 1 1 1
0 0 1 1 0 0 1 1
0 1 0 1 0 1 0 1
```

Of course, the result can be transposed if the encodings are wanted in rows instead of columns.

As a further example, the following matrix is encoded in binary. The result is a three-dimensional array in which the encodings of the matrix elements lie along the first dimension:

```
     M
0   1   2   3
4   5   6   7

     2 2 2TM
0 0 0 0
1 1 1 1

0 0 1 1
0 0 1 1

0 1 0 1
0 1 0 1
```

EXERCISES

6.9.1.　Write a function ∇ $V \leftarrow DIGITSOF$ N to compute a vector of the digits in a given integer N (positive, zero, or negative), as in these examples:

```
      DIGITSOF 170
1 7 0
      DIGITSOF ¯21056
2 1 0 5 6
      DIGITSOF 0
0
```

This function may use the function $DIGITSIN$ of Exercise 4.1.4 or 6.7.2 to determine the number of digits in the given number N.

6.9.2.　Write an expression using encode (and another function) to convert a given length M from meters to a three-element vector giving the length in yards, feet, and inches. (One meter is equal to 39.37 inches.) For example, if M is 10 meters, the result should be 10　2　9.7 (10 yards, 2 feet, and 9.7 inches).

6.9.3.　Write a function ∇ $B \leftarrow BINARYNUMBERS$ N to generate a matrix of the binary representations of the integers 0 through N, one number per row. Examples are

```
      BINARYNUMBERS 3
0  0
0  1
1  0
1  1
      BINARYNUMBERS 6
0  0  0
0  0  1
0  1  0
0  1  1
1  0  0
1  0  1
1  1  0
```

The matrix should have only as many columns as are needed to represent N without leading zeros.

6.9.4.　Write a function ∇ $H \leftarrow HEXADECIMAL$ N to convert a positive decimal (i.e., base-10) integer N to the corresponding base-16 ("hexadecimal") number. The result should be a character vector involving the characters '0123456789ABCDEF', which are the digits of the hexadecimal number system. Examples are

```
      HEXADECIMAL 10
A
      HEXADECIMAL 16
10
      HEXADECIMAL 255
FF
      HEXADECIMAL 26
1A
```

6.9.5.   Suppose cards in an ordinary deck of playing cards are represented by numbers 1 through 52, as in Exercise 6.6.2. Given a vector, *HAND*, of such card numbers, write an assignment statement to create a two-column matrix, *MHAND*, to represent the hand. Each row of *MHAND* should represent a card—the first element in the row representing the suit (1, 2, 3 or 4), and the second element representing the card's numeric value (1 through 13), as described in Exercise 2.13.10. The specific encoding should be such that

$HAND[J] = (13 \times (MHAND[J;1]-1)) + MHAND[J;2]$

Thus, if *HAND* is 21 12 27 52 1 then *MHAND* should be

```
2    8
1   12
3    1
4   13
1    1
```

6.9.6.   Redefine the *RANDOMSELECTION* function of Exercise 6.6.3 using the encode function, so that only one application of the roll function is needed to select a random subset of the given *VECTOR*. As before, each element of *VECTOR* should have a 50% chance of being included in the subset chosen, or (what amounts to the same thing) all subsets of *VECTOR* should be equally likely to be chosen. (Hint: Consider how each subset of *VECTOR* can be represented by a single number.)

The *decode* function (dyadic ⊥) is essentially the inverse of the encode function. The following are some examples of its use:

```
      10  10  10  10 ⊥ 2  8  3  0
2830
      0  24  60  60⊥20  8  42  4
1759324
      2⊥0  1  1  0  0  1
25
```

These should be compared with the examples of the use of encode at the beginning of this section. Notice that the left argument of the decode function can be a scalar. In that case, the scalar is, in effect, replicated to fill a vector of the same length as the right argument vector, as is usual in APL.

When *BASE* is a vector, it is generally true that the expression *BASE ⊤ BASE ⊥ CODE* has the same value as *CODE*. However, it is not always true that *BASE ⊥ BASE ⊤ NUMBER* has the same value as *NUMBER*, since encode may truncate an encoding on the left end, as in the example

```
      CODE←2  2  2⊤20
      CODE
1  0  0
      2  2  2⊥CODE
4
```

Decode can also have a matrix (or higher-dimensional array) as its right argument. Each column of a matrix is decoded separately, according to the left argument, and the result is a vector of the results for the columns. Thus, if M is the matrix

```
0   0   0   0   1   1   1   1
0   0   1   1   0   0   1   1
0   1   0   1   0   1   0   1
```

then the expression $2 \perp M$ yields the value 0 1 2 3 4 5 6 7 which results from converting each column of the matrix from binary to decimal. (In this case the scalar left argument 2 is replicated to match the number of rows in the matrix.)

When $BASE$ is a vector, the expression $BASE \perp CODE$ has the same value as the expression

$$(\phi \times \backslash 1 , \phi 1 \downarrow BASE) + . \times CODE$$

Notice that, although the vector $BASE$ must have as many elements as $CODE$ has elements (or rows), the first element of $BASE$ is not actually used in the computation.

The operation of the decode function can be understood better after tracing some examples by hand, using the equivalent expression above. The following trace is for the expression 0 24 60⊥20 8 42:

Expression	Value
$BASE$	0 24 60
$CODE$	20 8 42
$1 \downarrow BASE$	24 60
$\phi 1 \downarrow BASE$	60 24
$1 , \phi 1 \downarrow BASE$	1 60 24
$\times \backslash 1 , \phi 1 \downarrow BASE$	1 60 1440
$\phi \times \backslash 1 , \phi 1 \downarrow BASE$	1440 60 1
$(\phi \times \backslash 1 , \phi 1 \downarrow BASE) + . \times CODE$	29322

Another way of looking at decode is in terms of a diagram similar to the one used for encode:

Vector to be decoded:	20	8	42
	+	+	+
Decoding vector:	0	24	60
	×	×	×
Partial results:	0 → 20 →488 → 29322

Result of decoding

When $BASE$ is a scalar, the decode function evaluates a polynomial involving powers of the $BASE$ with coefficients given by the right-argument vector. That is, the $POLYVALUE$ function of Exercise 6.5.1 can be defined as follows using decode:

```
        ∇   V←X POLYVALUE COEFFS
[1]        V←X⊥⌽COEFFS
        ∇
```

(Notice the reversal of the coefficient vector.) As an example,

        2 *POLYVALUE* 0 6 ‾13 8 2 ‾6 3 yields
56

which is the value of the polynomial

$$6x - 13x^2 + 8x^3 + 2x^4 - 6x^5 + 3x^6$$

evaluated for x equal to 2.

Since encode and decode are essentially inverses of one another, and since their APL symbols are so similar, it is easy to get them confused. Some mnemonic devices are helpful to keep straight which is which. First, think of converting a number to a vector of binary digits: The vector is the "code"; encode converts from the number to the code, and decode converts from the code back to the number. Secondly, think of the symbol ⊤ or ⊥ as a thumbtack: When it points downward, it is being pushed in (encode); when it points upward, it has been pulled out (decode).

EXERCISES

6.9.7.   Write an expression to reverse the conversion done in Exercise 6.9.2. That is, given a three-element numeric vector *LENGTH* which represents a length in yards, feet, and inches, write an expression to compute the length in meters.

6.9.8.   Suppose *B* is a Boolean vector (containing only zeros and ones). Explain in English what the following expressions compute:

B ⊥ 1

B ⊥ *B*

6.9.9.   Write a function ∇ *D←HEXTODECIMAL H* to convert a character string *H* which represents a hexadecimal number (as in Exercise 6.9.4) to the corresponding decimal number. Examples are:

        HEXTODECIMAL 'A'
10
        HEXTODECIMAL '10'
16
        HEXTODECIMAL 'FF'
255
        HEXTODECIMAL '1A'
26

6.9.10.   Write an assignment statement to do the reverse of the task in Exercise 6.9.5. That is, given a matrix *MHAND* representing a hand of

cards, the statement should compute the corresponding vector representation, *HAND*, of the hand.

6.9.11.   Redo Exercise 4.5.6 using the decode function.

6.9.12.   Redo Exercise 3.8 (the function ∇ *V←M ELEMENTS P*) using
decode.

The decode and encode functions can be used to convert English words (or
other character strings) to and from numeric encodings, in a manner suggested
by Hagamen, Linden, Long, and Weber (see the Bibliography). The idea is to
treat a string of letters and blanks as a number in base 27, where blank is zero,
A is 1, *B* is 2, ... and *Z* is 26. The encoding of a string is done by converting the
base-27 number to base 10. The maximum length of string that can be converted depends on the maximum number precision in the particular version of
APL which is being used. The examples used here are for an implementation
that can represent decimal numbers with up to 18 digits of precision. In that
case, since

$$⌊27⊛1E18 \qquad \text{yields}$$

12

(i.e., the floor of the base-27 logarithm of 1,000,000,000,000,000,000 is 12), and
hence 27*12 is less than or equal to 10*18, any string of up to 12 letters
and blanks can be encoded uniquely as a number with 18 or fewer digits.

The following two functions do the encoding and decoding of a string. The
names *INCODE* and *UNCODE* have been used to avoid confusion with the encode and decode functions themselves. (Notice that *INCODE* uses the decode
function and *UNCODE* uses the encode function.)

```
     ∇   CODE←INCODE STRING
[1]      CODE←27⊥27|'ABCDEFGHIJKLMNOPQRSTUVWXYZ'ι12↑STRING
     ∇

     ∇   STRING←UNCODE CODE
[1]      STRING←' ABCDEFGHIJKLMNOPQRSTUVWXYZ'[1+(12ρ27)⊤CODE]
     ∇
```

The examples below were produced after setting $\Box PP \leftarrow 18$, so that all 18 digits of the numeric codes would be displayed:

```
      INCODE ' '
0
      INCODE 'A'
5559060566555523
      UNCODE ¯1+27*12
ZZZZZZZZZZZZ
      CODE←INCODE 'TEST STRING'
      CODE
112361209592248989
      UNCODE CODE
TEST STRING
      CODE←INCODE 'X-RAY'
      CODE
133555258290428874
      UNCODE CODE
X RAY
```

Notice that characters other than letters are treated identically by *INCODE*, and that all such characters are decoded as blanks by *UNCODE*. Also, the result of *UNCODE* is always a string of 12 characters, regardless of the length of the string originally given to *INCODE*.

The encoding done by the *INCODE* function is order preserving. That is, if one string is less than another string in lexicographic order (see Exercise 4.8.7), then the numeric code for the first string is less than the code for the second string (provided that both strings contain only letters and blanks). That property of the encoding can be used for sorting words: The words can first be encoded as numbers. The vector of resulting numbers can be sorted using grade up or grade down, and then the numbers can be converted back to strings. That method is particularly useful in versions of APL which do not permit grade up and grade down to be applied to character data or to matrices.

Hagamen, Linden, Long, and Weber also discuss a further encoding step, which they call "superencoding" and which can be useful for compressing text to save storage space. The details may be found in their original paper.

EXERCISES

6.9.13.   Write a function ∇ *CODE←MINCODE MATRIX* to convert a character matrix of up to 12 columns, which contains one word in each row, left-justified (as in Exercise 4.5.6), into a vector *CODE* of numbers. Each row of the matrix should be encoded as in the *INCODE* function. *MINCODE* should be a generalization of *INCODE* to a matrix argument. Do not use branch.

6.9.14.   Generalize the function *UNCODE* to a function

   ∇ *MATRIX←MUNCODE CODE* which will undo the coding specified in Exercise 6.9.13.

6.9.15.   Write a function ∇ *M←MSORT MATRIX* to sort a matrix of words into ascending order, using the *MINCODE* and *MUNCODE* functions of the preceding exercises.

6.9.16.   The game of Nim is played with counters such as coins or match sticks grouped into rows or piles. A typical starting configuration is

Group 1: ○

Group 2: ○ ○ ○

Group 3: ○ ○ ○ ○ ○

Group 4: ○ ○ ○ ○ ○ ○ ○

Such a configuration may be represented by a vector (1 3 5 7) which gives the number of counters in each group, and a function like *BARPLOT* (Exercise 6.4.2 or 6.7.8) can be used to display the configuration.

Two players take turns removing counters from the groups. On each turn a player may remove any number (at least one) of counters from any one group. The player who takes the last counter wins the game. (There is also a version of the game in which the player who is forced to take the last counter loses the game.)

For example, from the starting configuration above, play might proceed as follows:

Player	Move	New configuration
1	3 from group 4	1 3 5 4
2	3 from group 2	1 0 5 4
1	2 from group 3	1 0 3 4
2	2 from group 4	1 0 3 2
1	1 from group 1	0 0 3 2
2	1 from group 3	0 0 2 2
1	1 from group 3	0 0 1 2
2	1 from group 4	0 0 1 1
1	1 from group 3	0 0 0 1
2	1 from group 4	0 0 0 0

(player 2 wins)

Winning and losing configurations in Nim can be determined as follows (see Bĕck, Bleicher, and Crowe, pp. 340–356):

a.   Convert the numbers of counters in each group to binary numbers, forming a matrix with one group number in each row. Examples are:

1:	0	0	1		1:	0	0	1
3:	0	1	1		3:	0	1	1
5:	1	0	1		4:	1	0	0
7:	1	1	1		5:	1	0	1

b. For each column, determine whether or not the column contains an odd number of ones:

```
1:   0  0  1        1:   0  0  1
3:   0  1  1        3:   0  1  1
5:   1  0  1        4:   1  0  0
7:   1  1  1        5:   1  0  1
    -----              -----
     0  0  0           0  1  1
```

    (All columns have an   (Two columns have an
    even number of ones)   odd number of ones)

c. If no column has an odd number of ones, then the configuration is a "losing configuration." Any move will change it to a winning configuration for the other player. The configuration on the left above is an example of a losing configuration.

d. If some column has an odd number of ones, the configuration is a "winning configuration" because there is a move which will change it into a losing configuration for the other player. The winning move is whatever move will leave a configuration such that all columns in the binary representation have an even number of ones. For example, the configuration on the right above is a winning configuration: Removing all three counters from the second group produces the losing configuration

```
1:   0  0  1
0:   0  0  0
4:   1  0  0
5:   1  0  1
    -----
     0  0  0
```

for the other player.

Suppose $CONFIG$ is a vector representing a configuration of Nim. Write a function ∇ $R \leftarrow WINNING$ $CONFIG$ to determine whether or not the given configuration is a winning one. Do not use branch in this problem.

6.9.17. Suppose $CONFIG$ is a vector representing a Nim configuration, as in Exercise 6.9.16. Write a function ∇ $M \leftarrow WINNINGMOVE$ $CONFIG$ to produce a vector which indicates the winning move for the configuration, if a winning move exists. $M[1]$ should give the group number for the move, and $M[2]$ should give the number of counters to be removed from that group. If the configuration is a losing configuration, M should be returned empty. Try to use branch as little as possible in this problem; do not code any explicit loops.

6.9.18. (Project) Create a self-starting workspace, using the function $WINNINGMOVE$ and other user-defined functions, to play the game of Nim described in Exercises 6.9.16 and 6.9.17. Try to make the game as attractive as possible, with instructions, randomly chosen starting configurations, various levels of difficulty, and so on.

6.10   Matrix Inverse and Matrix Division (⌹)

The overstruck symbol ⌹, called the *domino* symbol, represents a monadic function for computing the inverse of a matrix. It also represents a dyadic function for performing division by a matrix. To see how it is used, consider a system of simultaneous linear equations such as

$$0.95x + 0.05y + 0.05z = 31780.2$$
$$0.85y + 0.05z = 36037.3$$
$$0.05x + 0.1y + 0.9z = 39630.5$$

which is to be solved for x, y, and z. If A is the matrix of coefficients

```
0.95    0.05    0.05
0       0.85    0.05
0.05    0.1     0.9
```

and C is the vector

```
31780.2 36037.3 39630.5
```

then the equations can be represented in terms of an inner product as

```
A +.× B = C
```

where B is a vector whose components are the unknown values x, y, and z.

To solve for the vector B, one multiplies (conceptually) both sides of the inner-product equation by the inverse of matrix A

```
(⌹A)+.×(A+.×B)  =  (⌹A)+.×C
```

and regroups the left-hand side (since matrix multiplication is associative) as

```
((⌹A)+.×A)+.×B  =  (⌹A)+.×C
```

which (since $((⌹A)+.×A)$ is an identity matrix) reduces to the assignment statement

```
B←(⌹A)+.×C
```

which yields

```
B
29342 40165 37941
```

Hence, the value of x is 29,342, the value of y is 40,165, and the value of z is 37,941. As a check, notice that $A+.×B$ yields the original value of vector C:

```
A+.×B
31780.2 36037.3 39630.5
```

Alternatively, the equations can be solved by using the dyadic domino function to perform matrix division, dividing the vector C by the matrix A:

```
B←C⌹A
B
29342 40165 37941
```

Although detailed discussion of matrix inversion and its applications is beyond the scope of this book, a few things should be noted about it:

1. The product of a matrix with its inverse is, by definition, an identity matrix. However, because numbers are represented in computers with only a limited number of digits of precision, the computation of matrix inverse is not always exact. For the matrix

```
        A
0.95              0.05              0.05
0                 0.85              0.05
0.05              0.1               0.9
```

and its inverse

```
      AI←⊞A
      AI
 1.055555556      ¯0.05555555556    ¯0.05555555556
 0.003472222222    1.184027778      ¯0.06597222222
¯0.05902777778    ¯0.1284722222      1.121527778
```

the inner product

```
      AI+.×A            yields
 1.000000000E0     ¯2.710505431E¯20    2.710505431E¯20
¯8.470329473E¯22    1.000000000E0      2.043466985E¯20
 1.355252716E¯20   ¯4.828087799E¯20    1.000000000E0
```

which is close to, but not exactly equal to, an identity matrix. Similarly, the inner product

```
      A+.×AI            yields
 1.000000000E0     2.710505431E¯20  0
 8.470329473E¯22   1.000000000E0    0
¯1.355252716E¯20   2.541098842E¯20  1.000000000E0
```

which is also not quite an identity matrix.

2. Not all matrices have inverses. If the rows (or columns) of a matrix are "linearly dependent," the matrix has no inverse. For example, in the following matrix

```
       M
 1.8              ¯4.2              0              9
¯3                 0                1              2.5
 0.8              ¯0.2              0              0
 0.5              ¯2                0              4.5
```

the first row is equal to the third row plus two times the fourth row:

```
      M[3;]+2×M[4;]
1.8  ¯4.2  0  9
```

So, since **one row** is a linear combination of other rows, the matrix has no inverse, and **attempting** to compute its inverse results in an error message:

```
    ⊞M
DOMAIN ERROR
    ⊞M
    ∧
```

Although ⊞ is normally applied with a square matrix as its right argument, it can also be **applied** to nonsquare matrices, as well as to scalars and vectors. However, **the details** are outside the scope of this book.

Chapter 7

Making APL Expressions Look Like English

Although one of the advantages of APL is its considerable lack of bias toward any particular natural language, it is possible to make APL expressions look like sentences of English (or of other natural languages which use the Roman alphabet). Several aspects of APL make this fairly easy to do. Chief among them is the fact that APL uses infix notation for calling user-defined functions, rather than having the name of a function followed by its arguments in parentheses, as in most other programming languages. Also, the right-to-left precedence rule of APL turns out to be appropriate for many English-language phrases. The fact that APL is an interpreted language that can be used in an immediate-execution (i.e., calculator) mode makes it easy to implement applications that use conversational English commands in APL. Finally, the APL workspace, which provides an easy way to save a collection of related functions and global variables, is a natural device for organizing the vocabulary of user-defined functions and global variables which make up an English-language application system.

In this chapter, techniques for making APL look like English are illustrated in an extended example which involves a simple system for composing and editing pages of text. That example was chosen for two reasons:

1. It is a nontrivial application, which gives a good idea of the complexity of English sentences and phrases that can be handled by the techniques used.

2. It is an application which is easily understood and whose basic data structures (pages and lines of text) are easily represented and manipulated in APL. That allows the presentation to concentrate on the syntactic and semantic aspects of the system, without a lengthy preliminary discussion of its "pragmatic" aspects (i.e., its purpose and its conceptual domain of application).

The reader should keep in mind that the chapter is intended to be primarily about the techniques used in the text-editing system, rather than about the text-editing system itself. Fairly full details of the text editor are given for completeness. However, the chapter can be read quickly to obtain the main ideas without checking all of the details. Similar ideas can be used to implement other, often smaller and simpler application systems which use English-language commands. A suggested project for another application of the same techniques is given in the exercises at the end of the chapter.

7.1 Specifications for a Simple Text Editor

The system to be designed is intended for use in composing and editing text one page at a time. It should be suitable for occasional use on small volumes of text by users who have minimal training in the use of computers. The commands for the system are to be as close to natural English as possible. Although that will make the commands considerably longer than the brief, cryptic commands of most other text-editing systems, it will also make the system easier to learn and to remember than other text-editing systems. (Section 7.5 will show how to define abbreviations for the commands, if desired.)

In order to keep the presentation as short as possible, a fairly minimal system will be described and implemented here. Some possible, and desirable, extensions to it are suggested in the exercises at the end of the chapter.

A minimal system for text editing ought to give the user at least the following capabilities:

1. Ability to begin a new page of text.
2. Ability to add lines of text to the end of the page.
3. Ability to display the page, with optional line numbers for reference.
4. Ability to insert lines between specified lines of the page.
5. Ability to delete specified lines of the page.

The system to be developed here will also provide the following features:

6. Optional column numbers when a page is displayed.
7. Ability to display lines of the page which are specified by line number.
8. Acceptance of block input text with spacing preserved exactly as typed.
9. Acceptance of paragraph input text in arbitrary form, which the system will break between words at appropriate places so as to fill lines as fully as possible to a specified width.
10. Optional centering of text horizontally.
11. Ability to add or insert specified numbers of blank lines.
12. Ability to ask the current length and width of the page.
13. Ability to copy lines of text from one part of the page to another place in the page.

A page or other segment of text can be represented in APL by a character matrix. The catenation function provides an easy way of joining segments of text together, and subscripting and compression can be used for selecting and deleting lines. Thus, the only difficult aspect of developing the system is designing and implementing an English-like command language for it.

7.2   A Set of English-like Commands for the Text Editor

APL's right-to-left evaluation rule is well suited to processing imperative statements in English, which usually begin with the main verb. If each word in commands like

```
BEGIN A PAGE OF WIDTH 65
ADD A PARAGRAPH ENDING AT '='
INSERT A BLOCK AFTER LINE 8
DELETE LINES 3, 5 AND 7
DISPLAY LINES 2 THRU 10
```

is implemented as an APL user-defined function, so that a whole command is an APL expression, then the function that corresponds to the imperative verb at the beginning of a command will automatically be evaluated last when the command is interpreted. Before that, the other functions in the command can accumulate data in global variables that the imperative verb function can work on.

Functions corresponding to imperative verbs at the beginning of commands will have to be monadic, since they can have no left arguments. Likewise, commands will have to end with constants, variables, or niladic functions. Other words in a command can be variables or niladic, monadic, or dyadic functions.

The command set that follows was developed for the text-editor application in keeping with the foregoing considerations. A further constraint was that a user-defined function name cannot be used both monadically and dyadically, as many primitive function symbols can be. A user-defined function must have a fixed number of arguments (0, 1, or 2). For that reason, a command like

```
SPACE 3
```

is included instead of the possibly more natural command

```
ADD 3 BLANK LINES
```

because the use of other commands, like

```
DISPLAY LINES 2 THRU 7
```

requires *LINES* to be at least monadic, while *ADD 3 BLANK LINES* would require *LINES* to be niladic.

The initial command set for the text editor is shown on page 194 expressed in a notation originally designed for describing the syntax of the COBOL programming language. Words and phrases written above one another in brackets are alternatives, one of which is to be chosen when a command is selected. Items in curly brackets, or braces, are mandatory, and items in square brackets are optional. As you can see, because of the many choices and optional elements, a large number of different commands are possible. The following are some examples:

```
BEGIN A PAGE OF WIDTH 65
ADD CENTERED 'CHAPTER 1'
SPACE 3
ADD A PARAGRAPH ENDING AT '≠'
```

(Here the system will accept input text typed by the user.)

```
ADD A CENTERED BLOCK OF WIDTH 50
```

(Again the system waits to accept input text.)

```
DISPLAY THE PAGE WITH HEADER AND LINE NUMBERS
DELETE LINES 2 3 AND 5
```

(The effect of the deletion on line numbering will be immediate, since the line numbers that are used are consecutive integers specifying the relative positions of lines from the beginning of a page.)

```
DISPLAY LINES 1 THRU 6 WITH NUMBERS
INSERT LINES 5 AND 6 BEFORE LINE 4
DELETE LINES 7 AND 8
HOW LONG IS THE PAGE
HOW WIDE
SPACE 1 AFTER LINE 1
PRINT THE PAGE
BEGIN A PAGE
ADD A CENTERED PARAGRAPH OF WIDTH 40 WITH BREAK AT '+'
```

(The system accepts input until a plus character is typed.)

```
PRINT LINE 5
INSERT 'SECTION 2' BEFORE LINE 5
SPACE 1 AFTER LINE 5
```

$$BEGIN\ A\ PAGE\ [OF\ WIDTH\ number]$$

$$ADD \left\{ \begin{array}{l} A\ [CENTERED] \left\{ \begin{array}{l} BLOCK \\ PARAGRAPH \end{array} \right\} [OF\ WIDTH\ number] \left[\left\{ \begin{array}{l} ENDING \\ WITH\ BREAK \end{array} \right\} [AT]\ '*' \right] \left[\left[\left\{ \begin{array}{l} BEFORE \\ AFTER \end{array} \right\} LINE \right] number \right] \\ [CENTERED]\ 'string' \end{array} \right.$$

$$\left\{ \begin{array}{l} DISPLAY \\ PRINT \end{array} \right\} \left\{ \begin{array}{l} THE\ PAGE \\ LINE\ number \\ LINES\ vector\ [AND\ number] \\ LINES\ number\ THRU\ number \end{array} \right\} \left[WITH \left\{ \begin{array}{l} [HEADER\ AND]\ [LINE]\ NUMBERS \\ [[LINE]\ NUMBERS\ AND]\ HEADER \end{array} \right\} \right]$$

$$INSERT \left\{ \begin{array}{l} A\ [CENTERED] \left\{ \begin{array}{l} BLOCK \\ PARAGRAPH \end{array} \right\} [OF\ WIDTH\ number] \left[\left\{ \begin{array}{l} ENDING \\ WITH\ BREAK \end{array} \right\} [AT]\ '*' \right] \left[\left\{ \begin{array}{l} BEFORE \\ AFTER \end{array} \right\} LINE\ number \right] \\ [CENTERED]\ 'string' \\ LINE\ number \\ LINES\ vector\ [AND\ number] \\ LINES\ number\ THRU\ number \end{array} \right.$$

$$DELETE \left\{ \begin{array}{l} LINE\ number \\ LINES\ vector\ [AND\ number] \\ LINES\ number\ THRU\ number \end{array} \right\}$$

$$SPACE\ number \left[\left\{ \begin{array}{l} BEFORE \\ AFTER \end{array} \right\} LINE\ number \right]$$

$$HOW \left\{ \begin{array}{l} LONG\ [IS\ THE\ PAGE] \\ WIDE \end{array} \right\}$$

*Any character can be used as a break character, in place of the asterisks shown above.

The following list is the vocabulary of the set of commands. Beside each word is shown the type of function that is syntactically appropriate for it.

A	monadic
ADD	monadic
AFTER	dyadic
AND	dyadic
AT	monadic
BEFORE	dyadic
BEGIN	monadic
BLOCK	niladic
BREAK	monadic
CENTERED	monadic
DELETE	monadic
DISPLAY	monadic
ENDING	dyadic
HEADER	niladic
HOW	monadic
INSERT	monadic
IS	dyadic
LINE	monadic
LINES	monadic
LONG	niladic
NUMBERS	niladic
OF	dyadic
PAGE	niladic
PARAGRAPH	niladic
PRINT	monadic
SPACE	monadic
THE	monadic
THRU	dyadic
WIDE	niladic
WIDTH	monadic
WITH	dyadic

Notice that most of the prepositions, the conjunction *AND*, and the verb *IS* are dyadic, as one might expect from their normal use as connectives in English syntax. Final nouns like *PAGE*, *BLOCK*, and *PARAGRAPH* are niladic, and adjectives and adjectival nouns are mostly monadic.

In general, the APL requirement that a function name have a fixed number of agruments will cause potential problems in the case of nouns which can be used both as final nouns and as modifiers of other nouns. It will also cause problems with adjectives which may be used either as modifiers of nouns (e.g., a WIDE page) or as predicate adjectives (e.g., the page is WIDE). In such cases a choice must be made of the most useful alternative for the particular application which is being implemented. The command set chosen for the text editor satisfies the constraint that each word must have a fixed number of arguments.

The function types chosen for words in the command set will cause the command

DISPLAY LINES 2 THRU 5 WITH HEADER AND LINE NUMBERS

to be "parsed" by the APL expression interpreter in the manner indicated by the following diagram, which shows the relationships between functions and their arguments in the expression:

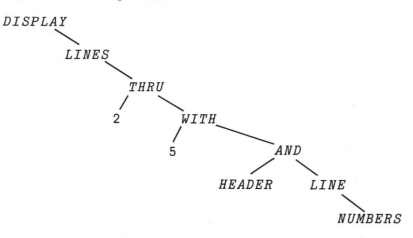

In keeping with the right-to-left precedence rule, the expression will be evaluated upward from the bottom right corner of the diagram, with the functions and constants being evaluated in the following order:

```
NUMBERS
LINE
HEADER
AND
5
WITH
2
THRU
LINES
DISPLAY
```

Notice that the left argument, 5, of *WITH* really belongs with *THRU*, according to normal English syntax, but it is forced to go with *WITH* in APL syntax. Such a violation of English syntax can be essentially corrected if the value of *WITH* can be made the same as the value of its left argument. In fact, as we shall see later, the definition of *WITH* in the text-editing system can be simply the function

```
     ∇   R←S WITH N
[1]      R←S
     ∇
```

7.3 Semantics of the Text Editor

The meanings of words in the command language for the text editor will be represented by APL functions which may set values of global variables, test values of global variables, request input, produce output, and/or pass values to other functions in a command expression. In order to interpret correctly the "verbs" of commands (*BEGIN, ADD, DISPLAY, PRINT, INSERT, DELETE, SPACE,* and *HOW*), the system will need to "know" the following things, which can be kept as values of the global variables indicated: (All variables and functions in the system which are not intended to be used directly by the user of the system will have names beginning with Δ to minimize the chance of the user accidentally typing one of them.)

ΔPAGE	—the current contents of the page being edited
ΔWIDTH	—the width to be used for a new page, block, or paragraph of text
ΔBREAK	—the break character which will signal the end of a block or paragraph of text entered by the user
ΔCENTER	—a value indicating whether or not a piece of input text (block, paragraph, or quoted string) is to be centered between the left and right margins of the page before it is added or inserted into the page
ΔAFTER	—the line number (between zero and the length of the page, inclusive) after which an insertion is to be made in the page
ΔLINES	—a vector of line numbers for existing lines of the page to be displayed, deleted, or inserted elsewhere in the page
ΔNUMBERS	—a value indicating whether or not line numbers are to be displayed when part or all of the page is displayed
ΔHEADER	—a value indicating whether or not column numbers are to be displayed when part or all of the page is displayed
ΔTYPE	—a value indicating the kind of text piece to be added, inserted, or displayed; in the implementation of the system the following codes will be used:

'B'—a Block of input text
'R'—a paRagraph of input text
'Q'—a Quoted string of input text
'L'—one or more existing Lines of the page
'G'—the current contents of the entire paGe

Consider, for example, the command

> *INSERT A CENTERED BLOCK OF WIDTH 50 BEFORE LINE 1*

By the time the *INSERT* function is executed during interpretation of the command, the following values will have had to be set by other functions in the command:

> Δ*AFTER*←0   because of the phrase *"BEFORE LINE 1"*
> Δ*WIDTH*←50
> Δ*TYPE*←'B' because a *BLOCK* of text is to be inserted
> Δ*CENTER*←1 because the block is to be centered before insertion.

Also, some break character, Δ*BREAK*, will have to be used to signal the end of the block of input text which the user is about to type. Since no break character is specified in the example command, some default value of Δ*BREAK* will have to be used.

Similarly, the command

> *DISPLAY LINES 2 THRU 5 WITH HEADER AND LINE NUMBERS*

will have to set the following values of global variables by the time the *DISPLAY* function is executed:

> Δ*TYPE*←'L'   because existing lines of the page are to be
>   displayed
> Δ*LINES*←2 3 4 5   indicating the specific lines to be displayed
> Δ*HEADER*←1   because a header line of column numbers is to
>   be displayed above the lines of the page
> Δ*NUMBERS*←1   because line numbers are to be displayed
>   alongside the lines displayed.

In summary, the meanings of commands for the text-editing system will be interpreted as follows: The word at the beginning of each command will be a function to perform the command according to the settings of certain global variables, as indicated above. Other words in a command will simply test and set values of the global variables, and perhaps pass a value to the main (leftmost) function in the command.

7.4 Implementation Details of the Text Editor

Probably the best way to begin the implementation of the text-editing system is to consider the requirements of the functions *BEGIN, ADD, DISPLAY, PRINT, INSERT, DELETE, SPACE,* and *HOW*, since those functions perform the actual work of the editor, and all other functions in the system merely assist them. By studying the command set and the global variables specified in Sections 7.2 and 7.3, one can determine which of the global variables each of the main "verb" functions needs to use, and what values of the global variables are appropriate for it:

—*BEGIN* expects:

$\Delta WIDTH$ to be a single positive integer (possibly a default
value, since the phrase "$OF\ WIDTH$ number" is optional)
$\Delta TYPE = 'G'$ (since the command must be "$BEGIN\ A\ PAGE$
...")

—ADD expects:

$\Delta PAGE$ to be a two-dimensional character array (possibly with
0 rows)
$\Delta WIDTH$ to be a single positive integer not greater than the
width of $\Delta PAGE$ (and possibly a default value)
$\Delta TYPE \in 'BRQ'$ (since only a block, paragraph, or quoted
string of input can be added to the page by the ADD
command)
$\Delta BREAK$ to be a single character (possibly a default value) if
$\Delta TYPE \in 'BR'$
$\Delta CENTER$ to be 0 or 1
$\Delta AFTER$ to be empty or to be a single integer between 0 and
the number of lines in $\Delta PAGE$, inclusive

—$DISPLAY$ and $PRINT$ expect:

$\Delta PAGE$ to be a two-dimensional character array (possibly with
0 rows)
$\Delta TYPE \in 'GL'$ (since only the full page or specified lines of it
can be displayed or printed)
$\Delta LINES$ to be a vector of valid line numbers of $\Delta PAGE$ if
$\Delta TYPE = 'L'$
$\Delta NUMBERS$ to be 0 or 1
$\Delta HEADER$ to be 0 or 1

—$INSERT$ expects:

$\Delta PAGE$ to be a two-dimensional character array (possibly with
0 rows)
$\Delta WIDTH$ to be a single positive integer (possibly a default
value) not greater than the width of $\Delta PAGE$
$\Delta TYPE \in 'BRQL'$ (since a block, paragraph, quoted string, or
specified lines of the page may be inserted into the page)
$\Delta BREAK$ to be a single character (possibly a default value) if
$\Delta TYPE \in 'BR'$
$\Delta CENTER$ to be 0 or 1 if $\Delta TYPE \in 'BRQ'$
$\Delta LINES$ to be a vector of valid line numbers of $\Delta PAGE$ if
$\Delta TYPE = 'L'$

$\triangle AFTER$ to be a single integer between 0 and the number of lines in $\triangle PAGE$, inclusive

—$DELETE$ expects:

$\triangle PAGE$ to be a two-dimensional character array with at least one row
$\triangle TYPE = 'L'$ (since only specified existing lines of the page can be deleted)
$\triangle LINES$ to be a vector of valid line numbers of $\triangle PAGE$

—$SPACE$ expects:

$\triangle PAGE$ to be a two-dimensional character array (possibly with 0 rows)
$\triangle AFTER$ to be either a default value (since the phrase "$BEFORE\ LINE$ number" or "$AFTER\ LINE$ number" is optional), or a single integer between 0 and the number of lines in $\triangle PAGE$, inclusive
(The number of blank lines to be inserted will be given by the argument of $SPACE$, not by the value of a global variable.)

—HOW expects:

$\triangle TYPE = 'G'$ or a default value (since the phrase "$IS\ THE\ PAGE$" is optional).

The foregoing consideration of the needs of the main verb functions suggests that the global variables should be reinitialized to certain default values between commands. The variables should be reinitialized as follows:

$\triangle WIDTH$ to the current width of $\triangle PAGE$, on the assumption that if the phrase "$OF\ WIDTH$ number" is omitted from a $BEGIN$, ADD, or $INSERT$ command, the new page, block, or paragraph is intended to have the same width as the current page
$\triangle BREAK$ to its current value (i.e., left unchanged), on the assumption that if the phrase "$ENDING\ AT$ 'character'" or "$WITH\ BREAK\ AT$ 'character'" is omitted from an ADD or $INSERT$ command, the user intends to keep using the same break character used previously
$\triangle CENTER$ to 0 on the assumption that centering will always be specified explicitly if desired
$\triangle AFTER$ to empty ($\iota 0$) as the default value for ADD and $SPACE$ commands (in which case text is to be added to the

end of $\Delta PAGE$), and also so that the $INSERT$ verb can
detect when the user has failed to specify an insertion point

$\Delta LINES$ to empty, so that the $DISPLAY$, $PRINT$, $INSERT$,
and $DELETE$ verbs can detect when the user has failed to
specify line numbers required for a command

$\Delta NUMBERS$ to 0 on the assumption that line numbers are to be
displayed or printed only if requested explicitly

$\Delta HEADER$ to 0 on the assumption that column numbers are to
be displayed or printed only if requested explicitly

$\Delta TYPE$ to $'Q'$, since if none of the words $PAGE$, $BLOCK$,
$PARAGRAPH$, $LINE$, or $LINES$ is used in a command to
refer to a piece of text, a quoted string is usually the text item
to be used. (An exception is the HOW command, for which the
piece of text is assumed always to be the entire page.)

These reinitializations can be performed by requiring each main verb function
to invoke the following function after the verb has done its other work:

```
       ∇    ΔREINITIALIZE
[1]        ΔWIDTH←¯1↑ρΔPAGE
[1]        ΔCENTER←ΔNUMBERS←ΔHEADER←0
[3]        ΔAFTER←ΔLINES←ι0
[4]        ΔTYPE←'Q'
       ∇
```

Before the very first command is entered by the user, after the text editor
workspace has been loaded, the global variables should all have some initial
values, so that the system will not just fail in case the user neglects to begin
with the command

$BEGIN$ A $PAGE$ OF $WIDTH$ number

The initial values for $\Delta CENTER$, $\Delta NUMBERS$, $\Delta HEADER$, $\Delta AFTER$, and
$\Delta LINES$ can be the same as those assigned by the $\Delta REINITIALIZE$ function. However, there are no reasonably natural values that can be used as de-
faults for $\Delta WIDTH$ and $\Delta BREAK$, and although $\Delta PAGE$ should naturally have
0 rows initially, there is no natural default value for its initial number of columns (just as there is no natural default value for $\Delta WIDTH$). Consequently,
$\Delta PAGE$, $\Delta WIDTH$, and $\Delta BREAK$ are probably best initialized to empty values,
so that if the user neglects to initialize them by proper use of the commands,
the system can provide prompting messages. Finally, the $\Delta TYPE$ variable
should probably be initialized to $'Q'$ as in $\Delta REINITIALIZE$, even though
the $BEGIN$ command is not supposed to contain a quoted string; that will
allow the $BEGIN$ function to detect whether the command correctly includes
the word $PAGE$. The initial values of the global variables can be assigned by
executing the following function, which saves the text editor as a self-starting
workspace and performs the initializations whenever it is loaded:

```
        ∇   ΔINITIALIZE
[1]         ⍕')SAVE'
[2]         ΔPAGE←ΔBREAK←''
[3]         ΔWIDTH←ΔAFTER←ΔLINES←ιΔCENTER←ΔNUMBERS←ΔHEADER←0
[4]         ΔTYPE←'Q'
        ∇
```

The *ERROR* function from Section 5.6 will be used for error handling in the text-editing system. However, it will be modified by making its name begin with Δ and by including a call to *ΔREINITIALIZE* in it:

```
        ∇   MESSAGE ΔERROR CONDITION
[1]         →(~CONDITION)/0
[2]         MESSAGE
[3]         ΔREINITIALIZE
[4]         →
        ∇
```

We can now begin to write the functions that define the meanings of the words in the commands for the text editor. Because the main verb functions are the most complicated, they will be left until later. We will begin with the definitions of some of the simpler words.

Simplest of all to define are the meanings of the words *A*, *AT*, *IS*, *OF*, *THE*, and *WITH*, which have no tasks to perform in the system except to act as connectives between other words:

A

> The word *A* occurs only in the phrases *"A PAGE ..."*, and *"A [CENTERED] BLOCK ..."* or *"A [CENTERED] PARAGRAPH ...."* It can simply pass its value on toward the left:
>
> ```
>         ∇ R←A S
> [1]     R←S
>         ∇
> ```

AT

> *AT* occurs only in the phrase *"ENDING AT ..."* or *"WITH BREAK AT ..."* and may be defined like *A*:
>
> ```
>         ∇ R←AT S
> [1]     R←S
>         ∇
> ```

IS

> *IS* occurs only in the *HOW* command (*"HOW LONG IS THE PAGE"* or *"HOW WIDE IS THE PAGE"*). Because *LONG* and *WIDE* must be niladic (since the phrase *"IS THE PAGE"* is optional), *IS* must be dyadic. Its value can be just the value of its left argument:
>
> ```
>         ∇ R←S IS T
> [1]     R←S
>         ∇
> ```

OF

> *OF* occurs only in the phrase *"OF WIDTH* number." As noted in Section 7.2, it must be dyadic. Its definition can be:
>
> ```
>       ∇ R←S OF T
> [1]   R←S
>       ∇
> ```

THE

> *THE* is used only in the phrase *"THE PAGE."* It can be defined like *A*:
>
> ```
>       ∇ R←THE S
> [1]   R←S
>       ∇
> ```

WITH

> *WITH* occurs in the phrases *"WITH BREAK AT '*'*,"* *"WITH [HEADER AND] [LINE] NUMBERS,"* and *'WITH [[LINE] NUMBERS AND] HEADER."* It must be dyadic and can be defined simply as:
>
> ```
>       ∇ R←S WITH N
> [1]   R←S
>       ∇
> ```

Notice that the definitions of the words *A*, *AT*, and *THE* make those words completely redundant and allow commands to be used without them. The following are examples of abbreviated commands that are possible:

```
BEGIN PAGE OF WIDTH 50
ADD PARAGRAPH ENDING '≠'
PRINT PAGE
```

Next in simplicity of meaning (for this system) are the words *BLOCK*, *BREAK*, *CENTERED*, *ENDING*, *HEADER*, *NUMBERS*, *PAGE*, *PARAGRAPH*, and *WIDTH*, whose jobs are to set values of global variables.

BLOCK

> *BLOCK* merely sets the global *ΔTYPE* variable to indicate that the command refers to a block of text (with spacing preserved exactly as the user types it). It returns the empty string, which will be used for error detection by other functions.
>
> ```
>       ∇ R←BLOCK
> [1]   ΔTYPE←'B'
> [2]   R←''
>       ∇
> ```

BREAK

BREAK sets the global $\Delta BREAK$ variable:

```
      ∇ R←BREAK C;M
[1]    M←'ONE CHARACTER SHOULD BE USED TO BREAK INPUT TEXT'
[2]    M ΔERROR(ΔNUMERIC C)∨1≠ρ,C
[3]    R←ΔBREAK←C
      ∇
```

Notice that the *BREAK* and *AT* functions together provide a new short command for the system: *BREAK AT* '*', which can be used to reset the break character without using an *ADD* or *INSERT* command. The function $\Delta NUMERIC$ in line 2 of *BREAK* is from Exercise 4.8.1 (with a Δ added).

CENTERED

CENTERED can simply set the $\Delta CENTER$ variable to true (1) and then pass the value of its argument along to the left. It must pass the value of its argument because the argument can be a quoted string, as in the phrase "*ADD CENTERED* '*PAGE 2*'."

```
      ∇ R←CENTERED S
[1]    ΔCENTER←1
[2]    R←S
      ∇
```

ENDING

Since *ENDING* has the same role as the pair of words *WITH BREAK*, its definition combines aspects of both *WITH* and *BREAK*:

```
      ∇ R←S ENDING C;M
[1]    M←'ONE CHARACTER SHOULD BE USED TO END INPUT TEXT'
[2]    M ΔERROR(ΔNUMERIC C)∨1≠ρ,C
[3]    ΔBREAK←C
[4]    R←S
      ∇
```

HEADER

HEADER sets the value of the global variable $\Delta HEADER$ to true and passes an empty vector as its value:

```
      ∇ R←HEADER
[1]    ΔHEADER←1
[2]    R←ι0
      ∇
```

NUMBERS

NUMBERS is similar to *HEADER*. Its job is just to indicate that line numbers are to be included when a piece of text is displayed:

```
      ∇ R←NUMBERS
[1]    ΔNUMBERS←1
[2]    R←ι0
      ∇
```

PAGE

> *PAGE* sets $\Delta TYPE$ to indicate that the entire page has been referred to. It passes an empty character vector as its value, to be used by other functions for detection of invalid commands like *"DELETE THE PAGE."*

```
      ∇ R←PAGE
[1]     ΔTYPE←'G'
[2]     R←''
      ∇
```

PARAGRAPH

> *PARAGRAPH* is similar to *PAGE*. It sets $\Delta TYPE$ to indicate that a paragraph of input text has been called for, and it returns an empty vector to be used by other functions for detection of invalid commands like *"INSERT A BLOCK BEFORE THE PARAGRAPH."*

```
      ∇ R←PARAGRAPH
[1]     ΔTYPE←'R'
[2]     R←''
      ∇
```

WIDTH

> The *WIDTH* function checks that its argument has a suitable value before setting the value of $\Delta WIDTH$:

```
      ∇ R←WIDTH W;M
[1]     M←'WIDTH SHOULD BE A SINGLE NUMBER'
[2]     M ΔERROR(~ΔNUMERIC W)∨1≠ρ,W
[3]     M←'WIDTH SHOULD BE A POSITIVE WHOLE NUMBER'
[4]     M ΔERROR(W≤0)∨W≠⌊W
[5]     R←ΔWIDTH←W
      ∇
```

The *LONG* and *WIDE* functions, used in the *HOW* command, will measure the current value of $\Delta PAGE$ and pass the appropriate result directly to the *HOW* function (not through a global variable). However, both *LONG* and *WIDE* must make sure that $\Delta PAGE$ has a value other than its initial empty value.

LONG

```
      ∇ R←LONG
[1]     'NO PAGE HAS BEEN STARTED' ΔERROR 2≠ρρΔPAGE
[2]     R←1↑ρΔPAGE
      ∇
```

WIDE

```
      ∇ R←WIDE
[1]     'NO PAGE HAS BEEN STARTED' ΔERROR 2≠ρρΔPAGE
[2]     R←¯1↑ρΔPAGE
      ∇
```

The words *AND* and *THRU* are used to produce vectors of line numbers. *AND* is also used in the phrases *"WITH HEADER AND LINE NUMBERS,"* *"WITH LINE NUMBERS AND HEADER,"* and their variants. Both *AND* and *THRU* expect numeric arguments; since the *NUMBERS* and *HEADER* functions have already been defined to return empty numeric vectors, they will cause no trouble for the *AND* function.

AND

```
     ∇ R←A AND B;M
[1]    M←'''AND'' SHOULD NOT BE USED WITH STRINGS'
[2]    M ΔERROR(~ΔNUMERIC A)∨~ΔNUMERIC B
[3]    R←A,B
     ∇
```

Having determined that its arguments are numeric, *AND* simply catenates them. For phrases such as *"WITH HEADER AND LINE NUMBERS"* the actual value returned by *AND* is unimportant, but in a phrase like *"LINES 2 AND 6"* it is important. This definition of *AND*, plus the fact that the comma is the catenation function in APL and that elements of a numeric vector are written with spaces between them, permits such fancy commands as

DISPLAY LINES 2, 3 AND 4 WITH HEADER
DELETE LINES 3 6 8 AND 4 7 9
INSERT LINES 4 3 AND 2 BEFORE LINE 1
PRINT LINES 3 AND 5 AND 9 WITH NUMBERS

Notice that line numbers need not be specified in increasing order. If they are not, the assumption will be that lines to be displayed, printed, or inserted elsewhere in the page are to be taken from the page in the order indicated by the command. (In the case of *DELETE* the order of line numbers will not be significant, since the lines will be deleted simultaneously.)

THRU

The *THRU* function is the function of Exercise 4.1.5. It should check that its arguments are single numbers. The version of *THRU* from Exercise 4.1.5 should permit phrases like *"LINES 2, 3 AND 9 THRU 12"* (which should yield the vector of line numbers 2 3 9 10 11 12), but it will not permit a phrase like *"LINES 2 THRU 5 AND 9 THRU 12"* because the right argument of the left *THRU* will be a vector (5 9 10 11 12). An improved version of *THRU* is suggested in an exercise at the end of this chapter.

Only the functions *AFTER, BEFORE, LINE,* and *LINES* remain to be defined before we get to the main verb functions. Of these, *LINE* is somewhat tricky, since it has three different uses in the system:

1. *LINE* can refer to a specific line of the page to be displayed, deleted, or inserted elsewhere in the page, as in

    DELETE LINE 5

2. *LINE* can be used with *AFTER* or *BEFORE* to indicate a point in the page for insertion of text, as in

    INSERT 'THIS STRING' AFTER LINE 5

3. *LINE* can optionally modify *NUMBERS* in the phrase *"WITH HEADER AND LINE NUMBERS"* and its variants.

Only in the first of these cases should *LINE* be permitted to set $\Delta TYPE \leftarrow 'L'$ and $\Delta LINES$ to the value of its argument. The trouble is, however, that the *LINE* function itself cannot always determine how it is being used. In case (3) it can do so, because the *NUMBERS* function will pass an empty vector to it. But in case (2) it is up to the *AFTER* or *BEFORE* function to detect how *LINE* is being used.

The situation concerning *LINE* is further complicated by the fact that *LINE* can be used in two different senses in the same command, as in

INSERT LINE 5 *AFTER LINE* 8

That command, which should yield the global variable settings

$\Delta TYPE \leftarrow 'L'$
$\Delta LINES \leftarrow, 5$
$\Delta AFTER \leftarrow 8$

contrasts with such commands as

INSERT A BLOCK AFTER LINE 8

and

INSERT 'THIS STRING' AFTER LINE 8

which should yield, respectively, the global variable settings

$\Delta TYPE \leftarrow 'B'$	and	$\Delta TYPE \leftarrow 'Q'$
$\Delta AFTER \leftarrow 8$		$\Delta AFTER \leftarrow 8$

The foregoing considerations suggest the following definitions:

LINE

```
       ∇ R←LINE L;M
[1]    R←L
[2]    →(0=ρ,L)/0  - in case of 'LINE NUMBERS'
[3]    M←'A LINE MUST BE REFERRED TO BY NUMBER'
[4]    M ΔERROR~ΔNUMERIC L
[5]    ΔTYPE←'L'
[6]    ΔLINES←,L
       ∇
```

LINES

```
      ∇ R←LINES L;M
[1]     M←'LINES MUST BE REFERRED TO BY NUMBER'
[2]     M ∆ERROR~∆NUMERIC L
[3]     ∆TYPE←'L'
[4]     R←∆LINES←,L
      ∇
```

AFTER

```
      ∇ R←A AFTER B;M
[1]     M←'A SINGLE LINE NUMBER SHOULD BE SPECIFIED WITH ''AFTER'''
[2]     M ∆ERROR(~∆NUMERIC B)∨1≠ρ,B
[3]     ∆AFTER←B
[4]     ∆LINES←ι0
[5]     R←A
[6]     →(∨/'L'≠∆TYPE)/0
[7]     ∆TYPE←'Q'
      ∇
```

Line 4 assumes that ∆*LINES* has been set, incorrectly, by the word
LINE or *LINES* following *AFTER*. It reinitializes ∆*LINES* to
empty. Lines 6 and 7 cause ∆*TYPE* to be reinitialized to '*Q*' only if
it is still set to '*L*'. That is because for a command such as

INSERT A BLOCK AFTER LINE 7

the *BLOCK* function will have changed ∆*TYPE* to '*B*' before the
AFTER function is executed, and the latter should not reset it to
'*Q*'. However, if ∆*TYPE* is still '*L*', *AFTER* must reset it to '*Q*'
in order to handle commands like

INSERT 'THIS STRING' AFTER LINE 7

Finally, notice that the definition of *AFTER* makes the word *LINE*
optional after it. Since *AFTER* uses its right argument directly, one
can use such commands as

INSERT LINE 5 AFTER 7
INSERT A PARAGRAPH AFTER 26

BEFORE

BEFORE is essentially the same as *AFTER*, except for the value that
it assigns to ∆*AFTER*:

```
      ∇ R←A BEFORE B;M
[1]     M←'A SINGLE LINE NUMBER SHOULD BE SPECIFIED WITH ''BEFORE'''
[2]     M ∆ERROR(~∆NUMERIC B)∨1≠ρ,B
[3]     ∆AFTER←B-1
[4]     ∆LINES←ι0
[5]     R←A
[6]     →(∨/'L'≠∆TYPE)/0
[7]     ∆TYPE←'Q'
      ∇
```

We are now ready to define the main verb functions.

BEGIN

```
     ∇ BEGIN P;M
[1]    M←'THE COMMAND SHOULD BE ''BEGIN A PAGE OF WIDTH...'''
[2]    M ∆ERROR ∆TYPE≠'G'
[3]    'NO WIDTH HAS BEEN SPECIFIED' ∆ERROR 1≠ρ,∆WIDTH
[4]    ∆PAGE←(0,∆WIDTH)ρ' '
[5]    ∆REINITIALIZE
     ∇
```

HOW

Most of the work of *HOW* has already been done by *LONG* or *WIDE*.

```
     ∇ HOW
[1]    R
[2]    ∆REINITIALIZE
     ∇
```

DELETE

```
     ∇ DELETE L;M
[1]    NO PAGE HAS BEEN STARTED' ∆ERROR 2≠ρρ∆PAGE
[2]    M←'LINES TO BE DELETED SHOULD BE SPECIFIED BY NUMBER'
[3]    M ∆ERROR~∆NUMERIC L
[4]    M←'SOME OF THOSE LINE NUMBERS ARE NOT IN THE PAGE'
[5]    M ∆ERROR~∧/Lει1↑ρ∆PAGE
[6]    ∆PAGE←(~(ι1↑ρ∆PAGE)εL)/[1]∆PAGE
[7]    ∆REINITIALIZE
     ∇
```

Notice that the validity check in line 5 will detect invalid fractional
line numbers as well as integer numbers which are not valid line
numbers for the current page.

SPACE

```
     ∇ SPACE N;M
[1]    'NO PAGE HAS BEEN STARTED' ∆ERROR 2≠ρρ∆PAGE
[2]    M←'GIVE THE NUMBER OF BLANK LINES WANTED AFTER ''SPACE'''
[3]    M ∆ERROR(~∆NUMERIC N)∨1≠ρ,N
[4]    N←(N,⁻1↑ρ∆PAGE)ρ' '
[5]    →(1≠ρ,∆AFTER)/ATEND
[6]    M←'THE PLACE FOR INSERTION IS NOT IN THE PAGE'
[7]    M ∆ERROR~∆AFTERε0,ι1↑ρ∆PAGE
[8]    ∆PAGE←((∆AFTER,⁻1↑ρ∆PAGE)↑∆PAGE),[1]N,[1](∆AFTER,0)↓∆PAGE
[9]    →END
[10]   ATEND:∆PAGE←∆PAGE,[1]N
[11]   END:∆REINITIALIZE
     ∇
```

Lines 6 through 8 handle insertion of spaces before or after a specified
line of the page, while line 10 handles insertion of spaces at the end of
the page.

The *ADD* and *INSERT* functions are very similar. The differences are (1) that *ADD* expects new text to be entered by the user (it cannot be used to insert existing lines of the page elsewhere in the page), and (2) the use of *BEFORE* or *AFTER* to specify an insertion point is optional with *ADD* (if no insertion point is specified, the new text is to be added to the end of the page). Consequently, it should be possible to define one of the functions *ADD* or *INSERT* in terms of the other. Since *INSERT* is the more general of the two, it is easiest to define *ADD* in terms of *INSERT*:

ADD

```
      ∇ ADD TEXT;M
[1]     M←'USE ''INSERT'', NOT ''ADD'' TO INSERT EXISTING LINES'
[2]     M←M,' OF THE PAGE ELSEWHERE IN THE PAGE'
[3]     M ΔERROR ΔTYPE='L'
[4]     →(1=ρ,ΔAFTER)/READY
[5]     ΔAFTER←1↑ρΔPAGE
[6]   READY:INSERT TEXT
      ∇
```

(For efficiency of execution, *ADD* could be defined without use of *INSERT* and optimized for its main use, which is to add new text to the end of the current page.)

INSERT will use special functions *ΔGETBLOCK*, *ΔGETPARA*, and *ΔGETLINES* to get the input block, input paragraph, or existing lines of the page which are to be inserted into the page. The *ΔGETLINES* function will also be used by the *DISPLAY* and *PRINT* functions. *INSERT* will also use a function called *ΔCENTERED*, which is like the function of Exercise 4.9.6, for centering text.

INSERT

```
      ∇ INSERT TEXT;M;PAGEWIDTH;TEXTWIDTH;PAGELENGTH
[1]     'NO PAGE HAS BEEN STARTED' ∆ERROR 2≠ρρ∆PAGE
[2]     PAGELENGTH←1↑ρ∆PAGE;PAGEWIDTH←¯1↑ρ∆PAGE
[3]     M←'INSERTION POINT HAS NOT BEEN SPECIFIED '
[4]     M←M,'OR IS NOT IN THE PAGE'
[5]     M ∆ERROR(1≠ρ,∆AFTER),~∆AFTER∊0,ιPAGELENGTH
[6]     M←'TEXT TO BE ADDED OR INSERTED CANNOT BE '
[7]     M←M,'WIDER THAN THE PAGE; TRY AGAIN'
[8]     →(∆TYPE≠'Q')/NONQUOTE
[9]     'ONLY CHARACTER STRINGS CAN BE INSERTED' ∆ERROR ∆NUMERIC TEXT
[10]    M ∆ERROR PAGEWIDTH<ρTEXT←,TEXT
[11]    TEXT←(1,ρTEXT)ρTEXT
[12]    →CENTER
[13]   NONQUOTE:M ∆ERROR ∆WIDTH>PAGEWIDTH
[14]    ⍎'→CASE',∆TYPE
[15]   CASEG:M←'THE PAGE CANNOT BE ADDED OR INSERTED INTO ITSELF'
[16]    M ∆ERROR 1
[17]   CASEB: TEXT←∆GETBLOCK
[18]    →CENTER
[19]   CASER:TEXT←∆GETPARA
[20]    →CENTER
[21]   CASEL:TEXT←∆GETLINES
[22]   CENTER:→(~∆CENTER)/PAD
[23]    TEXT←PAGEWIDTH ∆CENTERED TEXT
[24]    →IN
[25]   PAD:→(PAGEWIDTH=TEXTWIDTH←¯1↑ρTEXT)/IN
[26]    TEXT←TEXT,((1↑ρTEXT),PAGEWIDTH-TEXTWIDTH)ρ' '
[27]   IN:→(∆AFTER=PAGELENGTH)/ADDON
[28]    ∆PAGE←((∆AFTER,PAGEWIDTH)↑∆PAGE),[1]TEXT,[1](∆AFTER,0)↓∆PAGE
[29]    →END
[30]   ADDON:∆PAGE←∆PAGE,[1]TEXT
[31]   END:∆REINITIALIZE
      ∇
```

Lines 3 through 5 check that an appropriate insertion point has been specified.
Lines 9 through 11 deal with a quoted string which is to be inserted. They
check that it is actually a character string no wider than the current page, and if
so they reshape it into a one-row matrix. Line 14 uses the execute function to
implement a multiway branch according to the value of *∆TYPE*; the appropriate case in lines 15 through 21 gets the text to be inserted. Line 23 centers the
input text, if required. Line 26 pads the text on the right with blanks if necessary to make it the same width as the current page. Line 28 inserts text anywhere except at the end of the page, and line 30 adds text to the end of the
page.

In this implementation of the text editor, the *DISPLAY* and *PRINT* functions will be the same except for their names. In another version they might
differ according to where they send their output: *DISPLAY* could send output
to a screen, and *PRINT* could send output to a printer.

DISPLAY

DISPLAY will need a row of column numbers for use when a command calls for a *HEADER*. The same row of column numbers can be used by the △*GETBLOCK* function (which is yet to be defined) to provide a guide for the user when entering a block of text. Hence, a new global variable △*HEADERLINE* is introduced to have a vector of column numbers as its value: (It should be included in the △*INITIALIZE* function.)

```
      △HEADERLINE←'12345678-1-2345678-2-2345678-3-2345678-4-'
      △HEADERLINE←△HEADERLINE,'2345678-5-2345678-6-2345678-7-'
      △HEADERLINE←△HEADERLINE,'2345678-8-2345678-9-2345678-0'
      ∇  DISPLAY P;M;TEXT
[1]    'NO PAGE HAS BEEN STARTED' △ERROR 2≠ρρ△PAGE
[2]    M←'ONLY THE PAGE OR SPECIFIED LINES IN IT '
[3]    M←M,'CAN BE DISPLAYED OR PRINTED'
[4]    M △ERROR~△TYPE∈'GL'
[5]    →(△TYPE='L')/LINES
[6]    TEXT←△PAGE;△LINES←ι1↑ρ△PAGE
[7]    →HEADER
[8]    LINES:TEXT←△GETLINES
[9]    HEADER:→(~△HEADER)/NUMBERS
[10]   □ ←((3×△NUMBERS)ρ' '),(¯1↑ρTEXT)ρ△HEADERLINE
[11]   NUMBERS:→(~△NUMBERS)/OUT
[12]   TEXT←(0 1 ↓ 4 0 ⍕1000+((ρ,△LINES),1)ρ△LINES),TEXT
[13]   OUT:□ ←TEXT
[14]   △REINITIALIZE
      ∇
```

Line 10 prints the header line, if requested. It inserts three blanks at the beginning of the header line if line numbers have also been requested, so that the header line will be aligned correctly over the columns of the output text. Line 12 adds three-digit line numbers, if requested, to the left side of the text which is to be displayed.

PRINT

```
      ∇ PRINT P
[1]    DISPLAY P
      ∇
```

Finally, we must define the functions △*GETBLOCK*, △*GETPARA*, △*GETLINES*, and △*CENTERED* which are used by *INSERT* and/or *DISPLAY*. As has already been mentioned, △*CENTERED* is the subject of Exercise 4.9.6. △*GETPARA* is left as an exercise. △*GETLINES* is simple:

```
      ∇ S←△GETLINES;M
[1]    M←'THE LINES SPECIFIED ARE NOT ALL IN THE PAGE'
[2]    M △ERROR~∧/△LINES∈ι1↑ρ△PAGE
[3]    S←△PAGE[(,△LINES);]
      ∇
```

$\Delta GETBLOCK$ displays a row of column numbers of the width specified by $\Delta WIDTH$. It then accepts lines of input text and accumulates them in a matrix of specified width until a line is encountered whose last character is the break character $\Delta BREAK$. If the last line, without the break character, is nonempty, it is added to the end of the matrix; otherwise the last line is ignored. $\Delta GETBLOCK$ refuses to accept any input line whose width is greater than $\Delta WIDTH$; in such cases it asks the user to type a shorter line.

```
     ∇    B←ΔGETBLOCK;L;M
[1]       M←'NO BREAK CHARACTER HAS BEEN SPECIFIED'
[2]       M ΔERROR 1≠ρ,ΔBREAK
[3]       B←(0,ΔWIDTH)ρ' '
[4]       ☐ ←ΔWIDTHρΔHEADERLINE
[5]       →GETLINE
[6]    RETRY:☐ ←'LINE IS TOO LONG; TRY AGAIN'
[7]    GETLINE:L←,▯
[8]       →(ΔBREAK=¯1↑L)/LOOPEND
[9]       →(ΔWIDTH<ρL)/RETRY
[10]      B←B,[1]ΔWIDTH↑L
[11]      →GETLINE
[12]   LOOPEND:→(0=ρL←¯1↓L)/0
[13]      →(ΔWIDTH<ρL)/RETRY
[14]      B←B,[1]ΔWIDTH↑L
     ∇
```

Implementation of the text-editing system is now finished, except for definition of the functions $\Delta CENTERED$ and $\Delta GETPARA$ which have been left as
exercises. The following is an example of using the system. (Lines typed by the
user have been underlined.)

```
      BEGIN A PAGE OF WIDTH 40
      ADD CENTERED 'SAMPLE PAGE'
      ADD A PARAGRAPH ENDING AT '≠'
      THIS IS THE FIRST PARAGRAPH FOR THE PAGE. NOTICE HOW WORDS ARE
REARRANGED TO FILL OUT LINES AS FULLY AS POSSIBLE.≠
      ADD A CENTERED BLOCK OF WIDTH 10
12345678-1
THIS BLOCK
    IS
  TO BE
  SPACED
EXACTLY AS IT
LINE IS TOO LONG; TRY AGAIN
EXACTLY AS
  TYPED
≠
      DISPLAY THE PAGE WITH HEADER AND LINE NUMBERS
   12345678-1-2345678-2-2345678-3-2345678-4
001                SAMPLE PAGE
002      THIS IS THE FIRST PARAGRAPH FOR THE
003PAGE.  NOTICE HOW WORDS ARE REARRANGED
004TO FILL OUT LINES AS FULLY AS POSSIBLE.
005
006              THIS BLOCK
007                  IS
008                TO BE
009                SPACED
010             EXACTLY AS
011                 TYPED
```

    SPACE 2 AFTER LINE 1
    SPACE 1
    ADD A PARAGRAPH
   THIS IS THE SECOND PARAGRAPH FOR THE PAGE.   IT SHOULD BE ADDED
AFTER THE CENTERED BLOCK.≠
    HOW LONG IS THE PAGE
18
    HOW WIDE
40
    PRINT LINE 18

    PRINT THE PAGE WITH NUMBERS
001   *SAMPLE PAGE*
002
003
004   *THIS IS THE FIRST PARAGRAPH FOR THE*
005*PAGE.   NOTICE HOW WORDS ARE REARRANGED*
006*TO FILL OUT LINES AS FULLY AS POSSIBLE.*
007
008   *THIS BLOCK*
009   *IS*
010   *TO BE*
011   *SPACED*
012   *EXACTLY AS*
013   *TYPED*
014
015   *THIS IS THE SECOND PARAGRAPH FOR*
016*THE PAGE.   IT SHOULD BE ADDED AFTER THE*
017*CENTERED BLOCK.*
018
    ADD CENTERED 'THE END'
    INSERT LINES 9 8 10 13 12 11 AFTER LINE 13
    DELETE LINES 8 THRU 13
    HOW LONG
19
    PRINT LINES 7 THRU 14 WITH NUMBERS
007
008   *IS*
009   *THIS BLOCK*
010   *TO BE*
011   *TYPED*
012   *EXACTLY AS*
013   *SPACED*
014
    DELETE LINE 10

```
     PRINT THE PAGE
             SAMPLE PAGE


     THIS IS THE FIRST PARAGRAPH FOR THE
PAGE.  NOTICE HOW WORDS ARE REARRANGED
TO FILL OUT LINES AS FULLY AS POSSIBLE.

                 IS
         THIS BLOCK
             TYPED
         EXACTLY AS
           SPACED

     THIS IS THE SECOND PARAGRAPH FOR
THE PAGE.  IT SHOULD BE ADDED AFTER THE
CENTERED BLOCK.

             THE END
```

7.5 Extensions and Limitations of the Text Editor

Once implemented, the text-editing system can be extended easily in various ways. For example, synonyms can be defined for existing words in the vocabulary of the system:

```
     ∇ START P
[1]    BEGIN P
     ∇

     ∇ R←A THROUGH B
[1]    R←A THRU B
     ∇

     ∇ P←PARA
[1]    P←PARAGRAPH
     ∇

     ∇ N←NUMBER
[1]    N←NUMBERS
     ∇
```

Those definitions immediately extend the system to accept such commands as

```
     START A PAGE OF WIDTH 65
     ADD A PARA WITH BREAK AT '*'
     PRINT LINES 3 THROUGH 7
     DISPLAY LINE 6 WITH LINE NUMBER AND HEADER
```

For those who like a less verbose set of commands, abbreviated commands can be defined in terms of the existing commands. The following suggested abbreviations are only some of the possibilities:

```
      ∇   NEW N
[1]       BEGIN PAGE OF WIDTH N
      ∇

      ∇   BR C
[1]       BREAK C
      ∇

      ∇   AB
[1]       ADD BLOCK
      ∇

      ∇   AP
[1]       ADD PARAGRAPH
      ∇

      ∇   AC S
[1]       ADD CENTERED S
      ∇

      ∇   HL
[1]       HOW LONG
      ∇

      ∇   HW
[1]       HOW WIDE
      ∇

      ∇   DP
[1]       DISPLAY PAGE WITH HEADER AND NUMBERS
      ∇

      ∇   DL N
[1]       DISPLAY LINES N WITH HEADER AND NUMBERS
      ∇

      ∇   PP
[1]       PRINT PAGE
      ∇

      ∇   PL N
[1]       PRINT LINES N
      ∇

      ∇   IPA N
[1]       INSERT PARAGRAPH AFTER N
      ∇
      ∇   IBA N
[1]       INSERT BLOCK AFTER N
      ∇
      ∇   SP N
[1]       SPACE N
      ∇
```

The following session illustrates the abbreviated commands:

```
    NEW 40
    AC 'SAMPLE PAGE'
    BR '≠'
≠
    AP
    THIS IS THE FIRST PARAGRAPH FOR THE PAGE.  NOTICE HOW WORDS ARE
REARRANGED TO FILL OUT LINES AS FULLY AS POSSIBLE.≠
    AC BLOCK OF WIDTH 10
12345678-1
THIS BLOCK
    IS
  TO BE
  SPACED
EXACTLY AS
  TYPED
≠
    HL
11
    DL 1 THRU 3
  12345678-1-2345678-2-2345678-3-2345678-4
001                 SAMPLE PAGE
002     THIS IS THE FIRST PARAGRAPH FOR THE
003PAGE.  NOTICE HOW WORDS ARE REARRANGED
    SP 2 AFTER 1
    PP
                SAMPLE PAGE


    THIS IS THE FIRST PARAGRAPH FOR THE
PAGE.  NOTICE HOW WORDS ARE REARRANGED
TO FILL OUT LINES AS FULLY AS POSSIBLE.

            THIS BLOCK
                IS
              TO BE
              SPACED
          EXACTLY AS
              TYPED
```

Other extensions may require the introduction of new global variables or a change in the way existing global variables are used. For instance, it might be desirable to add a command of the form

REPLACE LINE number $\begin{Bmatrix} BY \\ WITH \end{Bmatrix}$

$\begin{Bmatrix} A[CENTERED] \begin{Bmatrix} BLOCK \\ PARAGRAPH \end{Bmatrix} & [OF\ WIDTH\ \text{number}] & \begin{bmatrix} \begin{Bmatrix} ENDING \\ WITH\ BREAK \end{Bmatrix} [AT]\ '*' \end{bmatrix} \\ [CENTERED]\ \text{'string'} \\ LINE\ \text{number} \\ LINES\ \text{vector}\ [AND\ \text{number}] \\ LINES\ \text{number}\ THRU\ \text{number} \end{Bmatrix}$

For that to be done, the way in which the variables $\Delta TYPE$ and $\Delta LINES$ are used would have to be changed, so that the correct type (and possibly line numbers) for the piece of text to be inserted would be available to the *REPLACE* function. (In the current implementation, the *LINE* function just after *REPLACE* would wipe out whatever values of $\Delta TYPE$ and $\Delta LINES$ were assigned further to the right in the command.)

However the text editor is extended, it will always have limitations due to the fact that it understands only a subset of English. It will be possible for a user of the system to forget its limitations and to type a command which is outside the capabilities of the system.

Most incorrect commands will result in error messages being printed. For instance, if the user enters a command which contains an undefined word, the APL interpreter will detect the error and will display a *VALUE ERROR* message. Examples are

```
      INSERT 'THIS STRING' FOLLOWING LINE 7
VALUE ERROR
      INSERT 'THIS STRING' FOLLOWING LINE 7
                           ∧

      EXCHANGE LINE 3 AND LINE 4
VALUE ERROR
      EXCHANGE LINE 3 AND LINE 4
         ∧
```

Similarly, if the user types valid words in an incorrect sequence, the APL interpreter will issue a *SYNTAX ERROR* message, provided the command is invalid as an APL expression:

```
      INSERT AFTER LINE 5 A BLOCK OF WIDTH 30
SYNTAX ERROR
      INSERT AFTER LINE 5 A BLOCK OF WIDTH 30
                  ∧
```

Still other incorrect commands will be caught by the semantic checks built into the functions of the text-editing system, as the following examples illustrate:

```
      INSERT A BLOCK BEFORE THE PARAGRAPH
A SINGLE LINE NUMBER SHOULD BE SPECIFIED WITH 'BEFORE'
      DELETE THE PARAGRAPH
LINES TO BE DELETED SHOULD BE SPECIFIED BY NUMBER
```

(The functions *BEFORE* and *DELETE* expect numeric arguments, while *PARAGRAPH* returns an empty character matrix.)

Unfortunately, there are some invalid commands which will get by both the APL interpreter's checks and the text editor's checks and will actually be misunderstood by the editor. The following part of a session with the editor gives some examples:

```
      PRINT THE LINE NUMBERS OF THE PAGE
001      ONCE UPON A TIME THERE WERE THREE
002BEARS, WHO LIVED TOGETHER IN A LITTLE
003HOUSE IN THE FOREST.  THERE WAS A MAMA
004BEAR, A PAPA BEAR, AND A BABY BEAR.
005

      HOW LONG IS 'THIS STRING OF CHARACTERS'
5

      ADD A PARAGRAPH ENDING AT '*'
      ONE DAY THE THREE BEARS DECIDED TO GO FOR A WALK.
WHILE THEY WERE GONE, A LITTLE GIRL NAMED GOLDILOCKS
CAME WANDERING BY THEIR HOUSE.*
      PRINT LINES 1 AND 2 OF THE PARAGRAPH
      ONCE UPON A TIME THERE WERE THREE
BEARS, WHO LIVED TOGETHER IN A LITTLE
```

Notice that *"PRINT THE LINE NUMBERS OF THE PAGE"* is interpreted as if it were *"PRINT THE PAGE WITH LINE NUMBERS,"* which is not a disastrous misinterpretation. However, *"HOW LONG IS 'THIS STRING OF CHARACTERS'"* reports the length of the current page, not the length of the quoted string and *"PRINT LINES 1 AND 2 OF THE PARAGRAPH"* causes lines 1 and 2 of the current page, not of the paragraph just added, to be printed. Misunderstandings like the last two examples, which cause the system to supply misinformation, can be annoying and puzzling to a casual user of the system. (It might be an improvement for the system to give fuller replies to some commands. For example, when asked *"HOW LONG IS THE PAGE,"* it might reply with *"45 LINES"* instead of just *"45,"* to reduce the chance of misunderstanding.)

Particular misunderstandings can be eliminated by making changes to the system. However, it would be difficult, if not impossible, to eliminate all potential misunderstandings. Performing more thorough syntactic and semantic checks on commands would make the system larger and slower than it is now. In any case, many of the error checks which are already in the system are unnecessary for users who have gained experience using the system. In building such a system driven by English commands one must seek a suitable compromise between error detection and cost. The error checks that are most desirable may be determined best from the experience of persons using the system.

In conclusion, the following general remarks apply to systems like the text editor which are designed to understand commands in English:

1. The relative ease of learning and remembering commands for such a system is paid for by the extra cost of interpreting the commands and by the extra keystrokes needed to type them, compared with shorter, more cryptic commands.

2. Such systems are most suitable for applications which are run infrequently and/or are used by persons with minimal training.

3. The semantics of such a system should be kept simple and the set of commands should be kept fairly small, so that the user can remember the commands easily and thus will not be likely to enter invalid commands.

4. Enough error checking should be built into such a system to eliminate probable misunderstandings. Which misunderstandings are likely can be determined best from the experience of persons actually using the system.

If these guidelines are kept in mind, the techniques illustrated in this chapter can be quite useful for implementing easy-to-use application systems in APL.

EXERCISES

7.1   Write the function ∇ $P \leftarrow \Delta GETPARA$ for the text-editing system. It should accept input lines of arbitrary width and shape them into a paragraph of specified width, $\Delta WIDTH$, by filling each line of the paragraph with as many words as possible. The first line of the paragraph should be indented just as the user has indented the first line of input. Multiple spaces the user types within a line (e.g., two spaces after a period) should not be squeezed out, unless they happen to cross from one line to the next line in the paragraph. Assume that the user will end the paragraph by typing the break character ($\Delta BREAK$) at the end of the last line of input. Add one blank line at the end of the paragraph.

7.2   Add a function END to the text editor, so that commands like the following ones can be used:

$DISPLAY\ LINES$ 10 $THRU\ THE\ END$
$DELETE\ THE\ END$
$SPACE$ 2 $BEFORE\ THE\ END$

where $THE\ END$ refers to the last line of the page. (Note: Although this new function is useful, it may cause misunderstandings. For example, some people may understand the command "$SPACE$ 2 $BEFORE\ THE\ END$" to mean, in ordinary English, that two blank lines are to be inserted after the last line, rather than before the last line, or that one blank line is to be inserted two lines before the end of the page.)

7.3.   Rewrite the $THRU$ function so that it will permit phrases like the following ones to be used in commands, with appropriate meanings:

$LINES$ 2 $THRU$ 5 AND 9 $THRU$ 12
$LINES$ 4, 6, 8 $THRU$ 15 AND 27

That is, $THRU$ should accept a vector as its right argument (and possibly as its left argument, too).

7.4.   Modify the text editor so that a command like

HOW LONG IS 'THIS CHARACTER STRING'

produces an appropriate answer, rather than the incorrect answer which the current version of the system produces.

7.5.   Add a *REPLACE* command to the system, with the form suggested in Section 7.5.

7.6.   Add to the text editor a *JUSTIFY* command of the form

$$JUSTIFY\begin{cases} LINE \ \ \text{number} \\ LINES \ \text{vector} \ AND \ \text{number} \\ LINES \ \text{number} \ THRU \ \text{number} \end{cases}$$

to right-and left-justify specified lines of the page. (See Exercise 6.3.8.)

7.7.   Learn about the facilities for reading and writing permanent files in a version of APL which you have access to, and revise the text editor so that it can save and retrieve pages of text as named files, using commands like

$$SAVE\begin{cases} THE \ PAGE \\ LINE \ \text{number} \\ LINES \ \text{vector} \ AND \ \text{number} \\ LINES \ \text{number} \ THRU \ \text{number} \end{cases} AS \ FILE \ \text{'filename'}$$

GET FILE 'filename'

$$ADD \ FILE \ \text{'filename'}\left[\begin{cases} BEFORE \\ AFTER \end{cases} LINE \ \text{number}\right]$$

$$INSERT \ FILE \ \text{'filename'} \begin{cases} BEFORE \\ AFTER \end{cases} LINE \ \text{number}$$

The *GET* command should begin a new page which contains the contents of a specified file. (The width of the page should be equal to the width of the widest line in the file.) The *ADD* and *INSERT* commands should add or insert lines of text from a specified file into the current page.

7.8.   In the current version of the text editor, if the *BEGIN* command at the very beginning of a session does not specify a *WIDTH*, the system replies with an error message:

```
    BEGIN A PAGE
NO WIDTH HAS BEEN SPECIFIED
```

However, the following sequence can also occur at the very beginning of a session with the editor:

```
    ADD A PARAGRAPH ENDING AT '*'
NO PAGE HAS BEEN STARTED
    BEGIN A PAGE
    HOW WIDE IS THE PAGE
0
```

That is, failure to specify a *WIDTH* in the *BEGIN* command in this case does not cause an error message to appear. Instead, the system begins a page of width zero. Why does that happen? Modify the text editor in as simple and general a way as possible so that the sequence would, instead, cause the following error messages to be printed at the beginning of a session:

```
    ADD A PARAGRAPH ENDING AT '*'
NO PAGE HAS BEEN STARTED
    BEGIN A PAGE
NO WIDTH HAS BEEN SPECIFIED
```

7.9.   (Project) Implement a system for keeping track of named items and one-line descriptions indexed by keywords, as illustrated by the following example session. The items described in the example are files. Lines typed by the user have been underlined and explanatory comments have been added. The full set of commands for the system is listed after the example session.

```
    ADD 'TOR82'        —adding an item to the index

ENTER DESCRIPTION OF THE ITEM:
DATA FROM SURVEYS IN TORONTO

ENTER KEYWORDS FOR THE ITEM:
PROJECT1 DATA TORONTO 1982
  10:14:07 10-AUG-84 31 BLKS INDEX —indicates that the workspace
                            has been saved automatically

    ADD 'NY82'          —adding another item to the index
```

ENTER DESCRIPTION OF THE ITEM:
DATA FROM SURVEYS IN NEW YORK

ENTER KEYWORDS FOR THE ITEM:
PROJECT1 DATA NEWYORK 1982
  10:14:39 10-AUG-84 31 BLKS INDEX

        ADD 'LA83'

ENTER DESCRIPTION OF THE ITEM:
DATA FROM SURVEYS IN LOS ANGELES

ENTER KEYWORDS FOR THE ITEM:
PROJECT1 DATA LOSANGELES 1983
  10:15:08 10-AUG-84 31 BLKS INDEX

        ADD 'TOR83'

ENTER DESCRIPTION OF THE ITEM:
DATA FROM SURVEYS IN TORONTO

ENTER KEYWORDS FOR THE ITEM:
DATA TORONTO PROJECT2 1983
  10:15:57 10-AUG-84 31 BLKS INDEX

        ADD 'NY82'
AN ITEM WITH THAT NAME ALREADY EXISTS

        ADD 'NY84'

ENTER DESCRIPTION OF THE ITEM:
DATA FROM SURVEYS IN NEW YORK

ENTER KEYWORDS FOR THE ITEM:
1984 NEWYORK PROJECT2 DATA
  10:16:49 10-AUG-84 31 BLKS INDEX

        ADD 'PROJ1'

ENTER DESCRIPTION OF THE ITEM:
PROGRAMS FOR ANALYZING DATA FROM PROJECT 1 SURVEYS

ENTER KEYWORDS FOR THE ITEM:
PROGRAMS PROJECT1 1983
  10:17:36 10-AUG-84 31 BLKS INDEX

        ADD 'PROJ2'

ENTER DESCRIPTION OF THE ITEM:
PROGRAMS FOR ANALYZING DATA FROM PROJECT2 SURVEYS

ENTER KEYWORDS FOR THE ITEM:
PROGRAMS PROJECT2 1984
  10:18:22 10-AUG-84 32 BLKS INDEX

  LIST THE ITEMS

LA83   NY82   NY84   PROJ1   PROJ2   TOR82   TOR83

  LIST THE KEYWORDS

DATA   NEWYORK   PROJECT1   TORONTO   1983
LOSANGELES   PROGRAMS   PROJECT2   1982   1984

   LIST ITEMS WITH KEYWORD '1983'

LA83   PROJ1   TOR83

   LIST ITEMS WITH KEYWORDS INCLUDING '1983 DATA'

LA83   TOR83   —only items that have both of the keywords
                          "data" and "1983" are listed

   LIST ITEMS WITH KEYWORDS AMONG '1983 DATA'

LA83   NY82   NY84   PROJ1   TOR82   TOR83
                          —items that have either or both of the
                          keywords "data" and "1983" are listed

    LIST THE ITEMS WITH KEYS INCLUDING 'TORONTO DATA' —"keys" is
                          accepted as an abbreviation for "keywords"

TOR82   TOR83

   LIST ITEMS WITH KEYS AMONG 'TORONTO NEWYORK'

NY82   NY84   TOR82   TOR83

   LIST THE ITEMS WITH KEYS INCLUDING 'TORONTO NEWYORK'

THERE ARE NONE

   DESCRIBE 'LA83'

DATA FROM SURVEYS IN LOS ANGELES

KEYWORDS ARE:
   DATA   LOSANGELES   PROJECT1   1983

   DESCRIBE THE ITEMS WITH KEYWORD 'NEWYORK'

ITEM: NY82

DATA FROM SURVEYS IN NEW YORK

KEYWORDS ARE:
   DATA   NEWYORK   PROJECT1   1982

ITEM: NY84

DATA FROM SURVEYS IN NEW YORK

KEYWORDS ARE:
   DATA   NEWYORK   PROJECT2   1984

      DESCRIBE 'PROJ1'

PROGRAMS FOR ANALYZING DATA FROM PROJECT 1 SURVEYS

KEYWORDS ARE:
   PROGRAMS   PROJECT1   1983

         CHANGE THE KEYWORDS OF 'PROJ1' TO 'APL PROGRAMS PROJECT1 1983'

OLD KEYWORDS:
PROGRAMS   PROJECT1   1983
 10:22:60 10-AUG-84 32 BLKS INDEX

         EDIT THE DESCRIPTION OF 'PROJ1'

PROGRAMS FOR ANALYZING DATA FROM PROJECT 1 SURVEYS
///////B3
               FOR ANALYZING DATA FROM PROJECT 1 SURVEYS
APL FUNCTIONS

  10:23:58 10-AUG-84 32 BLKS INDEX
         LIST ITEMS

LA83   NY82   NY84   PROJ1   PROJ2   TOR82   TOR83

         LIST KEYS

APL   LOSANGELES PROGRAMS   PROJECT2   1982   1984
DATA   NEWYORK   PROJECT1   TORONTO   1983

         FORGET 'LA83'   —removing an item from the index
  10:25:06 10-AUG-84 31 BLKS INDEX

         LIST THE ITEMS

NY82   NY84   PROJ1   PROJ2   TOR82   TOR83

         LIST THE KEYS

APL   NEWYORK   PROJECT1   TORONTO   1983
DATA   PROGRAMS   PROJECT2   1982   1984

         CHANGE THE NAME OF 'PROJ1' TO 'PROG1'
  10:26:36 10-AUG-84 32 BLKS INDEX

         CHANGE THE NAME OF 'PROJ2' TO 'PROG2'
  10:26:49 10-AUG-84 32 BLKS INDEX

         DESCRIBE 'PROJ1'

I KNOW OF NO SUCH ITEM

         DESCRIBE ITEMS WITH KEYS INCLUDING 'PROJECT1 PROGRAMS'

ITEM: PROG1

APL FUNCTIONS FOR ANALYZING DATA FROM PROJECT 1 SURVEYS

KEYWORDS ARE:
   APL   PROGRAMS PROJECT1   1983

The following is the set of commands for the system:

ADD 'itemname'—Add an item to the index. The system should prompt for the description and keywords for the item.

FORGET 'itemname'—Remove an item from the index.

LIST THE ITEMS—List the names of all items currently in the index. The word "the" is optional in this and other commands.

LIST THE KEYWORDS—List all keywords currently associated with one or more items in the index. The word "keywords" can be abbreviated to "keys" in this and other commands.

LIST THE ITEMS WITH THE KEYWORD 'word'—List the names of all items in the index which have the given word as one of their keywords. The word "keyword" can be abbreviated as "key."

LIST THE ITEMS WITH KEYWORDS AMONG 'list of words'—List the name of each item in the index which has one or more of the given words among its keywords.

LIST THE ITEMS WITH KEYWORDS INCLUDING 'list of words'—List the name of each item in the index which has all of the given words among its keywords.

DESCRIBE 'itemname'—Display the description and keywords for the specified item.

DESCRIBE THE ITEMS—Display the name, description, and keywords for each item currently in the index.

DESCRIBE THE ITEMS WITH KEYWORD 'word'—Display the name, description, and keywords for each item associated with the specified keyword.

DESCRIBE THE ITEMS WITH KEYWORDS AMONG 'list of words'—Display the name, description, and keywords for each item that has one or more of the given words among its keywords.

DESCRIBE THE ITEMS WITH KEYWORDS INCLUDING 'list of words'—Display the name, description, and keywords for each item which has all of the given words among its keywords.

CHANGE THE NAME OF 'itemname' *TO* 'newname'

CHANGE THE DESCRIPTION OF 'itemname' *TO* 'new description'

CHANGE THE KEYWORDS FOR 'itemname' *TO* 'new keywords'
In all commands the words *OF* and *FOR* are interchangeable. If the *OF*, *TO*, or *FOR* phrase is omitted from a *CHANGE* command, the system should prompt for the values needed.

EDIT THE NAME OF 'itemname'

EDIT THE DESCRIPTION OF 'itemname'

EDIT THE KEYWORDS OF 'itemname'

The editor to be used is the one described in Exercise 6.3.9.

Descriptions of items can be stored as rows of a matrix or, better, as records in a direct-access file if your version of APL supports such files. (Consult your reference manual for details.) The relationship between item names and keywords can be represented by a Boolean matrix in which item names correspond, say, to rows and keywords correspond to columns. If the length of item names and keywords is restricted, they can be encoded as numbers by use of the functions *INCODE, UNCODE, MINCODE*, and *MUNCODE* from Section 6.9. Among others, the functions *SQUEEZE* (Exercise 4.8.4) and *WORDLIST* (Exercise 5.5.4) are useful for this project.

The APL Keyboard and Character Set

The keyboard of an APL terminal has the following characters, usually in the positions shown:

¨	¯	<	≤	=	≥	>	≠	∨	∧	−	÷
1	2	3	4	5	6	7	8	9	0	+	×

?	ω	∈	ρ	~	↑	↓	ι	○	⋆	→
Q	W	E	R	T	Y	U	I	O	P	←

α	⌈	⌊	$\underline{F}$	∇	∆	∘	'	⎕	(	)
A	S	D	F	G	H	J	K	L	[	]

⊂	⊃	∩	∪	⊥	⊤	|	;	:	\
Z	X	C	V	B	N	M	,	.	/

Newer terminals also have keys for the characters

$ ◇   ⊢   ⊣   {   }

In addition to the foregoing characters, there are a number of *overstruck* characters, which are created by typing a pair of characters on top of one another, in either order, using the BACKSPACE key.

APL characters are named in various ways: by their conventional typographical names (e.g., "tilde" for ~), by their shapes (e.g., "domino" for ⌹), or by their functions in APL. Some are called by several different names.

229

The following table shows the APL special characters, including overstruck characters. It also gives the names of the characters and numbers of the sections of this book in which they are principally discussed.

Character	Name	Section
)	Right parenthesis	1.3, 2.10, 2.13, Appendix B
⍝ (∩ ∘)	Lamp; comment	1.4, 3.1
←	Left arrow; assignment	2.1
Δ	Delta	2.1, 3.7
_	Underscore; underline	2.1
.	Decimal point; dot	2.2, 6.4, 6.5
‾	Raised negative sign; high minus; overbar	2.2
−	Minus; subtraction; hyphen	2.2, 2.4
'	Quote; apostrophe	2.3
+	Plus; addition	2.4
×	Times; multiplication; signum	2.4, 4.1
÷	Division; reciprocal	2.4, 4.1
⋆	Star; asterisk; power; exponential	2.4, 4.1
<	Less than	2.5
≤	Less than or equal to	2.5
=	Equal; equivalence	2.5, 4.3
≥	Greater than or equal to	2.5
>	Greater than	2.5
≠	Not equal; inequivalence; exclusive or	2.5, 4.3
ρ	Rho; shape; reshape	2.6
,	Comma; catenate; ravel; laminate	2.8, 2.9, 2.12
⍪ (, ‾)	Comma-bar	2.9
(	Left parenthesis	2.10
ι	Iota; index generator; index	2.11, 4.7
[	Left bracket; open subscript	2.13, 3.1, 3.2, 3.7
]	Right bracket; close subscript	2.13, 3.1, 3.2, 3.7
;	Semicolon	2.13, 3.5, 5.2
∇	Del	3.1, 3.2, 3.7
⎕	Quad; window; box	3.2, 3.7, 5.1, Appendix B
/	Slash; reduction; compression	3.7, 4.4, 4.5
⌊	Down-stile; floor; minimum	4.1, 4.2
⌈	Up-stile; ceiling; maximum	4.1, 4.2
|	Stile; stroke; vertical bar; absolute value; residue	4.1
⍟ (○ ⋆)	Circle-star; logarithm	4.1

Character	Name	Section
! (' .)	Exclamation; shriek; factorial; binomial	4.1
o	Circle	4.1
∧	Caret; and	4.3
∨	Inverted caret; or	4.3
~	Tilde; not	4.3
⍲ (∧ ~)	Not-and; nand	4.3
⍱ (∨ ~)	Not-or; nor	4.3
≠ (/ −)	Slash-bar	4.4, 4.5
∈	Epsilon; membership	4.6
↑	Up-arrow; take	4.8
↓	Down-arrow; drop	4.8
⌽ (o |)	Circle-stile; circle-stroke; reverse; rotate	4.9
⊖ (o −)	Circle-bar	4.9
⍉ (o \ )	Circle-backslash; transpose	4.10
⍞ (' ☐)	Quote-quad	5.1
◇	Diamond	5.2
	(sometimes also accepted as < on > or ∨ on ∧)	
→	Right-arrow; branch	5.3, 5.4
\	Backslash; slope; scan; expansion	6.1, 6.3
⍀ (\ −)	Backslash-bar; slope-bar	6.1, 6.3
⍋ (∆ |)	Delta-stile; grade up; upgrade	6.2
⍒ (∇ |)	Del-stile; grade down; downgrade	6.2
∘	Small circle; jot	6.4
?	Question mark; query; roll; deal	6.6
⍕ (⊤ ∘)	Thorn; format	6.7
⍎ (⊥ ∘)	Hydrant; execute	6.8
⊤	Top; encode	6.9
⊥	Base; decode	6.9
⌹ (☐ ÷)	Domino; matrix inverse; matrix division	6.10

Other symbols which are accepted as legal characters and may have meanings in some versions of APL, but which are without current standard uses, are:

Character	Name
α	Alpha
ω	Omega
$ (or S on |)	dollar sign
¨	Dieresis
∩	Cap
∪	Cup
⊃	Right cap; right shoe; left union
⊂	Left cap; left shoe; right union

Character	Name
⊢	Left tack
⊣	Right tack
{	Left brace
}	Right brace
I (⊥ ⊤)	I-beam

(In some older versions of APL I-beam functions are used instead of the system functions discussed in Appendix B.)

Appendix B

SYSTEM COMMANDS, SYSTEM VARIABLES, AND SYSTEM FUNCTIONS

This appendix summarizes important system commands, system variables, and system functions of APL. System variables and system functions have replaced the I-beam functions used in older versions of APL. Most versions of APL include the commands, variables, and functions listed here, as well as others that are less standard. Details vary somewhat among different implementations of the language. When in doubt, check the reference manual for the particular version of APL which you are using.

A *system command* consists of a special keyword, which begins with a right parenthesis, possibly followed by a list of arguments, which are separated by blanks. Examples are:

```
)LOAD WORK
)ERASE FUNCTION1 FUNCTION2 FUNCTION3
)SAVE
```

System commands are normally executed as soon as they are typed, even in function definition mode. They cannot be included in user-defined functions unless they are put into quoted strings (to which the execute function (⍎) can be applied.) Versions of APL differ as to exactly which system commands can be executed from within user-defined functions.

System variables and *system functions* have names that begin with the quad symbol (□) to distinguish them from the names of user-defined variables and functions. Since they are interpreted like normal variables and functions, they can be included in user-defined functions.

A system variable has a value assigned to it initially by the APL system. That value is called its *default* value. However, a new value can be assigned to it at any time by use of the left arrow symbol (←) in the normal manner. An example is the *index origin* variable □IO mentioned in Section 2.11. When a workspace is saved, the current settings of its system variables are saved with it.

A system function can be niladic, monadic, or dyadic. It may perform some system action and it usually returns a value, but its definition cannot be changed by the user. The $\square LC$ function discussed in Section 5.6 is an example.

System Commands

)CLEAR
restores the active workspace to its usual initial state. All functions and variables are erased from the workspace, and system variables are reset to their default values.

)CONTINUE
saves the active workspace under a special name ($CONTINUE$) in the user's library. Then it signs the user off from APL. Hence, its action is equivalent to that of the pair of commands

)SAVE CONTINUE
)OFF

The next time the user signs on, the $CONTINUE$ workspace is loaded automatically to become the initial active workspace. System failures sometimes cause the $CONTINUE$ workspace to be saved automatically. As the name suggests, the)$CONTINUE$ command is intended as a device for easily interrupting an APL session and continuing it later.

)COPY
copies global variables and/or functions (or groups of global variables or functions) from a workspace in the library into the active workspace. It differs from)$LOAD$ by not destroying or changing variables and functions which are already in the active workspace, except ones with the same names as those being copied in. Thus,)$COPY$ provides a way to combine items from different workspaces into a single workspace.

The name of the workspace from which items are to be copied goes after the)$COPY$ keyword, followed by the names of items to be copied. For example, the command

)COPY WORK1 FUN1 FUN2 VAR1 FUN3
will copy items named $FUN1$ $FUN2$ $VAR1$ and $FUN3$ from workspace $WORK1$. If a workspace name is given but no items in it are named (e.g.,)$COPY$ $WORK1$), all of the global variables and functions in the specified workspace are copied into the active workspace.

)DIGITS
is an old system command whose job is being taken over by the $\square PP$ system variable discussed below. Without an argument, the)$DIGITS$ command displays the current "print precision" value: the maximum number of significant digits displayed when numbers are formatted by monadic Φ or are printed without use of the format function. If a number is used as argument of the)$DIGITS$ command, it sets the print precision to a new value. Thus,)$DIGITS$ 12 is equivalent to the assignment $\square PP \leftarrow 12$.

`)DROP`	removes a workspace from the user's library. The name of the workspace to be dropped is given as the argument of the command: e.g., `)DROP WORK1`.
`)ERASE`	removes global variables and user-defined functions from the active workspace. The names of the items to be erased are given as arguments of the command, as in the example

`)ERASE FUN1 VAR1 FUN2`

`)FNS`	displays the names of all user-defined functions in the active workspace.
`)GROUP`	collects specified variables and/or user-defined functions in the active workspace into a "group" which can be referred to by a single "group name." The primary use of groups is with the `)COPY` and `)PCOPY` functions, since all of the items in a group can be copied by naming the group. The group name is given after the `)GROUP` keyword and is followed by the names of the members to be put into the group. An example is

`)GROUP GP1 FUN1 VAR1 FUN2`
A command like `)GROUP GP1` with only a group name causes the group, if it exists, to be emptied, or "dispersed."

`)GRP`	displays the names of the members of a specified group. The group to be listed is given as the argument of the command: e.g., `)GRP GP1` (Caution: Be careful not to use `)GROUP GP1` when you want `)GRP GP1`!)
`)GRPS`	displays the names of all groups in the active workspace.
`)LIB`	displays the names of all workspaces in the user's library.
`)LOAD`	causes a specified workspace from the library to become the active workspace. The name of the workspace to be loaded is given as the argument of the command: e.g., `)LOAD WORK2`.
`)OFF`	terminates an APL session and either returns the user to the command level of the operating system or signs the user off from the computer, depending on the particular version of APL being used.
`)ORIGIN`	is an older command whose job is being taken over by the $\Box IO$ system variable discussed below. `)ORIGIN` used without an argument causes the current value of the index origin to be displayed. Use of an argument 0 or 1 with `)ORIGIN` causes the value of the index origin to be changed to the value indicated.
`)PCOPY`	("protected copy") works like the `)COPY` command, except that `)PCOPY` does not copy items that have the same names as items that are already in the active workspace. Thus it protects all existing global variables and functions in the active workspace from being changed by the copying process.

)SAVE	saves the current active workspace in the user's library. If no argument is given in the *)SAVE* command, the workspace is saved under the name given by its "workspace ID" (see the *)WSID* command). However, if a name is given as argument of the command (e.g., *)SAVE MYWORK*), that name is used as the name of the saved workspace.
)SI	causes the contents of the state indicator stack to be displayed. That is, it lists the names of all suspended and pendent functions, in the reverse of the order in which they were invoked. (See Section 5.5.)
)SINL or *)SIV*	acts like *)SI* and also displays the names of the local variables for each function in the state indicator stack.
)VARS	displays the names of all global variables in the active workspace. In some versions of APL, local variables of functions currently on the state indicator stack are also listed.
)WSID	without an argument displays the current "workspace ID," or name, of the active workspace. Using a name as argument for the command (e.g., *)WSID NEW*) changes the workspace ID to the name specified.

System Variables and System Functions

□AI	(Account Information) is a niladic system function that returns a vector of accounting information, usually including, among other things:

the user's identification number
the central processing unit (CPU) time used so far in the
 current session
the "connect time" (essentially the amount of clock time)
 so far for the current session

The times are usually given in milliseconds.

□AV	(Atomic Vector) is a niladic system function which provides a vector of all APL characters, including overstruck characters and usually including many unprintable characters such as control characters or characters not yet defined. The characters are given in the order that corresponds to the binary character code that is used by the particular version of APL in question. The dyadic index function (ι) can be used to find the position of any character in the atomic vector. That can be useful for sorting character data in versions of APL which do not allow the grade up and grade down

functions to be applied to character data: Instead of
sorting characters directly, one can sort by their positions
in the $\square AV$ vector. (However, since the sequence of
characters in $\square AV$ depends on the version of APL being
used, functions that use $\square AV$ for sorting character data
may give different results on different APL systems.)

$\square CR$ (Canonical Representation) is a monadic system function
which converts the definition of a specified user-defined
function to a character matrix which is called the *canonical
representation* of the function. Each row of the matrix
contains one line of the definition of the function,
without a line number. The argument of $\square CR$ should be
a character vector containing the name of the function to
be converted. For example, the canonical representation
of the $INPUTSTRING$ function from Section 5.4 is
computed as shown below:

```
        ∇INPUTSTRING[□]∇
    ∇   S←INPUTSTRING BREAK;LINE;POS
[1]     S←''
[2]    READLOOP:LINE←,⍞
[3]     POS←LINE⍳BREAK
[4]     →(POS≤ρLINE)/LOOPEND
[5]     S←S,LINE
[6]     →READLOOP
[7]    LOOPEND:S←S,(POS-1)↑LINE
    ∇

        M←□CR 'INPUTSTRING'
        ρM
8  28
        M
S←INPUTSTRING BREAK;LINE;POS
S←''
READLOOP:LINE←,⍞
POS←LINE⍳BREAK
→(POS≤ρLINE)/LOOPEND
S←S,LINE
→READLOOP
LOOPEND:S←S,(POS-1)↑LINE
```

Conversion to canonical representation allows the
definitions of user-defined functions to be operated on
(e.g., edited) by other functions. The conversion can be
reversed by use of the $\square FX$ system function described
below.

$\square CT$ (Comparison Tolerance, or "Fuzz" value) is a system
variable. Its default value is a very small positive number

(e.g., $1E^-13$); the exact value depends on the particular version of APL being used. If two numbers differ by at most $\square CT$, they are considered equal. That means that very small round-off errors in computations are, in effect, ignored. $\square CT$ can be set to 0 or to small positive values. Functions affected by $\square CT$ include comparisons (< ≤ = ≥ > ≠), floor and ceiling, membership, and index. The following examples show the effect of nonzero $\square CT$ values:

```
        □CT
1.136864040E¯13 —default value of the comparison tolerance
        A←.99999999994
        B←.99999999996
        A=1
0
        B=1
0
        A=B
0
        B<1
1
        □CT←5E¯11 —changing the comparison tolerance
        A=1
0
        B=1
1
        A=B
1
        A<1
1
        B<1
0
        ⌊A
0
        ⌊B
1
        A∈⍳3
0
        B∈⍳3
1
        2 1 3⍳A
4
        2 1 3⍳B
2
```

$\square DL$ (Delay) is a monadic function which is used to cause a time delay, usually during execution of a user-defined

function. The argument is the number of seconds of
delay desired. The delay produced is only approximate,
but is at least as much as specified by the argument. The
value returned by $\Box DL$ is the actual amount of the delay,
in seconds.

$\Box EX$ (Expunge) is a monadic function which erases variables or
functions from the active workspace (like the $)ERASE$
command). The names of the items to be erased are given
in the argument of $\Box EX$, which is either a character
vector containing a single name or a character matrix
containing one name in each row. $\Box EX$ returns a Boolean
vector in which 1's correspond to items that were
expunged, or were not found, and 0's correspond to
items in the argument array which were not valid names
in APL or (for some reason) could not be erased. The
following example shows the use of $\Box EX$:

```
      )VARS
A         C         CODE        ERASEFUNCTIONS
          ERASEVARIABLES   NAMES
      )FNS
INCODE   INPUTSTRING    MATCH2   UNCODE
      ERASEVARIABLES
B
CODE
NAMES
      ERASEFUNCTIONS
INCOME
MATCH
UNCODE
      □EX ERASEVARIABLES
1 1 1
      □EX ERASEFUNCTIONS
1 1 1
      )VARS
A         C         ERASEFUNCTIONS   ERASEVARIABLES
      )FNS
INPUTSTRING       MATCH2
      □EX 'ERASEVARIABLES'
1
      □EX 'ERASEFUNCTIONS'
1
      )VARS
A         C
```

$\Box EX$ is useful with the $\Box NL$ function described below.

$\Box FX$ (Fix) is a monadic system function which converts a
character matrix containing the canonical representation

of a user-defined function (see $\Box CR$ above) into a definition of the function. If $\Box FX$ is successful, it returns the name of the function (as a character vector). If unsuccessful, it returns the number of the first line of the function (starting with 0 for the header line) in which an error occurred.

$\Box IO$ (Index Origin) is a system variable which specifies the starting value for subscripts, dimension numbers, values of the index generator function, and so on. Its default value is 1, which results in sequences 1 2 3 4 ... ; its alternative value is 0, which results in sequences 0 1 2 3 .... The setting of the index origin affects the behavior of such functions as index (dyadic ι), roll and deal ($?$), grade up and grade down (Δ and ∇), and functions like catenation, lamination, reduction, compression, scan, expansion, and dyadic transpose, which involve dimension numbers. The following examples show some of the effects of setting $\Box IO$ to zero:

```
      □IO←0
      VEC←6?6
      VEC
4 3 5 2 0 1
      MAT←2 3ριό
      MAT
0 1 2
3 4 5

      ΔVEC
4 5 3 1 0 2
      VEC15
2
      VEC14
0
      VEC17
6
      +/[1]MAT
3 12
      +/[0]MAT
3 5 7
      MAT,[1]8
   0 1 2 8
   3 4 5 8

      MAT,[0]8
0 1 2
3 4 5
8 8 8
```

☐*LC*   (Line Counter) is a niladic system function whose value is a vector containing the current line numbers for all functions in the state indicator stack. ☐*LC*[1] is the line number of the function which is currently executing (if any); ☐*LC*[2] is the line number of the function which called the current one; and so on. See Section 5.6 for a use of ☐*LC*.

☐*LX*   (Latent eXpression) is a system variable whose value must be a character vector. Whenever a workspace is loaded, the value of ☐*LX* in that workspace is executed immediately (as if the execute function ♠ were applied to it). ☐*LX* provides a way of creating self-starting workspaces which is different from the method described in Section 6.8.

☐*NC*   (Name Classification) is a monadic system function which, when given a character vector or matrix, determines what kind of name the value of the vector, or each row of the matrix, represents. The result is one of the following numeric codes for each string tested:

0 if the string is a valid name not currently in use in the active workspace
1 if the string is a label name (e.g., in a suspended function or in the function currently executing)
2 if the string is the name of a variable in the active workspace
3 if the string is the name of a function in the active workspace
4 in all other cases

☐*NL*   (Name List) is a monadic system function which, when given a scalar or vector of code numbers 1 2 or 3 as described for ☐*NC* above, returns a matrix containing all of the names in the active workspace which match those code numbers. ☐*NL* is especially useful with the system function ☐*EX*. For example, the expression

☐*EX* ☐*NL* 2
will erase all global variables in the active workspace.
year month day hour (0-23) minute second millisecond

☐*PP*   (Print Precision) is a system variable that specifies the maximum number of significant digits to be included when a number is formatted with monadic ♇ or is printed without format control. The value of a number is rounded symmetrically into the least-significant digit displayed, as the following example illustrates:

```
      □PP
10
      VEC
5.55555  6.666660000E¯20  7.777770000E20  0.000555  0.000555555
      □PP←5
      VEC
5.5556  6.6667E¯20  7.7778E20  0.000555  0.00055556
```

Notice that leading zeros are not counted as significant digits.

□PW   (Print Width) is a system variable which specifies the number of columns in which output from the computer is to be displayed on the user's terminal.

□RL   (Random Link) is a system variable which gives the seed value for the pseudorandom number generator used by the roll and deal functions. Its default value and range of acceptable values depend on the particular version of APL being used. (See Section 6.6 for examples of its use.)

□TS   (Time Stamp) is a niladic system function which returns a vector giving the current date and time of day in the form
year   month   day   hour (0-23)   minute   second   millisecond
An example is

```
      □TS
1982  8  25  0  14  53  378
```

□WA   (Work Area) is a niladic system function which returns a number telling the amount of free space left in the active workspace. Whether the number represents bytes (characters) or words depends on the particular version of APL being used.

Appendix C

COMMON ERROR MESSAGES

This appendix includes some of the most common, and most standard error messages. Once again, details tend to vary from one version of APL to another, and most implementations also provide many other error messages.

DEFN ERROR	(Definition error) occurs if you attempt to define a function with the same name as one that already exists in the active workspace, if you type an invalid header line when defining a function, or if you attempt to list the definition of a function that has not been defined.
DOMAIN ERROR	occurs when an argument of the wrong type or wrong value is supplied to an APL primitive function. Examples are the use of a negative number as argument for the index generator function (ι) or the use of character data with logical or arithmetic functions.
INDEX ERROR	occurs when a subscript for an array is too large or too small for the dimension that is being subscripted.
LENGTH ERROR	occurs when one or both of the arguments for a primitive function have dimensions of inappropriate size. Such an error occurs, for instance, when an attempt is made to catenate horizontally two matrices which have different numbers of rows.
RANK ERROR	occurs when the number of dimensions (i.e., the rank) of an argument or arguments is inappropriate for a primitive function. An example is the attempt to laminate two arrays of different ranks (both greater than zero).
SI DAMAGE	(State Indicator damage) occurs when a suspended or pendent function is erased or is edited in certain ways. To avoid this error, check the state indicator stack (using

the system command) *SI*) and clear it if necessary (by typing → an appropriate number of times) before erasing or editing functions.

SYNTAX ERROR   occurs when an APL expression is ill-formed: for instance, when it has unbalanced parentheses or brackets or when a function in the expression has the wrong number of arguments.

VALUE ERROR   occurs when an attempt is made to use the value of a variable that has not had a value assigned to it, or to use the value of a user-defined function that does not return a value.

WS FULL   (Workspace full) occurs when there is no more free space in the active workspace. That commonly occurs for one of several reasons:

1. An attempt has been made to create one or more arrays which are larger than the workspace can accommodate.

2. Too many global variables (and their values) have accumulated in the active workspace, because not enough variables have been declared local to the functions that use them. The superfluous global variables should be erased and should be declared local to the functions in which they are used.

3. The state indicator stack has grown very large, either because the user has neglected to clear it (using →) after errors have occurred while executing user-defined functions, or because a recursive function has called itself over and over again without end. In either case the state indicator stack should be cleared before anything else is done.

WS NOT FOUND   (Workspace not found) occurs when an attempt is made to load a workspace that is not in the library.

ANSWERS TO SELECTED EXERCISES

For reasons of space, only bare answers are given here, without proper testing and commenting. Many of the exercises have other possible answers in addition to those given here.

2.6.1.	1 0 0 1 0 1 0 1 0 0 1
2.6.2.	The value of $\rho\rho\rho A$ is always 1, since ρA is always a vector and hence $\rho\rho A$ is always a one-element vector.
2.6.5.	4 4ρ1 0 0 0 0
2.6.7.	($\rho\rho M$)=2
2.8.1.	$A\quad LIST\ OF\quad WORDS$ (a vector of 20 characters)
2.9.1.	('*',[1](('*',C),'*')),[1]'*'
2.9.4.	$LIST\leftarrow((\rho LIST),1)\rho LIST$
2.10.2.	(2.9.1 redone) '*',[1]('*',C,'*'),[1]'*'
	(2.9.4 redone) same as before
2.11.1(a).	(ιN)*2 or (ιN)×(ιN)
2.12.1.	($\iota\rho DATA$),[1.5]$DATA$
2.13.1.	$V[\rho V]$
2.13.3.	'0123456789'[$DIGITS$+1]
2.13.6.	(2 5ρ'$FALSETRUE$ ')[N+1;ι5−N]
2.13.9.	M[.5×1+(ρM)[1];.5×1+(ρM)[2]]
2.13.16.	$PICTURE[ROW+{}^{-}1+\iota(\rho ELEMENT)[1];COL+{}^{-}1+\iota(\rho ELEMENT)[2]]\leftarrow ELEMENT$
3.2.	∇ $V\leftarrow A\ THRU\ B$
	[1] $V\leftarrow A,A+\iota B-A$
	∇
3.4.	∇ $BORDER\ CM$
	[1] '_',[1]('|',CM,'|'),[1]'$^{-}$'
	∇

245

4.1.2.
```
      ∇ R←INTEGER N
[1]   R←N=⌊N
      ∇
```

4.1.4.
```
      ∇ D←DIGITSIN N
[1]   D←1+⌊10⊛|N+N=0
      ∇
```

4.2.1.
```
      ∇ S←STRING CHOPTO LENGTH
[1]   S←(LENGTH⌊ρ,STRING)ρSTRING
      ∇
```

4.3.1.
```
      ∇ R←LEAPYEAR YEAR
[1]   R←(0=4|YEAR)∧(0≠100|YEAR)∨0=400|YEAR
      ∇
```

4.4.2.
```
      +/0<,ARRAY
```

4.4.7.
```
      ∧(1=(+/B),+/[1]B
```

4.5.2.
```
      ((VEC≥10)∧VEC≤60)/VEC
```

4.5.7.
```
      ∇ R←CH BLANKOUT S
[1]   R←,S
[2]   R[(R=CH)/⍳ρR]←' '
      ∇
```

4.5.12(a).
```
      2 1 2 1 2/[1]3 1 3 1 3/TICTACTOE
```

4.6.2.
```
      M←M×M∊⍳10
```

4.6.5.
```
      ∇ I←S INTERSECT T
[1]   I←(S∊T)/S
      ∇
```

4.7.1.
```
      STRING[⍳¯1+STRING⍳' ']
```

4.7.6.
```
      (∨/M=0)⍳1
```

4.7.7.
```
      ∇ D←DIGITVECTOR S
[1]   D←¯1+'0123456789'⍳S
      ∇
```

4.8.1.
```
      ∇ B←NUMERIC A
[1]   B←0=1↑0ρA
      ∇
```

4.8.6.
```
      ∇ ADDLINE;WIDTH
[1]   WIDTH←(ρ,LINE)⌈(ρPAGE)[2]
[2]   PAGE←((ρPAGE)[1],WIDTH)↑PAGE
[3]   LINE←WIDTH↑LINE
[4]   PAGE←PAGE,[1]LINE
      ∇
```

4.9.1.
```
      (1-(⌽STRING)⍳' ')↑STRING
```

4.9.4.
```
      ∧/1↓VECTOR>¯1⌽VECTOR
```

4.10.1.
```
      ,⍉(N,ρVEC)ρVEC
```

4.10.3.
```
      ∇ R←SYMMETRIC M
[1]   R←∧/,M=⍉M
      ∇
```

5.1.1. $1 \epsilon A$ should take much longer than $1 \epsilon \Delta TIME$, since the latter expression will use the scalar value of the local variable $\Delta TIME$ in the $TIMER$ function, rather than the vector value of the global variable $\Delta TIME$.

5.4.1. When the index origin is 0, the expression will exit from the function it is in when $CONDITION$ is 1. It will do nothing (i.e., there will be no branch) when $CONDITION$ is zero.

5.4.5. The output will be

THREE
SECOND
THIRD

$\rightarrow LABEL$ in $TEST2$ gets the value (3) of $LABEL$ from $TEST1$, but the branch will be to line 3 of $TEST2$, not to line 3 of $TEST1$.

5.5.1.

```
      ∇ POS←STRING MATCHFIRST SUBSTRING;TRY;LSUB;SUFFIX
[1]    STRING←,STRING
[2]    LSUB←ρSUBSTRING←,SUBSTRING
[3]    →(LSUB=0)/NOMATCH
[4]   ⍝ FIND POSITIONS WHERE FIRST CHAR. OF SUBSTRING MATCHES:
[5]    TRY←(STRING=SUBSTRING[1])/ιρSTRING
[6]   ⍝ TRY MATCHING THE SUBSTRING AT EACH SUCH POSITION:
[7]    LOOP:→(0=ρTRY)/NOMATCH
[8]    POS←TRY[1]
[9]    TRY←1↓TRY
[10]   SUFFIX←(POS-1)↓STRING
[11]   →(LSUB>ρSUFFIX)/NOMATCH
[12]   →(∧/SUBSTRING=LSUB↑SUFFIX)/0
[13]   →LOOP
[14]  NOMATCH:POS←0
      ∇
```

5.5.4.

```
      ∇ M←WORDLIST S
[1]    M←(SQUEEZE S) CUTAT ' '
      ∇
```

5.6.1.

```
      ∇ MESSAGE ERROR CONDITION
[1]    →(~CONDITION)/0
[2]    MESSAGE
[3]    REPEAT←ΔEND←ι0 —new line
[4]    →
      ∇
```

5.7.2. `'ABCDEF'[4 SUBSETS 6]`

5.7.6.

```
      ∇ M←K SUMSTO N;A;B
[1]    →(K>1)/CASE2
[2]    M← 1 1 ρN
[3]    →0
[4]   CASE2:→(N>0)/CASE3
[5]    M←(1,K)ρ0
[6]    →0
[7]   CASE3:A←0,(K-1)SUMSTO N
```

```
[8]      B←K SUMSTO N-1
[9]      B[;1]←B[;1]+1
[10]     M←A,[1]B
         ∇
```

6.1.1.   `(~∧\STRING=' ')/STRING`

6.1.4.   `(≤\VECTOR≠ELEMENT)/VECTOR`

6.2.1.   `⍒VECTOR` is the same as `⌽⍋VECTOR` if and only if all elements of *VECTOR* are different.

6.2.5.   `WORDS[⍋+/WORDS≠' ';]`

6.3.1.
```
         ∇ R←SPACEOUT STRING
[1]      R←(¯1↓(2×ρ,STRING)ρ1 0)\STRING
         ∇
```

6.3.3.
```
         ∇ B←NUMERIC A
[1]      B←0=0\0ρA
         ∇
```

6.4.1.
```
         ∇ M←DIAMOND SIZE;T
[1]      M←⍳SIZE
[2]      T←⌽M
[3]      M←((M[T]-⌊0.5×SIZE)∘.≤M⌊T
[4]      M←' *'[1+M]
         ∇
```

6.4.5.
```
         ∇ R←UNIQUE A
[1]      R←(1=+/A∘.=A)/A
         ∇
```

6.5.1.
```
         ∇ V←X POLYVALUE COEFFS
[1]      X←X*¯1+⍳ρ,COEFFS
[2]      V←X+.×COEFFS
         ∇
```

or, using scan instead of exponentiation, line 1 could be written

```
[1] X←1,×\(¯1+ρ,COEFFS)ρX
```

6.5.3.   `CASH+.×EXCHANGE`

6.6.1.
```
         ∇ TOTAL←DICE N
[1]      TOTAL←+/?Nρ6
         ∇
```

6.6.5.   (partial answer)
```
         ∇ CODE←KEY SCRAMBLE STRING
[1]      ⎕RL←KEY
[2]      CODE←(,STRING)[(ρ,STRING)?ρ,STRING]
         ∇
```

6.7.1.
```
         ∇ R←INTEGER N
[1]      R←~'.'∊⍕N
         ∇
```

6.7.7.   `0 1↓4 0⍕((ρ,V),1)ρ1000+V`

6.8.1.
```
         ∇ N←UNCOMMAFORM S
[1]      N←⍎(S≠',')/S
         ∇
```

6.9.1.
```
      ∇ V←DIGITSOF N
[1]     N←|N
[2]     V←1+⌊10⊛1⌈N
[3]     V←(Vρ10)⊤N
      ∇
```

6.9.5.
```
    MHAND←1+⍉4 13⊤HAND-1
```

6.9.8. $B\bot1$ gives the position of the rightmost zero in B, counting from the right end of the vector. If B has no zeros, $B\bot1$ is equal to ρ,B.

$B\bot B$ counts the number of 1's after the last (rightmost) zero in B. If B has no zeros, $B\bot B$ is equal to ρ,B.

6.9.13.
```
      ∇ CODE←MINCODE MATRIX
[1]     MATRIX←((ρMATRIX)[1],12)↑MATRIX
[2]     CODE←27⊥27|'ABCDEFGHIJKLMNOPQRSTUVWXYZ'⍳⍉MATRIX
      ∇
```

7.2.
```
      ∇ R←END
[1]     R←1↑ρ∆PAGE
      ∇
```

7.4. The following solution uses a new global variable $∆STRING$ to hold the value of a character string entered in the HOW command. (The same global variable can also be used in solving Exercise 7.5.) It should be initialized to a numeric value like ‾1 in $∆INITIALIZE$ and $∆REINITIALIZE$ so the HOW function can tell whether or not a quoted string has actually appeared in the command. The other function definitions modified are:

```
      ∇ R←LONG
[1]     R←'L'
      ∇

      ∇ R←WIDE
[1]     R←'W'
      ∇

      ∇ R←A IS B;M
[1]     M←'ONLY THE PAGE OR A GIVEN STRING CAN BE MEASURED'
[2]     M ∆ERROR ~∆TYPE∊'GQ'
[3]     R←A
[4]     →(∆TYPE='G')/0
[5]     ∆STRING←,B
      ∇

      ∇ HOW A;M
[1]     M←'I DON''T UNDERSTAND'
[2]     M ∆ERROR (1≠ρ,A)∨~(1↑,A)∊'LW'
[3]     M ∆ERROR ~∆TYPE∊'GQ'
[4]     →((∆TYPE='G')∨∆NUMERIC ∆STRING)/PAGE
[5]     (ρ,∆STRING);' CHARACTER',(1≠ρ,∆STRING)/'S'
[6]     →DONE
[7]   PAGE:'NO PAGE HAS BEEN STARTED' ∆ERROR 2≠ρρ∆PAGE
[8]     →(A='W')/WIDE
```

```
[9]     (1↑ρΔPAGE);' LINE',(1≠1↑ρΔPAGE)/'S'
[10]    →DONE
[11] WIDE:(¯1↑ρΔPAGE);' COLUMN',(1≠¯1↑ρΔPAGE)/'S'
[12] DONE:ΔREINITIALIZE
     ∇
```

BIBLIOGRAPHY

APLSF Language Manual, Digital Equipment Corporation, 1979.

Beck A., Bleicher, M.N., and Crowe, D.W., Excursions into Mathematics, Worth Publishers, Inc., 1969.

Berry, P., Sharp APL Reference Manual, I.P. Sharp Associates, Toronto, 1981.

COMSHARE APL Language and Operations Reference Manual, COMSHARE Limited, 1979.

Geller, D.P., and Freedman, D.P., Structured Programming in APL, Winthrop Publishers, Inc., 1976.

Gilman, L, and Rose, A.J., APL: An Interactive Approach, Third Edition, John Wiley & Sons, Inc., 1984.

Hagamen, W.D., Linden, D.J., Long, H.S., and Weber, J.C. Encoding verbal information as unique numbers, IBM Systems Journal, 1972, No. 4, pp. 278–315.

Iverson, K.E., A Programming Lanuage, John Wiley & Sons, Inc., 1962.

Keenan, D.J., Algorithm 134: String Searching, APL Quote Quad, Vol. 10, No. 1, Sept. 1979, pp. 20–21.

LePage, W.R., Applied APL Programming, Prentice–Hall, Inc., 1978.

Pakin, S., APL\360 Reference Manual, Science Research Associates, Inc., 1968.

Polivka, R.P., and Pakin, S., APL: The Language and Its Usage, Prentice–Hall, Inc., 1975.

VAX–11 APL Reference Manual, Digital Equipment Corporation, 1983.

Wiedmann, C., NOS Computing Service APL 2 Reference Manual, Control Data Corporation, 1978.

Index

Entries in this index refer only to the most important pages for each indexed item, particularly pages on which items are defined or explained. When several page references are given for an item, the main references are shown in italics.

Words beginning with special symbols are indexed under their first alphabetic characters. APL symbols themselves are indexed under their names and the names of the functions they represent. Appendix A provides an additional index of APL symbols.

The following abbreviations are used in the index:

ex   – exercise
ff   – and page or pages following
te   – user-defined function from the text-editing system in Chapter 7
udf – user-defined function given as an example (other than those in Chapter 7)